Vocabulary
for Achievement

Sixth Course

Margaret Ann Ríchek

GREAT SOURCE

WILMINGTON, MA

Author

Margaret Ann Richek

Professor of Education Emerita, Northeastern Illinois University; consultant in reading and vocabulary study; author of The World of Words *(Houghton Mifflin)*

Classroom Consultants

Beth Gaby
English Chair, Carl Schurz High School, Chicago, Illinois

Chris Hausammann
Teacher of English, Central Mountain High School, Lock Haven, Pennsylvania

Malisa Cannon
Teacher of Language Arts, Desert Sky Middle School, Tucson, Arizona

Stephanie Saltikov-Izabal
Teacher of Reading and English, At-Risk Specialist, Huntington Beach High School, Huntington Beach, California

Patricia Melvin
District Secondary Reading Specialist, Duval County Public Schools, Jacksonville, Florida

Sean Rochester
Teacher of English, Parkway Central High School, St. Louis, Missouri

Acknowledgments

Editorial: Ruth Rothstein, Victoria Fortune, Dan Carsen, Amy Gilbert

Design and Production: Mazer Corporation

Text Design and Production: Mazer Creative Services

Illustrations: Susan Aiello, Barbara Samanich, Toby Williams of Wilkinson Studios, LLC; George Cathey, Jerry Hoare, Ron Zalme of Langley Creative

Cover Design: Mazer Creative Services

Cover Photo: Stock Free/Mazer Creative Services

Definitions for the three hundred words taught in this textbook are based on Houghton Mifflin dictionaries—in particular, *The American Heritage High School Dictionary*—but have been abbreviated and adapted for instructional purposes.

All pronunciations are reproduced by permission from *The American Heritage Dictionary of the English Language, Fourth Edition,* copyright © 2000. Passages on pages 19–20 are from *Roget's II The New Thesaurus.* Copyright © 2003 by Houghton Mifflin Company. Reproduced by permission from *Roget's II The New Thesaurus,* Third Edition.

Printed in the United States of America

International Standard Book Number: 978-0-669-51760-6

15 16 17 - 0304 - 18 17 16
4500587672

Contents

COMPLETE WORD LIST FOR SIXTH COURSE

Words About Language

WORD LIST

cognate	inflection	orthography	paradigm	philology
phonology	rejoinder	rhetoric	succinct	syntax

This lesson includes words related to language. Some of the words describe language itself, such as *phonology* and *syntax.* Others describe various ways that language can be used, such as *rhetoric* and *rejoinder.*

1. cognate (kŏg′nāt′) from Latin *co-,* "together" + *gnatus,* "born"
   a. *noun* A word that looks like and is related to another word in a different language
   • *Clima* and *climate,* as well as *insecto* and *insect,* are two of the many thousands of pairs of **cognates** in Spanish and in English.
   b. *adjective* Having the same source, origin, or ancestor
   • The Hebrew greeting *shalom* and the Arabic *salaam* are **cognate** words derived from a Semitic root meaning "peace."
   c. *adjective* Similar in function and character
   • Cinema and television are **cognate** media.

2. inflection (ĭn-flĕk′shən) *noun* from Latin *in-,* "in" + *flectere,* "to bend"
   a. Alteration of pitch or tone of voice
   • In English, a rising **inflection** at the end of a sentence usually indicates a question.
   b. The addition of an affix to a word, or a change in the form of a word, to show the plural, tense, or another grammatical relationship
   • Past tense verbs are typically formed with the **inflection** *-ed.*

   inflect *verb* Speakers of Turkish **inflect** the word *baba,* or "father," to form *babam,* meaning "my father."

3. orthography (ôr-thŏg′rə-fē) *noun* from Greek *ortho,* "correct" + *graphein,* "to write"
   The study of the letters and spelling system of a language
   • Whereas English **orthography** is alphabetic, in Chinese **orthography,** each character typically represents a full word.

   orthographic *adjective* In English, **orthographic** representations of the *f* sound can also be spelled *gh* or *ph.*

English and Chinese orthographic representations for the word *love*

4. paradigm (păr′ə-dīm′) *noun* from Greek *para-,* "alongside" + *deiknunai,* "to show"
   a. The set of inflected forms of a word
   • The **paradigm** of the noun *sheep* is limited to *sheep* and *sheep's.*
   b. A model or framework that sets forth a way of viewing things, especially in an intellectual discipline
   • The "double-blind" study is a **paradigm** that helps avoid false results.

   paradigmatic *adjective* Einstein's theories resulted in **paradigmatic** shifts in the way physicists think about energy and matter.

5. philology (fĭ-lŏl´ə-jē) *noun* from Greek *philo-*, "love" + *-logy*, "study"
The study of the history of language
- Studies in **philology** trace the relationship between classical and Late Latin verbs.

philological or **philologic** *adjective* Miri's article was a **philological** analysis of slang terms.

6. phonology (fə-nŏl´ə-jē) *noun* from Greek *phon*, "sound" + *-logy*, "study".
The sound system of a language; the study of such a sound system
- The use of the article *a* or *an*, depending on the word that follows, is governed by rules of English **phonology**.

phonological or **phonologic** *adjective* The small child showed **phonological** awareness when he identified the word *man* as having three sound segments.

7. rejoinder (rĭ-join´dər) *noun* from Latin *re-*, "back" + *iungere*, "to join"
An often witty or critical response to a reply; an answer
- When the first candidate said, "I'm not certain," his opponent replied, "You're never certain," to which the first candidate gave the **rejoinder**, "You're certainly wrong!"

rejoin *verb* The defense lawyer **rejoined** the prosecution's most powerful point, thereby convincing the jury that her client was innocent.

8. rhetoric (rĕt´ər-ĭk) *noun* from Greek *rhetor*, "public speaker"
a. The study and art of using language effectively and persuasively
- Martin Luther King Jr.'s 1963 "I Have a Dream" speech is a fine example of **rhetoric.**
b. Speech that is elaborate, pretentious, or insincere
- The politician used moralistic **rhetoric** while secretly taking bribes.

rhetorical *adjective* In a **rhetorical** exaggeration, the lawyer called the seventeen-year-old defendant "a helpless child."

9. succinct (sək-sĭngkt´, sə-sĭngkt´) *adjective* from Latin *sub-*, "under" + *cingere*, "to support; to gird"
Clear and precise; expressed in few words
- When asked to describe the game, his **succinct** reply was, "We won."

10. syntax (sĭn´tăks´) *noun* from Greek *syn-*, "together" + *tassein*, "to arrange"
The arrangement of words to form grammatical sentences
- In English **syntax,** adjectives are placed before nouns.

syntactic or **syntactical** *adjective* Though Jenna was good at learning new Spanish vocabulary, she found it difficult to learn the **syntactic** rules for proper sentence structure.

WRITE THE CORRECT WORD

Write the correct word in the space next to each definition. Use each word only once.

orthography **1.** a spelling system

rejoinder **2.** a critical answer to a reply

Phonology **3.** the sound system of a language

Cognate **4.** a model

rhetoric **5.** the art of using language effectively

philology **6.** the study of language history

Paradigm **7.** of similar origin

syntax **8.** the arrangement of words

succinct **9.** clear and precise

Inflection **10.** a change in pitch or tone of voice

COMPLETE THE SENTENCE

Write the letter for the word that best completes each sentence.

_____ **1.** In English, -s is a common _____ added to a singular noun to form the plural.
    a. cognate   **b.** inflection   **c.** philology   **d.** rejoinder

_____ **2.** Actors who study _____ often can portray foreign accents quite convincingly.
    a. phonology   **b.** rhetoric   **c.** syntax   **d.** orthography

_____ **3.** American Sign Language has a different _____ from spoken English; for example, the question "What did you buy?" can be signed as "You bought what?"
    a. cognate   **b.** philology   **c.** rejoinder   **d.** syntax

_____ **4.** CB radio users are famous for their _____ phrases, like "ten four."
    a. rhetorical   **b.** succinct   **c.** orthographic   **d.** inflected

_____ **5.** In some ways, computers and typewriters are _____.
    a. cognate   **b.** paradigmatic   **c.** rejoined   **d.** syntactic

_____ **6.** Anyone who wants to be a public speaker should study classic _____ models.
    a. orthographic   **b.** phonological   **c.** rhetorical   **d.** inflected

_____ **7.** To learn to write Arabic, you must study the characters that compose its _____.
    a. rhetoric   **b.** orthography   **c.** paradigms   **d.** rejoinders

_____ **8.** Someone interested in both history and languages may enjoy a career in _____.
    a. inflection   **b.** philology   **c.** syntax   **d.** rhetoric

_____ **9.** His witty _____ silenced his accuser and amused the audience.
    a. rejoinder   **b.** phonology   **c.** orthography   **d.** inflection

_____ **10.** Persuading medieval scholars to believe Earth is round required a shift in _____.
    a. cognate   **b.** rhetoric   **c.** paradigm   **d.** philologist

Challenge: After their _____ teacher delivered a lengthy lecture on ancient Greek, the students were relieved when she then gave a very _____ presentation on Old English.
    a. rhetoric…orthographic   **b.** philology…succinct   **c.** phonology…inflected

The Great English Transition

To see how drastically the English language changed between the years 1000 and 1400, read the sentence "Have mercy on my son" in both Old and Middle English. In Old English, this phrase read, "Gemilitsa mimum suna," and a few centuries later, the same phrase in Middle English had changed to "Haue mercy on my sone."

(1) There are also vast differences in *orthography*. For example, the Old English letters æ and ᵹ were replaced by the letters *a* and *g*, respectively. **(2)** These are mirrored by changes in *phonology*. Middle English may be difficult for us to understand, but Old English is an entirely different language.

(3) Nouns and verbs were heavily *inflected* in Old English. The verb *fremman* (perform) had no less than ten endings; today, *perform* has only three: *-ed, ing*, and *-s*. **(4)** The many *paradigms* in Old English allowed one word to specify who, when, and how an action took place. **(5)** In contrast, much of Modern English's *syntax* depends on word order. **(6)** Inflections also made Old English relatively *succinct*. For example, the sentence "Have mercy on my son" in Old English has only three words, whereas in Middle English it has five.

As you can see, in a span of a few hundred years, the English language radically evolved. The Germanic Anglo-Saxon language of Old English transformed into Middle English, a language much closer to the one we speak today. What sparked this dramatic linguistic change?

In 1066, William the Conqueror from Normandy defeated England. **(7)** *Philologists* have shown that this victory of the French-speaking Normans over the Saxons, who spoke Old English, caused a chain of events that added thousands of new words to the English language.

William the Conqueror declared himself king of England and, along with his nobles, continued to speak French. **(8)** This foreign tongue became the language of the educated and was used in legal suits and in most writing—in short, wherever formal *rhetoric* was appropriate.

Why, then, didn't England end up speaking French? For one thing, the Norman English kings lost their lands in France, and became more solidly based in England. In addition, the common people continued to speak English, and the nobles interacted and intermarried with them. Gradually, these factors combined to form Middle English, which ultimately evolved into Modern English.

Not surprisingly, given the way in which the two languages merged, French words tend to be used in more literary and academic settings. Compare these word pairs, the first from Old English and the second from French: *king, royal; guts, courage; sweat, perspire*. **(9)** The more formal words—*royal, courage*, and *perspire*—all have *cognates* in French and, in fact, come from that language. For example, in French, a king is a *roi*, which is a cognate of *royal*.

(10) William the Conqueror may have won the English throne, but there is a simple *rejoinder* to anybody who feels that the king won the linguistic battle. A large study of English word frequency showed that Old English contributed almost all of the hundred most frequently used words. It seems that English-language speakers are very attached to their Anglo-Saxon roots.

Each sentence below refers to a numbered sentence in the passage. Write the letter of the choice that gives the sentence a meaning that is closest to the original sentence.

_____ 1. There are also vast differences in _____.
   a. meaning   **b.** voice modulation   **c.** responses   **d.** spelling

_____ 2. These are mirrored by changes in _____.
   a. frequency   **b.** pronunciation   **c.** appearance   **d.** spelling

_____ 3. Nouns and verbs were heavily _____ in Old English.
   a. added to   **b.** ordered   **c.** misspelled   **d.** rewritten

_____ 4. The complex _____ in Old English allowed one word to specify many things.
   a. metaphors   **b.** letter system   **c.** sets of word forms   **d.** related words

_____ **5.** In contrast, much of Modern English's _____ depends on word order.
    a. skillfulness   **b.** brevity   **c.** philosophy   **d.** grammar

_____ **6.** Inflections also made Old English relatively _____.
    a. short   **b.** persuasive   **c.** historical   **d.** affixed

_____ **7.** _____ have shown that this victory added thousands of new words to the English language.
    a. Legal analysts   **b.** Sound experts   **c.** Speech therapists   **d.** Language historians

_____ **8.** French became the language used wherever formal _____ was appropriate.
    a. similarity   **b.** alteration   **c.** speech   **d.** study

_____ **9.** The more formal words all have _____ in French.
    a. uses   **b.** abbreviations   **c.** plural forms   **d.** related words

_____ **10.** There is a simple _____ to anybody who feels that the king won the linguistic battle.
    a. reward   **b.** question   **c.** insult   **d.** response

Indicate whether the statements below are TRUE or FALSE according to the passage.

_____ **1.** After 1066, French replaced English completely as the new language of England.

_____ **2.** English includes thousands of words borrowed from the French language.

_____ **3.** Language sometimes undergoes great changes due to historical events.

WRITING EXTENDED RESPONSES

Because it incorporates aspects of two languages, English has a large vocabulary. Is this an advantage or a disadvantage? Choose the perspective of one type of person (for example, a writer, scientist, or second-language learner) and defend your point of view with at least two well-supported reasons. Your essay should be a minimum of three paragraphs long. Use at least three lesson words in your essay and underline them.

WRITE THE DERIVATIVE

Complete the sentence by writing the correct form of the word shown in parentheses. You may not need to change the form that is given.

_____ **1.** _____ research enhances our understanding of ancient cultures. (*philology*)

_____ **2.** Many languages use _____ verbs to change tenses. (*inflection*)

_____ **3.** Some educators are trying to make _____ changes to the cultural education program in the state. (*paradigm*)

4. The _____ system of the language of the Kalahari Bushmen in Africa includes clicking sounds as well as consonants and vowels. *(phonology)*

5. When the audience booed his joke, the comedian _____, "That's okay, I'll be laughing all the way to the bank." *(rejoinder)*

6. The _____ variations of the several languages on the Rosetta Stone helped researchers decode Egyptian hieroglyphics. *(orthography)*

7. In his address, the president asked _____, "Where is our country headed?" *(rhetoric)*

8. Even in the same language, accents and _____ differences vary from region to region. *(syntax)*

9. When participating in a timed debate, being _____ is essential. *(succinct)*

10. The French word *un* and the Spanish word *uno* are _____ for *one*. *(cognate)*

FIND THE EXAMPLE

Choose the answer that best describes the action or situation.

1. An example of Standard English *syntax*
  a. ain't got none **b.** he aren't **c.** a ice cream **d.** an hour

2. A *cognate* of the Spanish greeting "hola"
  a. goodbye **b.** hello **c.** si, Señor **d.** dictionary

3. The most likely source of *rhetoric*
  a. an orator **b.** a pilot **c.** a comic book **d.** a lifeguard

4. A quality of being *succinct*
  a. brevity **b.** vagueness **c.** humor **d.** criticism

5. An English *orthographic* representation
  a. rune **b.** hieroglyph **c.** letter **d.** picture

6. An *inflection* of the word "lobby"
  a. lobbied **b.** argue for **c.** hobby **d.** foyer

7. The most unlikely place to hear a *rejoinder*
  a. a debate **b.** a lecture **c.** a court trial **d.** military drill

8. A topic of *philology*
  a. stamps **b.** Latin **c.** typing **d.** philosophy

9. Another word for a *paradigm*
  a. copy **b.** dialogue **c.** perfection **d.** framework

10. The main focus of *phonology*
  a. word games **b.** word sounds **c.** telephones **d.** spelling

Honesty and Deception

WORD LIST

belie	clandestine	disingenuous	dissemble	forthright
nefarious	perfidious	probity	scrupulous	spurious

"One falsehood spoils a thousand truths," states an African proverb. The words in this lesson deal with different facets of honesty and deception.

1. **belie** (bĭ-lī´) *verb* from Old English *beleogan*, "to deceive with lies"
   To depict falsely; to misrepresent
   • The boss's easygoing manner **belies** her demand for perfection from employees.

2. **clandestine** (klăn-dĕs´tĭn) *adjective* probably from Latin *clam*, "in secret" + *intestinus*, "internal"
   Kept or done in secret, often to conceal an illegal or improper purpose
   • Witnesses reported **clandestine** meetings in the back room of the restaurant, so the police conducted a raid.

clandestine

3. **disingenuous** (dĭs´ĭn-jĕn´yoō-əs) *adjective* from Latin *dis-*, "not" + *ingenuus*, "honest; freeborn"
   Pretending to be unaware or unsophisticated; insincere or calculating; not telling the whole truth
   • With a **disingenuous** shrug, Maribel denied all knowledge of plans for a surprise party.

4. **dissemble** (dĭ-sĕm´bəl) *verb* from Old French *dis-*, "not" + *sembler*, "to appear; to seem"
   To disguise or conceal one's feelings or motives behind a false appearance
   • Beth was unable to **dissemble** her annoyance with her roommate for talking on the phone until midnight.

> *Dissemble* usually refers to the actions of hiding something negative under a falsely positive demeanor.

5. **forthright** (fôrth´rīt´) *adjective*
   Direct; with complete disclosure and honesty; without evasion
   • The accountant was completely **forthright** with his company about his plans to quit his job and become a math teacher.

   forthrightness *noun* I don't agree with your opinion, but I admire your **forthrightness** in stating it so boldly.

6. **nefarious** (nə-fâr´ē-əs) *adjective* from Latin *nefas*, "crime; transgression"
   Openly or notoriously wicked; infamous
   • In the sixteenth and seventeenth centuries, **nefarious** pirates kidnapped travelers and sold them as slaves.

   nefariousness *noun* The article reported on the **nefariousness** of the hacker's plot to infect millions of computers with a virus.

7. **perfidious** (pər-fĭd´ē-əs) *adjective* from Latin *per-*, "to destruction" + *fides*, "faith"
Disloyal; treacherous
- Ignoring all proxy votes would be a **perfidious** violation of the democratic process.

perfidy *noun* In an act of **perfidy,** Hitler attacked his former Russian allies during World War II.

8. **probity** (prō´bĭ-tē) *noun* from Latin *probus*, "upright; good"
Complete and confirmed integrity; uprightness
- To assure that his **probity** wouldn't be questioned, the president hired a firm to handle his personal finances during his term in office.

9. **scrupulous** (skrōō´pyə-ləs) *adjective* from Latin *scrupus*, "rough stone"
   a. Having strict principles; acting in strict regard for what is right or proper
   - The governor declared that she was **scrupulous** about not letting campaign donations influence her policies.
   b. Conscientious and exact; painstaking
   - The interior designer was known for his **scrupulous** attention to detail.

scruple *noun* Michael's **scruples** prevented him from accepting a lucrative position at a corporation known for exploiting laborers.

scruple *verb* To hesitate because of conscience or principle
- A person who would cheat his relatives would not **scruple** to betray his friends.

> *Unscrupulous,* meaning "dishonest," is the opposite of *scrupulous.*

10. **spurious** (spyŏŏr´ē-əs) *adjective* from Latin *spurius*, "illegitimate"
Not genuine; lacking authenticity or validity; false
- The judge dismissed the **spurious** malpractice suit, declaring that the physician had given excellent care.

spuriousness *noun* His **spuriousness** in trying to pass himself off as a professor was apparent the minute we engaged him in conversation.

WORD ENRICHMENT

Cicero's pebbles

The word *scrupulous* is derived from a word that meant "a small, sharp stone or pebble." The great Roman orator, Cicero, used the word figuratively, to indicate that doing something wrong would be a source of anxiety, just as having a pebble in one's shoe would cause discomfort. At first, *scrupulous* referred to a small unit of measurement. By the seventeenth century, though, the word had acquired the reference to one's conscience that Cicero previously had attributed to it.

WRITE THE CORRECT WORD

Write the correct word in the space next to each definition. Use each word only once.

_____ 1. total integrity

_____ 2. to misrepresent

_____ 3. conscientious

_____ 4. direct; honest

_____ 5. to hide motives behind
a false appearance

_____ 6. treacherous

_____ 7. wicked; infamous

_____ 8. not genuine

_____ 9. done in secret

_____ 10. pretending to be unaware

COMPLETE THE SENTENCE

Write the letter for the word that best completes each sentence.

_____ 1. The _____ criminal was known for selling forgeries of valuable paintings.
a. forthright   b. scrupulous   c. nefarious   d. probity

_____ 2. The homey atmosphere of the restaurant _____ the sophistication of
its cuisine.
a. perfidies   b. scruples   c. belies   d. probes

_____ 3. Hospital staff must be _____ in assuring that surgical instruments
are sanitized.
a. disingenuous   b. spurious   c. clandestine   d. scrupulous

_____ 4. The ball player had assured fans he would stay with the team, so when he signed
with another, they felt he was _____.
a. spurious   b. perfidious   c. forthright   d. clandestine

_____ 5. The rebels held a _____ meeting in an abandoned warehouse.
a. clandestine   b. disingenuous   c. dissembled   d. spurious

_____ 6. This _____ Italian antique was made in a modern factory.
a. scrupulous   b. belied   c. forthright   d. spurious

_____ 7. It is admirable to confront difficult situations in a _____ way.
a. dissembling   b. nefarious   c. disingenuous   d. forthright

_____ 8. Sonja was _____ when she claimed she hadn't heard her mother tell her to
come home early.
a. nefarious   b. disingenuous   c. perfidious   d. forthright

_____ 9. A good judge is characterized by _____.
a. perfidy   b. spuriousness   c. probity   d. disingenuousness

_____ 10. Despite his fears, the defendant _____, maintaining a calm demeanor.
a. dissembled   b. belied   c. scrupled   d. clandestined

Challenge: Displaying a complete lack of scruples, the _____ traitor passed critical
information to the enemy at a _____ rendezvous.
_____   a. spurious…dissembled   b. nefarious…spurious   c. perfidious…clandestine

The Big Bad Wolf?

(1) Language and folklore are filled with references to the *nefarious* wolf. Consider just a few popular phrases. To *keep the wolf from the door* means "to avoid poverty or hunger"; to *throw to the wolves* is "to abandon to danger"; even *wolfing down food* is an act most people disapprove of.

A vast folk tradition also depicts the animal as the wily essence of evil. The wolf is the villain in many tales. Sometimes, as in the story of the "Three Little Pigs," it plays the part openly. **(2)** In other tales, not content to be *forthright* about its wicked plans, this fanged beast assumes disguises. **(3)** Who can forget the wolf's *perfidy* in "Little Red Riding Hood"? **(4)** He *dissembles* shamelessly, pretending to be a loving grandmother. And then, there is the fable of the wolf in sheep's clothing. **(5)** In this story, the wolf becomes a metaphor for the *disingenuous* villain.

Much of this negativity can be attributed to the fact that wolves are, in actuality, predators of great strength. For instance, an adult timber wolf can chew through chain mail. Like dogs, they use their keen sense of smell to hunt prey. They also roam a territory of up to 120 square miles, creating a potential conflict with human populations.

There is no question that wolves have posed problems to people and livestock. However, left to flourish in the wild, wolves do little harm except to their natural prey.

In fact, they can be beneficial in controlling burgeoning wildlife populations. It is estimated that each year, in Wisconsin, wolves kill about 6,000 deer, many of them already sick and disabled.

The truth is that wolves have much more to fear from humans than humans do from wolves. Many states, such as Wisconsin and Minnesota, once put bounties on the animals, paying people to kill them. By the 1960s, wolves were close to extinction in Minnesota. However, when bounties were withdrawn and wolves received protection from the Endangered Species Act of 1973, the wolf population began to rise. In Minnesota, an estimated 2,500 wolves now roam freely.

But saving the wolf is not simply a matter of law. **(6)** People *clandestinely*—and illegally—continue to shoot them, sparked in part by the negative reputation of wolves. **(7)** Despite evidence to the contrary, these people argue *spuriously* that wolves pose a great danger to humans and so killing them is desirable. **(8)** Some even consider killing wolves an act of *probity*.

To help change attitudes, the International Wolf Center in Minnesota is hand-raising baby wolves. Volunteers feed the pups with bottles, stroke them, and even burp them. **(9)** The facility is *scrupulously* maintained. For example, caregivers must wash the soles of their shoes in a chlorine solution before entering the nursery. **(10)** The gentle gray-eyed pups, who *belie* the reputation of the "big bad wolf," may be viewed from behind glass or from webcam pictures. As they grow older, the animals are kept in a wildlife preserve.

Watching actual wolves grow in captivity can help to dispel the unreasonable prejudice against them. Gradually, the wolves are introduced into the wild to take their place among the increasing number of wild wolves roaming the northern woods.

Each sentence below refers to a numbered sentence in the passage. Write the letter of the choice that gives the sentence a meaning that is closest to the original sentence.

_____ **1.** Language and folklore are filled with references to the _____ wolf.
   a. secretive   **b.** wicked   **c.** playful   **d.** honest

_____ **2.** Not content to be _____ about its wicked plans, it assumes disguises.
   a. direct   **b.** insincere   **c.** sophisticated   **d.** simple

_____ **3.** Who can forget the wolf's _____ in "Little Red Riding Hood"?
   a. treachery   **b.** misrepresentation   **c.** concealment   **d.** disguise

_____ **4.** This animal _____ shamelessly, pretending to be a loving grandmother.
   a. expresses himself   **b.** lacks validity   **c.** gives affection   **d.** hides his motives

_____ **5.** In this story, the wolf becomes a metaphor for the _____ villain.

    a. aggressive   **b.** wicked   **c.** deceptive   **d.** hostile

_____ **6.** People _____ —and illegally—continue to shoot them, sparked in part by the negative reputation of wolves.

    a. secretly   **b.** directly   **c.** immorally   **d.** treacherously

_____ **7.** Despite evidence to the contrary, these people argue _____ that wolves pose a great danger to humans and so killing them is desirable.

    a. openly   **b.** insincerely   **c.** falsely   **d.** secretly

_____ **8.** Some even consider killing wolves an act of _____ .

    a. evil   **b.** honesty   **c.** integrity   **d.** disloyalty

_____ **9.** The facility is _____ maintained.

    a. illegally   **b.** painstakingly   **c.** expensively   **d.** directly

_____ **10.** The gentle gray-eyed pups, who _____ the reputation of the "big bad wolf," may be viewed from behind glass or from webcam pictures.

    a. secretly maintain   **b.** condemn harshly   **c.** try to evade   **d.** depict as false

Indicate whether the statements below are TRUE or FALSE according to the passage.

_____ **1.** There are now more wolves in the wild in Minnesota than there were in the 1960s.

_____ **2.** Left in the wild, wolves are doing tremendous harm to healthy deer.

_____ **3.** The reputation of wolves in language and folklore contributes to human aggression against them.

FINISH THE THOUGHT

Complete each sentence with a phrase that shows the meaning of the italicized word.

1. We made *clandestine* plans to _____

_____

2. The man's charming personality *belied* _____

_____

WRITE THE DERIVATIVE

Complete the sentence by writing the correct form of the word shown in parentheses. You may not need to change the form that is given.

_____ **1.** Leo's _____ sometimes alienates those he is trying to convince. *(forthright)*

_____ **2.** The smugglers _____ brought diamonds into the country. *(clandestine)*

_____ 3. On last year's climb, I _____ my fear beneath a show of courage. (*dissemble*)

_____ 4. The _____ of Benedict Arnold is recorded in many histories of the American Revolutionary War. (*perfidious*)

_____ 5. She had few _____ about stealing money from the club's treasury. (*scrupulous*)

_____ 6. _____ her utter terror, Natalie maintained a calm expression. (*belie*)

_____ 7. The _____ of their stock-market schemes earned them a long jail sentence. (*nefarious*)

_____ 8. Hector smiled _____ at his rival. (*disingenuous*)

_____ 9. The prime minister is a woman of indisputable _____. (*probity*)

_____ 10. The _____ of the art dealer's claim that the sculptures were created by Picasso was evident to the museum curator. (*spurious*)

FIND THE EXAMPLE

Choose the answer that best describes the action or situation.

_____ 1. A *perfidious* act
   a. hiding   **b.** voting   **c.** treason   **d.** marriage

_____ 2. A *nefarious* character in most folktales
   a. princess   **b.** dragon   **c.** prince   **d.** horse

_____ 3. A person most likely to have *clandestine* meetings regularly
   a. a school principal   **b.** a police officer   **c.** an office manager   **d.** a CIA agent

_____ 4. An expression or a gesture that would *belie* boredom
   a. loud yawn   **b.** glazed eyes   **c.** animated smile   **d.** constant fidgeting

_____ 5. How a *scrupulous* person treats a friend
   a. rudely   **b.** callously   **c.** thoughtlessly   **d.** kindly

_____ 6. A way to establish one's *probity*
   a. flaunt wealth   **b.** behave morally   **c.** write a novel   **d.** hire a bodyguard

_____ 7. A *forthright* answer to a parent's question "Where are you going?"
   a. Just out.   **b.** Don't know.   **c.** To Jonah's house.   **d.** To get something.

_____ 8. Something that would most likely reveal a *spurious* financial scheme
   a. a bank teller   **b.** a business course   **c.** an IRS audit   **d.** a marketing plan

_____ 9. Someone whose friendly remark would most likely be *disingenuous*
   a. a boss   **b.** a best friend   **c.** a sibling   **d.** an enemy

_____ 10. An event that is likely to require its planner to *dissemble*
   a. surprise party   **b.** tennis match   **c.** graduation party   **d.** educational lecture

Time

WORD LIST

| concomitant | eon | extant | hiatus | inure |
| irrevocable | millennium | perpetuity | pristine | transience |

History is measured in eras. Calendars track months and days. Seasons mark the periods for growing crops. Even our daily habits of eating and sleeping are connected to specific time periods. The words in this lesson relate to the many ways in which we measure time.

1. concomitant (kən-kŏmˊĭ-tənt) from Latin *con-*, "with" + *comitari*, "to accompany"
   a. *adjective* Occurring or existing at the same time; accompanying; following as a result
   • Heightened security measures have been **concomitant** with the growing use of computers in business transactions.
   b. *noun* Something or someone that occurs or exists at the same time as another thing
   • For a period of time, automobiles were **concomitants** of horse-drawn carriages.

   concomitance *noun* The **concomitance** of admitting that I broke the antique vase and hearing the thunderclap outside was unnerving.

2. eon (ēˊŏnˊ) *noun* from Latin *aeon*, "age"
   a. The longest division of geologic time, containing two or more eras
   • The Proterozoic **Eon**, which lasted almost two billion years, saw the emergence of multicellular life.
   b. An indefinitely long period of time; an age
   • The Grand Canyon was carved over **eons**, as rushing waters flowed over rock.

carved over eons

> The plural form *eons* is generally used when referring to an indefinite period of time.

3. extant (ĕkˊstənt) *adjective* from Latin *ex-*, "out" + *stare*, "to stand"
   Still in existence; not destroyed, lost, or extinct
   • The historian found that many manuscripts and diaries from the sixteenth century were still **extant**.

4. hiatus (hī-āˊtəs) *noun* from Latin *hiare*, "to gape"
   A gap or an interruption in space or time; a break
   • During the **hiatus** between semesters, Martin will complete a month-long internship with a magazine publisher.

> The plural of *hiatus* is either *hiatuses* or *hiatus*.

5. inure (ĭn-yŏŏrˊ) *verb* from Latin *in-*, "in" + *ure*, "use"
   To accustom to something undesirable, especially by prolonged subjection or exposure
   • Two years in the Marine Corps have **inured** Elsa to being away from her family.

6. **irrevocable** (ĭ-rĕv´ə-kə-bəl) *adjective* from Latin *in-*, "not" + *re-*, "back" + *vocare*, "to call"

Impossible to retract; irreversible
- The king's cruel decree was **irrevocable,** and many subjects were forced to leave the country.

7. **millennium** (mə-lĕn´ē-əm) *noun* Latin *mille*, thousand
   a. A span of one thousand years
      - The year 2000 was the last year of the second **millennium** A.D.
   b. A hoped-for period of joy, serenity, and prosperity
      - While we wait for the **millennium,** we must pursue policies of peace and justice.

> The plural of *millennium* is either *millennia* or *millenniums*. Note that we are now in the third millennium A.D. (not the second).

8. **perpetuity** (pûr´pĭ-tōō´ĭ-tē) *noun* from Latin *perpetuus*, "continuous"

Time without end; eternity
- The flame that burns in **perpetuity** at the grave of President John F. Kennedy Jr. symbolizes hope for all generations.

perpetual *adjective* Continuing without interruption
- By the end of the day, Diane was worn out by the **perpetual** questions from her five-year-old.

perpetuate *verb* Nirit and Barak will **perpetuate** the memory of their grandfather by establishing a foundation in his name.

9. **pristine** (prĭs´tēn´) *adjective* from Latin *pristinus*, "former; earlier; original"
   a. Unspoiled, untouched by civilization; remaining in a pure state
      - The first people to reach the peak of Mount Everest were taken aback by its **pristine** beauty.
   b. Free from dirt or decay; clean
      - The twenty-year-old carpet was in **pristine** condition.
   c. Typical of the earliest time or condition; original; primitive
      - The **pristine** ceiling, decorated with colorful hieroglyphic paintings, stunned the explorers as they entered the pharaoh's tomb.

10. **transience** (trăn´zē-əns) *noun* from Latin *trans-*, "over" + *ire*, "to go"
    a. A short life or existence; an impermanence
       - The **transience** of the pale blossoms adds to their delicate charm.
    b. A state of moving from place to place
       - The **transience** of migrant workers often prevents their children from receiving a good education.

transient *adjective* The **transient** burst of summerlike weather during Chicago's cold winter was soon replaced by snow.

WORD ENRICHMENT

Calling to irrevocable

The Latin root *voc*, which means "call," is used figuratively in many words, including *irrevocable*. For example, one's profession is often called a *vocation*, or, in an old-fashioned expression, "a calling." Similarly, a *convocation* is a meeting that is "called together." The word *invocation*, or "calling in," often refers to a prayer that begins a meeting.

WRITE THE CORRECT WORD

Write the correct word in the space next to each definition. Use each word only once.

_____ **1.** a gap; a break

_____ **2.** an impermanence

_____ **3.** unspoiled

_____ **4.** still in existence

_____ **5.** an infinitely long period of time

_____ **6.** an eternity

_____ **7.** one thousand years

_____ **8.** occurring at the same time

_____ **9.** irreversible

_____ **10.** to accustom to something undesirable

COMPLETE THE SENTENCE

Write the letter for the word that best completes each sentence.

_____ **1.** Our decision is _____; we will not change our minds.
  a. irrevocable   **b.** extant   **c.** concomitant   **d.** transient

_____ **2.** The original handwritten scripts of Shakespeare's plays are not _____.
  a. perpetuity   **b.** inured   **c.** extant   **d.** irrevocable

_____ **3.** Emma reflected on the _____ of a human life.
  a. hiatus   **b.** transience   **c.** millennium   **d.** perpetuity

_____ **4.** Did the year 1000 or 1001 mark the beginning of the second _____?
  a. eon   **b.** concomitance   **c.** millennium   **d.** extant

_____ **5.** Margo was thrilled to find an antique desk in _____ condition.
  a. pristine   **b.** extant   **c.** concomitant   **d.** transient

_____ **6.** In football, halftime provides the teams with a brief _____ from game action.
  a. eon   **b.** transience   **c.** hiatus   **d.** extant

_____ **7.** Few things exist in _____; even the sun will eventually exhaust its energy.
  a. eons   **b.** millennium   **c.** transience   **d.** perpetuity

_____ **8.** Dinosaurs became extinct _____ ago, during the Mesozoic Era.
  a. perpetuities   **b.** eons   **c.** concomitance   **d.** extants

_____ **9.** Laboring in mines often _____ workers to dangerous and difficult conditions.
  a. inures   **b.** perpetuates   **c.** eons   **d.** transience

_____ **10.** Sometimes an apparent relationship between two _____ events is a coincidence.
  a. hiatus   **b.** pristine   **c.** extant   **d.** concomitant

Challenge: Whenever _____ fossils and relics are uncovered from an archaeological dig, scientists gain new insights into what life may have been like _____ ago.
_____   **a.** extant…transience   **b.** irrevocable…millennia   **c.** pristine…eons

Two Turntables and a Mike

Hip-hop may be popular worldwide today, but few people know about this beat-driven music's humble beginnings. Rewind back to 1973, New York City, the West Bronx, in a housing project at Sedgwick Avenue. Clive Campbell, a nineteen-year-old from Jamaica, is setting up his turntable so he can DJ his sister's birthday party in the recreation room.

By the time the candles are blown out, Campbell is hooked on being a disc jockey, or DJ. He dubs himself DJ Kool Herc (after Hercules, a nickname he earned for his great skill at sports), and starts to DJ parties. **(1)** The future of American pop music will be *irrevocably* changed.

(2) Employing a trick he learned in Jamaica, Herc started using two turntables *concomitantly* to play the same record. This enabled him to play the best part of the song over and over again without pausing. He just cut back and forth between the two records.

The crowds loved it. Usually, Herc repeated the song portion that is called "the break," or the dance section without vocals. By extending the break, people could dance longer to their favorite beats, and this inspired the creation of new, acrobatic dance moves.

As people spun on their heads, stood on their hands, and swung their feet over the ground, Herc started calling these dancers "b-boys" for "break-boys." The style of dancing that they created was different from any at the time, and eventually it swept across the nation as "break dancing."

One day, Herc asked his friend Coke La Rock to pick up a microphone and "work the crowd." As master of ceremonies, or MC, La Rock did "shout-outs" to name friends he saw "in the house" and rhymed phrases to the break beat. Thus, he became the first hip-hop MC. As more MCs joined the hip-hop bandwagon, their spoken rhymes evolved into rap music.

Other DJs in the Bronx soon caught on. Joseph Sadler, also from Jamaica, started a group of hip-hop DJs known as Grandmaster Flash. He and his crew of five MCs are credited with several hip-hop inventions, including record scratching to create a beat. **(3)** Although scratching started as a mistake, Flash's crew turned it into an art form, which is now so popular that it might last, figuratively speaking, for *perpetuity*.

At first, though, record-company executives did not appreciate hip-hop. **(4)** They were used to *pristine* original songs played by a single band. Hip-hop's gritty vocals and scratched-together record clips were simply too messy. **(5)** Conservative record executives had yet to become *inured* to the strange new sound.

(6) In fact, for a time, it seemed as if hip-hop would be just another *transient* fad. Then, one day, former soul singer Sylvia Robinson heard Henry Jackson rapping behind a pizza counter. She owned a small record company and invited Jackson and two friends to record with her.

Jackson was not a rapper, so he borrowed rhymes from his friend Grandmaster Caz, and cut the record that would make him a star. The trio called themselves The Sugar Hill Gang, and their debut song, "Rappers Delight," was the first hip-hop record to hit the Top 40.

(7) After that, hip-hop grew in popularity without *hiatus*. Band after band signed recording contracts with Robinson, and, eventually, the big record labels also began to sign hip-hop artists.

(8) Hip-hop has survived into the current *millennium*, becoming a $1.5 billion industry. **(9)** Despite many predictions that it would soon go the way of the dinosaurs, it is *extant* and going strong. **(10)** And to think it all started—what seems like *eons* ago—with two turntables, a mike, and a guy named Herc.

Each sentence below refers to a numbered sentence in the passage. Write the letter of the choice that gives the sentence a meaning that is closest to the original sentence.

_____ **1.** The future of American pop music will be _____ changed.
   a. hardly   **b.** irreversibly   **c.** shortly   **d.** noticeably

_____ **2.** Herc started using two turntables _____ to play the same record.
   a. at the same time   **b.** carefully placed   **c.** quickly   **d.** temporarily

_____ 3. Scratching is now so popular that it might last, figuratively speaking, _____.
    a. for a thousand years **b.** forever   **c.** all night   **d.** for a decade

_____ 4. They were used to _____ original songs played by a single band.
    a. gritty   **b.** well-produced   **c.** clean   **d.** harmonious

_____ 5. Record executives had to become _____ the strange new sound.
    a. accustomed to   **b.** forced to hear   **c.** fond of   **d.** introduced to

_____ 6. It seemed as if hip-hop would be just another _____ fad.
    a. enduring   **b.** intriguing   **c.** worldwide   **d.** temporary

_____ 7. After that, hip-hop grew in popularity without _____.
    a. pause   **b.** promotion   **c.** second thought   **d.** following

_____ 8. Hip-hop has survived into the current _____.
    a. era   **b.** 1,000-year period   **c.** category   **d.** audience

_____ 9. Despite many predictions that it would go the way of the dinosaurs, it is _____.
    a. infinite   **b.** trendy   **c.** imagined   **d.** in existence

_____ 10. It all started—what seems like _____ ago—with two turntables, a mike, and a guy named Herc.
    a. 100 years   **b.** 1,000 years   **c.** ages   **d.** a few years

Indicate whether the statements below are TRUE or FALSE according to the passage.

_____ 1. The "break" is the portion of a song that does not have vocals.

_____ 2. Part of the popularity of hip-hop seems to come from its relationship to dance.

_____ 3. "Rappers Delight" was the first rap record to hit the Top 40.

WRITING EXTENDED RESPONSES

Hip-hop emerged within a short period of time, but other cultural trends can take far longer to develop. Think of another trend or process of events. You may choose a personal development, the development of an organization (such as a team), or a societal trend. In a descriptive essay of three or more paragraphs, create a timeline of the development of your trend or event. Use at least three lesson words in your essay and underline them.

WRITE THE DERIVATIVE

Complete the sentence by writing the correct form of the word shown in parentheses. You may not need to change the form that is given.

_____ 1. The closing of the factory _____ changed life for the townspeople. *(irrevocable)*

_____ 2. Moesha proudly kept her antique doll collection in _____ condition. *(pristine)*

_____ **3.** Although most hotels and motels have a _____ clientele, some cater to businesspeople who are living away from home for months or even years at a time. *(transience)*

_____ **4.** In the early 1900s, inventors strove to create manufacturing machines that would run _____, day and night. *(perpetuity)*

_____ **5.** It has been several _____ since the beginning of human settlement in the Americas. *(millennium)*

_____ **6.** During the large paleontology conference, several sessions ran _____. *(concomitant)*

_____ **7.** After a two-month period of _____ themselves to the conditions on the island, the castaways learned to live a pleasant, though hard-working, life. *(inure)*

_____ **8.** Students in the United States enjoy relatively lengthy _____ between the end of one school year and the beginning of another. *(hiatus)*

_____ **9.** There is only one _____ copy of this early postage stamp. *(extant)*

_____ **10.** The sun, the center of our solar system, was formed _____ ago. *(eon)*

FIND THE EXAMPLE

Choose the answer that best describes the action or situation.

_____ **1.** A traditional fairy tale character who lives in happiness for *perpetuity*
a. Big Bad Wolf   **b.** Evil Stepmother   **c.** Ogre   **d.** Prince Charming

_____ **2.** Something that is usually found in *pristine* condition
a. new book   **b.** used car   **c.** rented DVD   **d.** antique furniture

_____ **3.** The number of years it might take to make an *eon*
a. ten   **b.** five hundred   **c.** two billion   **d.** ten thousand

_____ **4.** The number of years it takes to make a *millennium*
a. one hundred   **b.** three hundred   **c.** five million   **d.** one thousand

_____ **5.** Entertainment that is most likely to have *concomitant* shows
a. baseball game   **b.** country fair   **c.** ballet   **d.** dramatic play

_____ **6.** How an *irrevocable* decision can be described
a. not binding   **b.** unchangeable   **c.** illegal   **d.** negotiable

_____ **7.** Something you would most likely NOT have to *inure* yourself to
a. your favorite food   **b.** tedious TV show   **c.** jealous remarks   **d.** least favorite vegetable

_____ **8.** Something you might enjoy a brief *hiatus* from
a. deep sleep   **b.** intense study   **c.** funny TV show   **d.** favorite video game

_____ **9.** Something that is NOT *extant*
a. chats   **b.** bubblegum   **c.** bicycles   **d.** stegosaurus

_____ **10.** Something most people would prefer to have on only a *transient* basis
a. full-time job   **b.** place to live   **c.** house guests   **d.** friendship

Using the Dictionary

Using a Dictionary or Thesaurus to Find Synonyms

Both the dictionary and a thesaurus provide resources to help you find synonyms for words, so that you can precisely express a particular shade of meaning.

Strategies

1. *Use a dictionary.* The dictionary contains synonym paragraphs for many words. These are usually listed under the most frequent of the words covered. For example, *difference, dissimilarly, unlikeness, divergence, variation, distinction,* and *discrepancy* are all listed under *difference.* The entry for each of the other words refers you to this synonym list at *difference.* Subtle differences in the usages of these words are also covered.

   SYNONYMS *difference, dissimilarity, unlikeness, divergence, variation, distinction, discrepancy* These nouns refer to a lack of correspondence or agreement. *Difference* is the most general: *differences in color and size; a difference of opinion. Dissimilarity* is difference between things otherwise alike or comparable: *a dissimilarity between the twins' personalities. Unlikeness* usually implies greater and more obvious difference: *an unlikeness among their teaching styles. Divergence* suggests an increasing difference: *points of divergence between British and American English. Variation* occurs between things of the same class or species; often it refers to modification of something original, prescribed, or typical: *variations in temperature; a variation in shape. Distinction* often means a difference in detail, determinable only by close inspection: *the distinction between "good" and "excellent."* A *discrepancy* is a difference between things that should correspond or match: *a discrepancy between words and actions.*

2. *Use a thesaurus.* A thesaurus is a resource devoted entirely to synonyms. It lists thousands of words and provides synonyms for each. (The word *thesaurus* comes from the Greek word for "treasury.") There are two forms of thesauri. In the first, each word is associated with a number. You begin by looking up the word in the *second* part of the thesaurus, called the Index. It gives a number where the concept is found. If the word has more than one meaning, a few numbers may be listed. You then decide the meaning you want. Finally, you look up the number in the *first* part of the book, called Categories. You can then find several synonyms that reference this meaning.

   In other thesauri, such as *Roget's II The New Thesaurus* (Houghton Mifflin, 2003) the words are simply arranged alphabetically. The entry for *difference* follows.

   difference *noun*
   1. The condition of being unlike or dissimilar : discrepance, discrepancy, disparity, dissimilarity, dissimilitude, distinction, divarication, divergence, unlikeness. *See* SAME. **2.** A marked lack of correspondence or agreement : disagreement, discrepance, discrepancy, disparity, gap, incompatibility, incongruity, inconsistency. *See* AGREE. **3.** The condition or fact of varying : variance, variation. *See* CHANGE, SAME. **4.** A state of disagreement and disharmony : clash, conflict, confrontation, contention, difficulty, disaccord, discord, discordance, dissension, dissent, dissentience, dissidence, dissonance, faction, friction, inharmony, schism, strife, variance, war, warfare. *See* CONFLICT.

   In this entry, the word is given, followed by the part of speech. Then four definitions appear, each definition followed by a colon and several synonyms. Finally references are made to additional entries that may also contain helpful synonyms (*same, agree, change, conflict*).

Practice

Below, you will find a synonym paragraph from a dictionary and a thesaurus entry. Read each item. Decide which of the three synonyms in parentheses fits most appropriately in each sentence, and write it in the space provided. To choose the correct answer, study both entries. You will need to take information from both types of paragraphs. Remember to choose the *best* word from the alternatives.

Dictionary:

Synonyms *grand, magnificent, imposing, stately, majestic, august, grandiose* These adjectives mean strikingly large in size, scope, or extent. Both *grand* and *magnificent* apply to what is physically or aesthetically impressive. *Grand* implies dignity, sweep, or eminence: *a grand hotel lobby with marble floors.* *Magnificent* suggests splendor, sumptuousness, and grandeur: *a magnificent cathedral.* *Imposing* describes what impressed by virtue of its size, bearing, or power: *mountain peaks of imposing height.* *Stately* refers principally to what is dignified and handsome: *a stately oak.* *Majestic* suggests lofty dignity or nobility: *the majestic Alps.* *August* describes what inspires solemn reverence or awe: *the august presence of royalty.* *Grandiose* often suggests pretentiousness, affectation, or pompousness: *grandiose ideas.*

Thesaurus:

grand *adjective*
1. Large and impressive in size, scope, or extent : august, baronial, grandiose, imposing, lordly, magnific, magnificent, majestic, noble, princely, regal, royal, splendid, stately, sublime, superb. *See* BIG, GOOD
2. Exceedingly dignified in form, tone, or style : elevated, eloquent, exalted, high, high-flown, lofty. *See* HIGH, STYLE. **3.** Raised to or occupying a high position or rank : august, elevated, exalted, high ranking, lofty. *See* RISE

1. The ——— speech impressed everyone in the audience. (stately, baronial, eloquent)

   _____

2. The ——— pyramids towered above us. (magnificent, princely, exalted)

   _____

3. Members of the court gathered reverently around the ——— emperor. (elevated, grandiose, august)

   _____

4. His plans were so unrealistically ——— that we knew they would never be realized. (princely, elevated, grandiose)

   _____

5. The ——— entranceway showed that it was an important government building. (high-flown, noble, imposing)

   _____

6. After his knighthood was conferred, he held a(n) ——— position. (exalted, grand, princely)

   _____

7. Our ——— patriarch stood silently watching over us as we greeted each other at the family reunion. (grandiose, high-flown, stately)

   _____

8. The ——— palaces at Versailles suggest the extent of riches and power of Louix XIV. (majestic, eloquent, high)

   _____

Humor

WORD LIST

buffoon	farce	irony	jocular	lampoon
levity	parody	raillery	regale	satirical

"Laughter is the best medicine," as the adage goes. Humor can make us forget our troubles, stop feeling sorry for ourselves, or see problems in a new light. The words in this vocabulary list are all related to different types of humor and comedy.

1. **buffoon** (bə-fōōn´) *noun* from Old Italian *buffare,* "to puff"
   a. A clown or jester, especially one who makes undignified, rude jokes
     • The **buffoon** was the king's favorite companion, until he told a rude joke about the queen and was banished from the castle.
   b. A ridiculous or stupid person
     • My favorite character was the **buffoon** who always tried to fix what wasn't broken and ended up destroying everything he touched.

   buffoonery *noun* At the cast party, several of the actors indulged in **buffoonery,** but no one took offense.

2. **farce** (färs) *noun* from Latin *farcire,* "to stuff"
   a. A comic play using exaggerated characters and improbable plots
     • In a famous **farce** from the silent-film era, the starving Charlie Chaplain sits down to eat his shoe with a knife and a fork.
   b. A mockery; an absurd show or pretense
     • With no agenda or business to discuss, the meeting was a **farce.**

   farcical *adjective* In a **farcical** portrayal of his character, the actor exaggerated his gestures to the point of absurdity.

3. **irony** (ī´rə-nē) *noun* from Greek *eironeia,* "pretended ignorance"
   a. A deliberate use of words to convey the opposite of their literal meaning
     • "Nice job cleaning," Mom said, with **irony,** as she stepped over the clothes that were scattered on the floor of my room.
   b. A contrast between what might be expected and what actually occurs
     • There's **irony** in the fact that the two ambassadors were discussing trade agreements while their countries were preparing for war.

   ironic *adjective* It was **ironic** that Angela snubbed the sibling who cared for her, but adored the one who ignored her.

4. **jocular** (jŏk´yə-lər) *adjective* from Latin *iocus,* "joke"
   Characterized by a joking manner
     • His remark was meant to be **jocular,** but the humor did not come through in the e-mail, and his friends took it seriously.

   jocularity *noun* My grandfather claims that he owes his **jocularity** to his birthday—April 1.

> The terms *irony, parody,* and *satire* are also used to describe the types of literature that employ these techniques for humorous or rhetorical effect.

jocular

5. lampoon (lăm-pōon´)
  a. *noun* A good-natured written piece that pokes fun at something or somebody
   • The students thought the **lampoon** in the school paper, mocking the new dress code, was hilarious, but the principal was not amused.
  b. *noun* A written attack, often using ridicule
   • The editorial was a **lampoon** that portrayed the governor as a lackey doing the bidding of his biggest campaign contributors.
  c. *verb* To satirize or ridicule
   • The comic strip **lampooned** the CEO, showing him with a long Pinocchio-like nose, and stating, "I didn't steal money from the company," while $100 bills were falling from his suit-coat pockets.

A *lampoon* may be good-natured or cruel.

6. levity (lĕv´ĭ-tē) *noun* from Latin *levis,* "light"
  A light and humorous manner or attitude, often when inappropriate
   • The **levity** of her speech at the funeral service shocked many of the mourners.

7. parody (păr´ə-dē) from Greek *para-,* "beside; parallel to" + *oide,* "song; ode"
  a. *noun* A comic imitation that exaggerates characteristics in order to poke fun
   • In a quick succession of one-liners, the standup comic delivered **parodies** of every candidate running for president.
  b. *noun* Something so bad as to seem like intentional mockery
   • The rigged election was a **parody** of democracy.
  c. *verb* To ridicule or make a mockery of
   • The office assistant was mortified to discover that her boss was standing behind her when she **parodied** him.

8. raillery (rā´lə-rē) *noun* from Old French *railler,* "to tease"
  Good-natured teasing or ridicule, particularly in a conversation
   • The star said, "Without my fans, I'd be no better than they are," and her assistant, indulging in **raillery,** answered, "You aren't."

9. regale (rĭ-gāl´) *verb* from Old French *galer,* "to make merry"
  To delight or give pleasure; to entertain
   • Margie **regaled** her guests with funny stories about her vacation.

10. satirical (sə-tĭr´ĭ-kəl) *adjective* from Latin *satur,* "well-fitted"
  Using sarcasm or sharp wit to expose human vice or weakness
   • In the **satirical** movie, the rock star is so obsessed with his wardrobe that he forgets to go on stage.

  satire *noun* In the author's **satire** on the excesses of the wealthy, the host refuses to admit guests who haven't brought expensive gifts.

WORD ENRICHMENT

Lightness and laughter

You have probably heard people refer to being "lighthearted" when they are happy and carefree. Such "weightlessness" is the origin of *levity.* The word *carnival* is also partially based upon the Latin word *levare,* "to raise."

WRITE THE CORRECT WORD

Write the correct word in the space next to each definition. Use each word only once.

_____ **1.** a light, often inappropriate, manner

_____ **2.** to entertain

_____ **3.** good-natured teasing

_____ **4.** sarcastic and witty

_____ **5.** a written piece that pokes fun at something

_____ **6.** a comic play, marked by exaggeration

_____ **7.** in a joking manner

_____ **8.** a rude clown or jester

_____ **9.** a comic imitation

_____ **10.** words that are deliberately used to mean their opposite

COMPLETE THE SENTENCE

Write the letter for the word that best completes each sentence.

_____ **1.** The editorial page often contains _____ cartoons that sarcastically poke fun at politicians.
   a. satirical   **b.** buffoonish   **c.** levity   **d.** farcical

_____ **2.** It's hard to take Hans seriously when he's always speaking in a _____ manner.
   a. lampooning   **b.** levity   **c.** jocular   **d.** regaled

_____ **3.** The _____ in the play was a loud, vulgar character.
   a. satire   **b.** lampoon   **c.** irony   **d.** buffoon

_____ **4.** When one is the object of a _____, the best response is often to laugh.
   a. lampoon   **b.** regale   **c.** jocularity   **d.** buffoon

_____ **5.** Mel Brooks's *Young Frankenstein* was a clever _____ of the classic 1930s film, *Frankenstein*.
   a. irony   **b.** parody   **c.** levity   **d.** buffoon

_____ **6.** "Nice shot," his golf partner said, with _____, as the ball hit a tree.
   a. farce   **b.** parody   **c.** irony   **d.** lampoon

_____ **7.** The explorer _____ the dinner guests with amusing tales of his African safari.
   a. lampooned   **b.** satirized   **c.** parodied   **d.** regaled

_____ **8.** Old friends frequently engage in _____ to show their affection for each other.
   a. parodies   **b.** lampoons   **c.** raillery   **d.** farces

_____ **9.** The woman who was looking for her lost dog did not appreciate her neighbor's _____.
   a. levity   **b.** satirical   **c.** regale   **d.** lampoon

_____ **10.** In the _____, the lead actor sets out to disguise herself as her neighbor's cat.
   a. irony   **b.** farce   **c.** raillery   **d.** regalement

Challenge: Mark Twain is famous for _____ American culture through characters like Aunt Polly, who is a(n) _____ of gullible, superstitious rural Americans at that time.

_____   **a.** regaling…raillery   **b.** lampooning…parody   **c.** satirizing…irony

Jesters and Fools

The importance of humor in people's lives is evidenced by the fact that comedy has existed in virtually every culture. The earliest accounts of the nobility employing professional comedians, called fools or jesters, date back to ancient Egypt and China, nearly 5,000 years ago. With a repertoire that included everything from coarse practical jokes to intellectual witticisms, the jesters continued to be a fashionable form of entertainment in royal courts throughout the Renaissance.

In ancient Greece, most jesters were freelance entertainers who congregated in public places, hoping for invitations to perform, but some were permanently employed by nobles. **(1)** They entertained guests by both *parodying* well-known figures or dancers at the gathering, and making impertinent remarks and observations about the individuals in the audience. **(2)** If their mimicry and *raillery* were appreciated, they were richly rewarded; if the host or the guests took offense, jesters were beaten.

A clever jester was often able to speak truths that other men could not. **(3)** Through a clever use of *irony,* a jester could show a ruler the error or folly of his ways. For example, the first emperor of China, Shi Huang Di, who had ordered the building of the Great Wall of China, decided that he wanted the wall to be painted. Many thousands of workers had already died during the wall's construction, and many more were sure to perish while painting it. The emperor's jester, however, jokingly convinced him to abandon the plan.

Some wealthy and powerful Romans collected slaves whose antics were considered amusing. **(4)** These jesters, or fools, were kept not only to *regale* their owners but also to bring them good luck. **(5)** The Romans believed that the jester, with his abusive *buffoonery,* would absorb the ill luck that might otherwise befall those he abused.

It was during the Middle Ages that the jester got his name. As a court minstrel, he sang of *gestes,* or heroic deeds. **(6)** But as the popularity of minstrels declined, these performers began telling *jocular* stories to amuse their audiences. In Italy, particularly, the role of court jester evolved into a highly skilled profession. Often, the court fool was a man of taste and imagination, talented in music and poetry, as well as in comedy.

During the fifteenth and sixteenth centuries, jesters played a significant role in the social life of most European countries. **(7)** There was a belief that nourishment taken amidst mirth and merriment produced a light and healthy blood; therefore, jesters were given license to *lampoon* the pretensions and self-deceptions of society, as long as their antics kept the dinner guests laughing.

(8) Dressed in a hood crowned by donkey's ears, a patchwork suit, and long, pointy shoes decorated with bells, the jester of the Renaissance era was often called upon to turn the seriousness of life at court into a spontaneous *farce.* The successful ones gained a reputation for humor and won the affections of their masters.

Toward the end of the seventeenth century, however, their popularity waned. **(9)** Serious statesmen began to view their influence as degrading, and some fools were banished for their *levity* and impudent wit. Before long, they disappeared from court and became relegated to the stage. **(10)** Comedians, the modern-day counterparts of court jesters, continue to play an important role in pointing out society's shortcomings and absurdities through *satire.*

Each sentence below refers to a numbered sentence in the passage. Write the letter of the choice that gives the sentence a meaning that is closest to the original sentence.

_____ **1.** They entertained guests by _____ well-known figures or dancers at the gathering.
    a. mocking   **b.** entertaining   **c.** teasing   **d.** humoring

_____ **2.** If their mimicry and _____ were appreciated, they were richly rewarded.
    a. playful teasing   **b.** rude jokes   **c.** sarcasm   **d.** comic imitations

_____ **3.** Through a clever use of _____, a jester could show a ruler the error of his ways.
    a. mockery   **b.** contrast   **c.** sharp wit   **d.** exaggeration

_____ **4.** These jesters, or fools, were kept not only to _____ their owners but also to
bring them good luck.
    a. imitate   **b.** ridicule   **c.** entertain   **d.** tease

_____ **5.** The Romans believed that the jester, with his abusive _____, would absorb the
ill luck that might otherwise befall those he abused.
    a. rude humor   **b.** ridicule   **c.** joking manner   **d.** sarcasm

_____ **6.** These performers began telling _____ stories to amuse their audiences.
    a. joking   **b.** exaggerated   **c.** literal   **d.** mocking

_____ **7.** Jesters were given license to _____ the pretensions and self-deceptions of society.
    a. contrast   **b.** imitate   **c.** characterize   **d.** ridicule

_____ **8.** The jester of the Renaissance era was often called upon to turn the seriousness
of life at court into a spontaneous _____.
    a. rude joke   **b.** comic exaggeration   **c.** written attack   **d.** human vice

_____ **9.** Some fools were banished for their _____ and impudent wit.
    a. imitations   **b.** sharp wit   **c.** inappropriate humor   **d.** rude jokes

_____ **10.** Comedians point out society's shortcomings through _____.
    a. entertainment   **b.** written attacks   **c.** exaggeration   **d.** sarcasm

Indicate whether the statements below are TRUE or FALSE according to the passage.

_____ **1.** Jesters first appeared in Renaissance Europe.

_____ **2.** In the fifteenth and sixteenth centuries, Europeans believed that laughing while
eating could make one healthier.

_____ **3.** Comics continue to play an important role in pointing out society's flaws.

FINISH THE THOUGHT

Complete each sentence so that it shows the meaning of the italicized word.

1. The *jocular* woman said _____

_____

2. It is *ironic* that _____

_____

WRITE THE DERIVATIVE

**Complete the sentence by writing the correct form of the word shown in
parentheses. You may not need to change the form that is given.**

_____ **1.** Slapstick comedy is a genre known for its _____ antics. *(farce)*

_____ **2.** In the United States, it is not against the law to _____ political figures. *(lampoon)*

_____ **3.** For the entire show last night, the well-known comedian _____ the audience with one hysterical line after another. *(regale)*

_____ **4.** The teacher chided the class saying that the seriousness of the issue left no room for _____ . *(levity)*

_____ **5.** In one last _____ statement from his death bed, Oscar Wilde is alleged to have said, "Either that wallpaper goes, or I do." *(irony)*

_____ **6.** In isolated instances, the _____ of college fraternity initiations has resulted in injury, and even death. *(buffoon)*

_____ **7.** Once you knew them, you realized that the couple's constant jabs at each other were simply _____ . *(raillery)*

_____ **8.** Swift's essay "A Modest Proposal" is a _____ on the superior attitudes the English had toward the Irish. *(satirical)*

_____ **9.** The store manager felt it was important for the "Santa Claus" to have a _____ demeanor. *(jocular)*

_____ **10.** Most controversial personalities readily lend themselves to _____ . *(parody)*

FIND THE EXAMPLE

Choose the answer that best describes the action or situation.

_____ **1.** Someone who is most likely to have a *jocular* manner
  a. strict teacher   **b.** drill sergeant   **c.** standup comedian   **d.** homicide detective

_____ **2.** Someone who is LEAST likely to be *lampooned*
  a. politician   **b.** movie celebrity   **c.** corporate bigwig   **d.** volunteer

_____ **3.** What a person who *regales* you would most likely do
  a. tell a funny story   **b.** give an order   **c.** give clear directions   **d.** verbally attack you

_____ **4.** A likely characteristic of the humor of a *buffoon*
  a. seriousness   **b.** crudeness   **c.** subtlety   **d.** gentleness

_____ **5.** Someone who is most likely to use *ironic* language on the job
  a. textbook author   **b.** ER nurse   **c.** opinion columnist   **d.** air-traffic controller

_____ **6.** The setting where you would most likely engage in *raillery*
  a. taking a test   **b.** facing a judge   **c.** studying alone   **d.** eating with friends

_____ **7.** A word that best characterizes a *farce*
  a. sad   **b.** clever   **c.** cruel   **d.** silly

_____ **8.** A place where you would be LEAST likely to find *satirical* writing
  a. TV comedy show   **b.** humor magazine   **c.** romance novel   **d.** comic novel

_____ **9.** A situation where *levity* would likely be most inappropriate
  a. celebrity party   **b.** rescue mission   **c.** family gathering   **d.** retirement dinner

_____ **10.** The word that would best characterize a *parody*
  a. angry   **b.** solemn   **c.** exaggerated   **d.** subtle

Clarity and Vagueness

WORD LIST

adumbrate	arcane	covert	educe	fathom
impenetrable	impervious	limpid	manifest	nebulous

Anyone who has tried to follow directions realizes the value of clarity and the frustration of vagueness. The words in this lesson will help you understand the many factors that go into making communication and situations clear—and unclear.

1. adumbrate (ăd´əm-brāt´) *verb* from Latin *ad-*, "to" + *umbra*, "shadow"

  a. To describe roughly or vaguely; to give a sketchy outline of
   • The general **adumbrated** his attack plans to the press, but refused to reveal details.

  b. To foreshadow; to give an indistinct hint of something that will happen
   • The critic's subdued manner after viewing the play **adumbrated** the negative review he would write.

  c. To overshadow; to shadow or obscure
   • Twilight **adumbrated** the bright colors of the street mural.

2. arcane (är-kān´) *adjective* from Latin *arcanus*, "secret"
Known or understood only by a few; mysterious
   • Only a few scholars understood the film's **arcane** references to ancient Sanskrit.

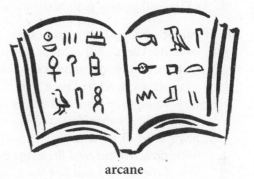

arcane

3. covert (kō´vərt, kō vûrt´) *adjective* from Old French *covrir*, "to cover"
Concealed or hidden; not openly practiced or shown
   • Spies are involved in **covert** activities to discover the secrets of enemy governments.

   covertness *noun* Planning a surprise party requires **covertness.**

4. educe (ĭ-dōōs´) *verb* from Latin *ex-*, "out" + *ducere*, "to lead"

  a. To draw or bring out; elicit
   • Firefighters were able to **educe** from the child that there were more people inside the building.

  b. To assume from evidence or facts; to deduce
   • The police **educed** the robber's identity from fingerprint evidence.

5. fathom (făth´əm) *verb* from Middle English *fathme*, "outstretched arms"
To understand or comprehend
   • Frank could easily **fathom** why his shy brother wouldn't be willing to go to the dance.

   unfathomable *adjective* Difficult or impossible to understand
   • It is **unfathomable** to me that one country would attack another without a good cause.

6. **impenetrable** (ĭm-pĕn´ĭ-trə-bəl) *adjective* from Latin *in-*, "not" + *penetrare*, "deeply"
   a. Impossible to pierce, break through, or enter
      • The football team was confident that its defense was **impenetrable.**
   b. Impossible to understand; incomprehensible
      • The article was filled with so much scientific jargon that most readers found it **impenetrable.**

7. **impervious** (ĭm-pûr´vē-əs) *adjective* from Latin *in-*, "not" + *per-*, "through" + *via*, "road; way"
   Incapable of being affected, harmed, or broken into
      • The supremely confident Miss Parker seemed **impervious** to criticism.

   imperviousness *noun* Built miles below Earth's surface, the shelter's **imperviousness** was never doubted.

8. **limpid** (lĭm´pĭd) *adjective* from Latin *limpidus*, "clear"
   a. Transparent; clear
      • We could see crabs and sea urchins at the bottom of the **limpid** waters.
   b. Calm, untroubled, and serene
      • With her **limpid** expression, the bride seemed relaxed, even though her wedding planner was frantic.
   c. Easily intelligible or understood
      • The book review praised the author's **limpid** prose.

9. **manifest** (măn´ə-fĕst´) from Latin *manifestus*, "obvious"
   a. *adjective* Clearly apparent or obvious
      • Signs of relief were **manifest** on the workers' faces when they heard that the contract had been signed.
   b. *verb* To show or demonstrate plainly; to reveal
      • The audience **manifested** its approval with thunderous applause.
   c. *noun* A list of passengers or cargo on a ship, plane, truck, or train
      • The detective checked the **manifests** of all international flights to see if the suspect had fled the country.

> We often use the verb form of *manifest* with a reflexive, as in "The disease *manifested itself* in a rash."

10. **nebulous** (nĕb´yə-ləs) *adjective* from Latin *nebula*, "cloud"
    a. Cloudy, misty, or hazy
       • Even with the most powerful telescope, the galaxy appeared **nebulous.**
    b. Vague; without defined form or limits
       • The defendant's **nebulous** answers to the prosecutor's questions made the jury suspect that he was hiding some facts.

WORD ENRICHMENT

Fathoming the ocean

The word *fathom* has been part of the English language since the year 800. Originally, the word meant "the length of a man's outstretched arms, or approximately six feet." A *fathom* is now a nautical measure that determines the depth of water by a sounding line. But in a more figurative use, it has come to mean "to get to the bottom of," or, in other words, "to understand."

WRITE THE CORRECT WORD

Write the correct word in the space next to each definition. Use each word only once.

_____ 1. impossible to pierce

_____ 2. to comprehend

_____ 3. to describe vaguely

_____ 4. calm and serene

_____ 5. understood only by a few

_____ 6. hidden or concealed

_____ 7. obvious; apparent

_____ 8. to draw out

_____ 9. cloudy; hazy

_____ 10. incapable of being affected

COMPLETE THE SENTENCE

Write the letter for the word that best completes each sentence.

_____ 1. The armor on the tank was built to be _____ to bullets.
  a. arcane   **b.** impenetrable   **c.** covert   **d.** manifest

_____ 2. Once she cleaned all the dirt from the window, the glass was absolutely _____.
  a. limpid   **b.** impervious   **c.** nebulous   **d.** unfathomable

_____ 3. I can't begin to _____ why we had four fire drills at school today.
  a. adumbrate   **b.** manifest   **c.** fathom   **d.** educe

_____ 4. The trouble _____ itself after the protestors started insulting one another.
  a. fathomed   **b.** adumbrated   **c.** manifested   **d.** coverted

_____ 5. Stu made a(n) _____ comment about an extinct lizard none of us had heard of.
  a. impervious   **b.** limpid   **c.** covert   **d.** arcane

_____ 6. Sheila wanted to know for certain if she was going to get the promotion, but her boss's response was quite _____.
  a. nebulous   **b.** limpid   **c.** educed   **d.** manifest

_____ 7. I've never seen Felipe's father smile; he seems completely _____ to humor.
  a. adumbrated   **b.** impervious   **c.** manifest   **d.** arcane

_____ 8. Maria could not discuss her _____ work for the government, even with her husband.
  a. impenetrable   **b.** unfathomable   **c.** covert   **d.** limpid

_____ 9. Since I sincerely value your opinion, I hope I can _____ a word of advice from you.
  a. educe   **b.** adumbrate   **c.** manifest   **d.** fathom

_____ 10. While the film director _____ a rough outline of how he wanted this scene to be filmed, he didn't give us specific details.
  a. fathomed   **b.** limpid   **c.** manifested   **d.** adumbrated

Challenge: The teacher hoped that her students would use _____ language in their essays, but sadly, she found most of the sentences to be downright _____.
_____   **a.** covert…educed   **b.** limpid…impenetrable   **c.** nebulous…manifest

Oodles of Doodles

It's a dog with a cheeky, irresistible personality, and it's intelligent, playful, and obedient. Is it a Labrador retriever? A poodle? No, it's a Labradoodle!

(1) Poodles, developed as water retrievers, have tight, curly coats that are virtually *impenetrable* to rain and cold weather. They are also famed for intelligence. **(2)** However, this can *manifest* itself in a bit too much independence. **(3)** Poodles that are not properly trained may be temperamental and *impervious* to the commands of their owners.

Labrador retrievers, on the other hand, are noted for friendliness and obedience. This makes them excellent guide and assistance dogs for the physically disabled. However, they are quite social and require a great deal of attention. **(4)** Being left alone often *educes* depression from these sensitive dogs. And, perhaps because labradors shed their coats so freely, humans with allergies can have difficulty with this breed.

How about a dog that combines the best features of both? Voilà! Breeders in Australia developed the Labradoodle after they received a request for a guide dog that would combine gentleness and obedience with reduced allergy triggers. The resulting Labradoodle was highly intelligent and cooperative. **(5)** The friendliness of the retriever seemed to *adumbrate* the willfulness of the poodle. **(6)** Its *limpid* eyes radiated agreeableness, combined with a love of play. Perhaps most important, the poodle heritage made the Labradoodle less prone than the retriever to cause allergic reactions in humans.

Thus, the Labradoodle has become a popular dog, fetching prices up to several thousand dollars. Other poodle combinations have followed, including the Pekepoo (pekingese/poodle), the Goldenpoo (golden retriever/poodle), and the Schnoodle (schnauzer/poodle). Owners attest to the intelligence and friendliness of the dogs and note fewer allergic reactions to them.

Some people also feel that mixed breeds are healthier than purebred dogs, which sometimes are a product of considerable inbreeding. **(7)** Yet, crossing one breed with another gives *nebulous* assurances, at best. If both breeds are prone to skeletal problems, they may have a greater tendency to pass on the trait to offspring. And future generations of mixed breeds may prove less healthy or endowed with desirable traits than the first generation. Additionally, the results of mixed breeding are not always reliable. For example, not all Labradoodles have allergy-reducing properties.

(8) In fact, some breeders of purebred dogs can't *fathom* why mixed breeds have become so popular. They feel that breeders of purebred dogs carefully monitor their parent dogs for personality and physical characteristics. **(9)** They even use such *arcane* technologies as genetic testing. **(10)** These breeders claim that the lack of quality control in mixed breeding invites *covert* activities. For instance, dishonest breeders may misrepresent the quality of mixed-breed dogs they offer.

Breeders of Labradoodles have responded to these challenges by founding the International Labradoodle Association. This society hopes to protect the future of the new dog. Eventually, the Labradoodle may develop into its own breed. Until that time, owners are enjoying dogs that, as one person testified, are so intelligent and obedient that they can respond to commands to turn on lights or remove specific items from a refrigerator!

Each sentence below refers to a numbered sentence in the passage. Write the letter of the choice that gives the sentence a meaning that is closest to the original sentence.

_____ **1.** Poodles have tight coats that are virtually _____ rain and cold weather.
   a. mysterious to   **b.** susceptible to   **c.** hidden from   **d.** unable to be entered by

_____ **2.** However, this can _____ itself in a bit too much independence.
   a. flatter   **b.** conceal   **c.** reveal   **d.** volunteer

_____ **3.** Poodles may be temperamental and _____ the commands of their owners.
   a. unaffected by   **b.** excited about   **c.** insulted by   **d.** eager to please

_____ **4.** Being left alone often _____ depression from these sensitive dogs.
       a. calms   **b.** clouds   **c.** draws out   **d.** hides

_____ **5.** The friendliness of the retriever seemed to _____ the willfulness of the poodle.
       a. draw out   **b.** overshadow   **c.** deplore   **d.** challenge

_____ **6.** Its _____ eyes radiated agreeableness, combined with a love of play.
       a. untroubled   **b.** bored   **c.** diseased   **d.** cloudy

_____ **7.** Yet, crossing one breed with another gives _____ assurances, at best.
       a. partial   **b.** enraged   **c.** obvious   **d.** vague

_____ **8.** Some breeders of purebred dogs can't _____ why mixed breeds have become
so popular.
       a. deny   **b.** comprehend   **c.** predict   **d.** appreciate

_____ **9.** They even use such _____ technologies as genetic testing.
       a. obvious to all   **b.** impractical   **c.** understood by few   **d.** clearly unethical

_____ **10.** These breeders claim that the lack of quality control in mixed breeding invites
_____ activities.
       a. playful   **b.** clearly apparent   **c.** sophisticated   **d.** hidden

Indicate whether the statements below are TRUE or FALSE according to the passage.

_____ **1.** Labrador retrievers are known for being a moody and temperamental breed.

_____ **2.** It is clear that mixed breeds are healthier than pure breeds.

_____ **3.** Not every Labradoodle has allergy-free properties.

WRITING EXTENDED RESPONSES

In this passage you have read about the development of mixed-breed dogs. If you were buying a dog from a breeder (as a pet for yourself or someone else), what background or traits would you look for? In an expository essay, explain what qualities you would look for. Your essay should consider your own personal wishes or the wishes of the person for whom you are buying the dog. Your essay should be three or more paragraphs in length. Use at least three lesson words in your essay and underline them.

WRITE THE DERIVATIVE

Complete the sentence by writing the correct form of the word shown in parentheses. You may not need to change the form that is given.

_____ **1.** The chess master's strategies were _____ to the beginning players. (*fathom*)

_____ **2.** Andrea stays so healthy, it's as though she possesses an _____ to germs. (*impervious*)

_____ **3.** Mozart's music is so _____ elegant that musicians can clearly hear the structure beneath the melodies. *(limpid)*

_____ **4.** We were amazed when Will uttered an _____ quotation. *(arcane)*

_____ **5.** As we walked through the forest, the canopy of thick branches _____ the bright sun shining above. *(adumbrate)*

_____ **6.** When my little sister asked me whether unicorns were real, I deliberately gave her a _____ response. *(nebulous)*

_____ **7.** The difficult times of World War II _____ heroism from innumerable ordinary people. *(educe)*

_____ **8.** The _____ fortress allowed the unit to hold out indefinitely against enemy attacks. *(impenetrable)*

_____ **9.** The nations have refused to trade with one another, a clear sign of how their quarrel is _____ itself. *(manifest)*

_____ **10.** Crimes are usually committed _____. *(covert)*

FIND THE EXAMPLE

Choose the answer that best describes the action or situation.

_____ **1.** An example of a *covert* activity
    a. painting   **b.** spying   **c.** eating   **d.** performing

_____ **2.** The animal most likely to be *impervious* to the attack of a spider
    a. baby robin   **b.** beetle   **c.** eagle   **d.** moth

_____ **3.** What toddlers might do when they want to *manifest* their frustration
    a. hiccup   **b.** fall asleep   **c.** clap their hands   **d.** cry

_____ **4.** A likely way to *adumbrate* an assigned research paper
    a. write a summary   **b.** write the paper   **c.** take notes   **d.** create a title

_____ **5.** An example of a *nebulous* remark
    a. It's my fault.   **b.** I totally agree.   **c.** This is awful!   **d.** Well, it's hard to say.

_____ **6.** The liquid most likely to be *limpid*
    a. oil   **b.** water   **c.** orange juice   **d.** milk

_____ **7.** Of the following, the most *arcane* lecture topic
    a. quantum theory   **b.** English grammar   **c.** history of jazz   **d.** pet care

_____ **8.** An *unfathomable* action by someone who has just won a prestigious award
    a. throwing a party   **b.** calling friends   **c.** jumping for joy   **d.** keeping it a secret

_____ **9.** An *impenetrable* object
    a. a leaf   **b.** bulletproof vest   **c.** heavy sweater   **d.** canvas tent

_____ **10.** Someone whose job is to *educe* the facts of a case
    a. judges   **b.** court clerks   **c.** detectives   **d.** witnesses

Relationships

WORD LIST

adjunct	amalgamate	compatriot	conclave	contiguous
diffuse	diverge	parity	synergy	transcend

The words in this lesson describe the connections, correlations, and interactions among the inhabitants and things in the world around us.

1. **adjunct** (ăj´ŭngkt´) from Latin *ad-*, "to" + *iungere*, "to join"
   a. *noun* Something or someone attached to another in a dependent or subordinate position
   • A thesaurus is a useful **adjunct** to the dictionary.
   b. *adjective* Added or connected in a subordinate, temporary, or auxiliary position
   • The **adjunct** professor of history had to share a cramped office with two other faculty members.

2. **amalgamate** (ə-măl´gə-māt´) *verb* from Greek *malagma*, "softening substance"
   To combine into a unified or an integrated whole; to unite
   • Three local businesses **amalgamated** to form a national corporation.

   amalgam or **amalgamation** *noun* The course was an **amalgam** of lectures on different subjects.

> In chemistry, to *amalgamate* means "to mix or alloy a metal with mercury."

3. **compatriot** (kəm-pā´trē-ət) *noun* from Latin *com-*, "together; with" + Late Latin *patriota*, "countryman"
   a. A person from one's own country
   • The Rosenfelds lived in Mexico City, surrounded by a small group of their **compatriots** from Hungary.
   b. A colleague
   • The coach and his **compatriots** held a meeting to iron out some problems in the league.

4. **conclave** (kŏn´klāv´) *noun* from Latin *com-*, "together; with" + *clavis*, "key"
   a. A secret or confidential meeting
   • One of the members leaked news of the **conclave** to the press.
   b. A meeting of family members or associates
   • The school faculty held a **conclave** to discuss making the curriculum more cohesive from grade to grade.

compatriots

5. **contiguous** (kən-tĭg´yoō-əs) *adjective* from Latin *com-*, "together" + *tangere*, "to touch"
   a. Sharing an edge or boundary; neighboring; adjacent
   • Unfortunately, the **contiguous** countries of Azerbaijan and Armenia have been involved in many territorial disputes.
   b. Connecting in time without a break; uninterrupted
   • President Franklin Delano Roosevelt served four **contiguous** terms in office.

6. **diffuse** from Latin *dis-*, "apart" + *fundere*, "to pour"
   a. *adjective* (dǐ-fyoos´) Widely spread or scattered; not concentrated
   • The theater's **diffuse** lighting created a warm atmosphere.
   b. *adjective* (dǐ-fyoos´) Wordy or unclear
   • I had a hard time getting used to the novelist's **diffuse** writing style.
   c. *verb* (dǐ-fyooz´) To pour out and cause to spread freely; to spread; to scatter
   • The Internet is a valuable tool for **diffusing** information.

   diffusion *noun* **Diffusion** is what causes an odor to spread in still air.

Note the different pronunciations of *diffuse* depending on its part of speech.

7. **diverge** (dǐ-vûrj´) *verb* from Latin *dis-*, "apart" + *vergere*, "to bend"
   a. To extend in different directions from a common point; to branch out
   • Robert Frost's poem "The Road Not Taken" muses on two paths that **diverge** in the woods.
   b. To differ in opinion or in manner
   • The two sisters **diverge** when it comes to politics.
   c. To depart from a set course or norm; to deviate
   • The company **diverged** from manufacturing into retail.

   divergent *adjective* The students had **divergent** opinions about the effectiveness of the new dress code.

8. **parity** (pǎr´ǐ-tē) *noun* from Late Latin *par*, "equal"
   Equality in amount, status, or value; functional equivalence
   • During much of 2003, the dollar maintained **parity** with the euro.

9. **synergy** (sǐn´ər-jē) *noun* from Greek *sunergos*, "working together"
   The interaction or cooperation of agents or forces so that their combined effect is greater than the sum of their individual effects
   • The **synergy** of a team of average players who know each other well often beats a team of individual superstars.

   synergetic *adjective* The Chicago mayor's trip to London proved to be a critical link in establishing the two cities' **synergetic** relationship.

10. **transcend** (trǎn-sěnd´) *verb* from Latin *trans-*, "across; beyond" + *scandere*, "to climb"
    a. To pass beyond the limits of; to be greater than; to surpass
    • Do family loyalties always **transcend** loyalties to friends?
    b. To exist above and independent of
    • Michael Jordon could jump so high and maneuver through the air so freely that at times he seemed to **transcend** gravity.

    transcendent *adjective* Latasha described the musical performance as "so beautiful and **transcendent** that I felt as though I had been transported into another world. "

WRITE THE CORRECT WORD

Write the correct word in the space next to each definition. Use each word only once.

_____ **1.** to differ

_____ **2.** equality

_____ **3.** connected

_____ **4.** a colleague

_____ **5.** the positive effect of two merged forces

_____ **6.** to combine

_____ **7.** a secret meeting

_____ **8.** to spread or scatter

_____ **9.** to surpass

_____ **10.** auxiliary; subordinate

COMPLETE THE SENTENCE

Write the letter for the word that best completes each sentence.

_____ **1.** Florida and Georgia are _____ states.
   a. adjunct   **b.** contiguous   **c.** amalgamated   **d.** diffuse

_____ **2.** The council held a _____ prior to the press conference.
   a. conclave   **b.** parity   **c.** compatriot   **d.** synergy

_____ **3.** Gwen _____ a physical handicap to become a successful athlete.
   a. diverged   **b.** amalgamated   **c.** transcended   **d.** diffused

_____ **4.** Lu demanded salary _____, insisting on the right to equal pay for equal work.
   a. synergy   **b.** compatriot   **c.** conclave   **d.** parity

_____ **5.** The special _____ that happens in great bands is rarely captured when members pursue solo careers.
   a. adjunct   **b.** parity   **c.** synergy   **d.** contiguous

_____ **6.** Oxygen is _____ through the body by means of the circulatory system.
   a. diffused   **b.** diverged   **c.** transcended   **d.** amalgamated

_____ **7.** Many foreign immigrants seek out _____ in their new country.
   a. conclaves   **b.** compatriots   **c.** amalgamates   **d.** adjuncts

_____ **8.** Strangely, the three eyewitness accounts of the incident _____ dramatically.
   a. transcended   **b.** amalgamated   **c.** diverged   **d.** diffused

_____ **9.** The two small companies _____, hoping to increase their resources.
   a. diffused   **b.** diverged   **c.** transcended   **d.** amalgamated

_____ **10.** In addition to the downtown office, several _____ offices throughout the city were convenient for people living in other neighborhoods.
   a. amalgamate   **b.** adjunct   **c.** conclave   **d.** parity

Challenge: A(n) _____ of many nations working in partnership would promote the _____ that usually results from sharing resources.

_____   **a.** adjunct…parity   **b.** conclave…diffusion   **c.** amalgamation…synergy

Wayne Lawrence: Music, Business, Family

A satisfying hobby, an interesting career, and a supportive family give Wayne Lawrence a busy and fulfilling life. The son of Jamaican immigrants who wanted him to have many talents, Lawrence had a childhood that revolved around music. He studied guitar and piano, and he joined a band as a teenager. He also showed an early knack for planning and organizing. For his band's shows, he set up club dates, rented space, distributed flyers, and arranged transportation.

His first job after college was in the music industry. As a publicity assistant for a small record label that featured hip-hop, reggae, funk, soul, and jazz artists, he met many famous musicians.

Later, however, Lawrence pursued a career that demanded he use more of his business skills. For the past ten years, Lawrence has worked in the "nerve center" of a large, international company—in its information technology (IT) division. Lawrence is part of a group that helps integrate and plan every aspect of the company's operations. Their efforts help the firm achieve billions of dollars of sales. A college degree in marketing and advertising and a master's degree in global technology prepared Lawrence for his important role.

Lawrence deals with issues ranging from where to build manufacturing plants to the selling of goods. **(1)** Since the company owns and sells more than 100 product brands, a lack of coordination could result in a *diffusion* of effort. Two of the company's products could even end up competing with each other. **(2)** Lawrence and his *compatriots*

work to assure that all areas of the company function efficiently. **(3)** Working within what's known as the Americas branch, he handles business in the United States and its *contiguous* countries, Canada and Mexico.

Interacting smoothly with others is important in Lawrence's job, for group brainstorming and teamwork are essential to decision making and implementation. **(4)** A proposal or plan of action is usually the result of many *conclaves*. **(5)** Lawrence's nine team members tend to have *parity* in expertise, which often results in agreement. **(6)** However, when they work with teams from the finance or sales divisions, they often deal with *divergent* opinions and perspectives. **(7)** In addition, they may call in *adjuncts* who have special expertise. Of course, sometimes there is friction. But if differing opinions are expected and respected, wide input often results in better decisions. **(8)** For example, if Lawrence's company wants to achieve *synergy* among its many branches, then teams might propose that one of the company's product divisions supply its raw materials to another. **(9)** Or separate advertising campaigns might be *amalgamated* into one.

Speaking of changes, Lawrence originally started out in the finance division. **(10)** But, eventually, he wanted a change and soon had to *transcend* an often-difficult adjustment to IT. Clearly, Lawrence has proved himself capable: The company trusts him enough to have him leading his own team.

Like most jobs, Lawrence's poses challenges. His travels, which consume about ten days per month, take him away from his family. But when he comes back, his wife and two young children enjoy hearing him strum his guitar.

Each sentence below refers to a numbered sentence in the passage. Write the letter of the choice that gives the sentence a meaning that is closest to the original sentence.

_____ **1.** A lack of coordination could result in a(n) _____ of effort.
    a. intense combination   **b.** important equality   **c.** softened standard   **d.** inefficient scattering

_____ **2.** Lawrence and his _____ work to assure that all areas of the company function efficiently.
    a. colleagues   **b.** staff   **c.** competitors   **d.** friends

_____ **3.** He handles business in the United States and its _____ countries, Canada and Mexico.
    a. amicable   **b.** combined   **c.** secretive   **d.** adjacent

_____ **4.** A proposal is usually the result of many _____.
      a. arguments   **b.** meetings   **c.** combinations   **d.** cryptic documents

_____ **5.** Lawrence's nine team members tend to have _____ in expertise.
      a. lacks   **b.** equality   **c.** combinations   **d.** smatterings

_____ **6.** However, when they work with teams from the finance or sales divisions, they often deal with _____ opinions.
      a. differing   **b.** ill-informed   **c.** management   **d.** subordinate

_____ **7.** In addition, they may call in _____ who have special expertise.
      a. equal colleagues   **b.** superior workers   **c.** expert scientists   **d.** auxiliary staff

_____ **8.** Lawrence's company wants to achieve _____ among its many branches.
      a. several goals   **b.** a combined effect   **c.** wide input   **d.** lack of competition

_____ **9.** Or separate advertising campaigns might be _____ into one.
      a. spread   **b.** surpassed   **c.** combined   **d.** devised

_____ **10.** He wanted a change and had to _____ the often-difficult adjustment to IT.
      a. wipe out   **b.** rise above   **c.** combine   **d.** ignore

Indicate whether the statements below are TRUE or FALSE according to the passage.

_____ **1.** Wayne Lawrence has clearly always known what career he wanted to pursue.

_____ **2.** Lawrence's team deals with many different aspects of the company.

_____ **3.** Lawrence has been in the IT section of the company since he started working there.

FINISH THE THOUGHT

Complete each sentence so that it shows the meaning of the italicized word.

1. In order to *transcend* _____

_____

2. Most of the doctor's *compatriots* _____

_____

WRITE THE DERIVATIVE

Complete the sentence by writing the correct form of the word shown in parentheses. You may not need to change the form that is given.

_____ **1.** A society that cannot tolerate _____ opinions is not truly democratic. *(diverge)*

_____ **2.** Critics praised the soprano's _____ aria. *(transcend)*

3. "World Music" is a term that describes an _____ of popular songs from many diverse nations. (*amalgamate*)

4. When the representatives discovered that a select few had held a _____ to decide the issue, the others were furious. (*conclave*)

5. The suspect and his two _____ entered the court in handcuffs. (*compatriot*)

6. Athletes in all-star games rarely display the _____ teamwork one might expect from those who play together all season. (*synergy*)

7. Because she was doing an excellent job, Laska served as chair of the committee for five _____ terms. (*contiguous*)

8. Exercise helps with the _____ of tension and stress. (*diffuse*)

9. Area health clinics serve as _____ to the region's main hospital. (*adjunct*)

10. There is a lack of _____ in taxing policies, as I pay twice the rate that my neighbors do. (*parity*)

FIND THE EXAMPLE

Choose the answer that best describes the action or situation.

_____ **1.** One example of an *amalgam*
    a. sugar   **b.** glass   **c.** fresh water   **d.** cookie dough

_____ **2.** Two U.S. states that are *contiguous*
    a. Texas, Utah   **b.** Illinois, Florida   **c.** Maine, Nevada   **d.** New York, Vermont

_____ **3.** A group of people who by law must hold a *conclave*
    a. a jury   **b.** labor union   **c.** sales force   **d.** school committee

_____ **4.** How your parents might feel if you *transcend* difficulties
    a. worried   **b.** proud   **c.** confused   **d.** embarrassed

_____ **5.** Something *compatriots* are most likely to share
    a. height   **b.** a wallet   **c.** language   **d.** pets

_____ **6.** Things that *diverge*
    a. river branches   **b.** building bricks   **c.** flagpoles   **d.** marble pillars

_____ **7.** Something that would most likely NOT be considered an *adjunct*
    a. personal assistant   **b.** field office   **c.** student teacher   **d.** main headquarters

_____ **8.** Something that always lacks *synergy*
    a. soloist   **b.** chorus   **c.** orchestra   **d.** string quartet

_____ **9.** A way to *diffuse* tension in a meeting
    a. bite your nails   **b.** give dirty looks   **c.** yell in anger   **d.** tell a joke

_____ **10.** A government system based on *parity*
    a. monarchy   **b.** tyranny   **c.** democracy   **d.** oligarchy

Reading and Reasoning

Three Types of Context Clues

The words, sentences, or paragraphs surrounding an unfamiliar word often provide clues to the meaning of that word. These clues are called *context clues.*

Strategies

Three types of context clues are common: *definition clues, opposite clues,* and *substitution clues.*

1. *Look for definition clues.* An author might actually define the word in the text.
   - Words or phrases set off by commas, parentheses, or dashes:
     > His *bombastic*—overblown and exaggerated—speech was out of place in the small group setting.
     > (A *bombastic* speech is overblown and exaggerated.)
     > This construction is often called an *appositive.*
   - The use of *or* or *and:*
     > A *protracted,* or long and drawn out, meeting can become boring.
     > (*Protracted* is long and drawn out.)
   - Defining by a list of examples:
     > The subphylum of *vertebrates* includes mammals, amphibians, reptiles, and bony fish but not, for example, amoebas.
     > (Since these are animals with backbones, *vertebrates* refers to animals with backbones.)
   - Definition by inclusion in a list of examples:
     > One part of the collection included a flute, harp, violin, and *balalaika.*
     > (Since the other items refer to musical instruments, it is reasonable to assume that a *balalaika* does, too. In fact, it is a stringed instrument.)

2. *Look for opposite clues.* Sometimes an author defines a word by giving its opposite.
   - The use of *not* or *no:*
     > With no thought of helping with the cleaning, Silvia *indolently* continued to lounge on the sofa.
     > (*Indolently* means in a lazy way.)
   - Words or prefixes signaling opposites, such as *but, nevertheless, despite, rather than, unless, despite, although, in spite of, regardless, in-, non-,* and *un-:*
     > One man became nervous, but the other maintained his *aplomb.*
     > (*Aplomb* means self confidence, poise.)
   - Words with negative senses, like *barely, only, never, hardly, nothing, merely:*
     > Only one performance was exciting, the others were *insipid.*
     > (*Insipid* means dull, lacking excitement.)
     > There was hardly any food, but there was a *superfluity* of beverages.
     > (*Superfluity* means oversupply.)

3. *Try substituting simpler words.* The meanings of some unfamiliar words can be found by substituting simpler words to see if they make sense.
   > With bad weather threatening crops, and the winter coming, the people in the village were carefully *husbanding* their food.
   > (The word *saving* makes sense. *Husbanding* means saving, conserving.)

Practice

Read each sentence to determine the meaning of the italicized word. Write the meaning you infer from the context clues. Then look up the word in the dictionary and write the most suitable formal definition.

1. The *impecunious* man was in love, but lacked any means of supporting a wife or family.

   My definition _____

   Dictionary definition _____

2. Although one brother was wise, humble, and prudent, the other was *fatuous*.

   My definition _____

   Dictionary definition _____

3. His nervous manner, downcast expression, and constant frown were symptoms of *angst*.

   My definition _____

   Dictionary definition _____

4. The man's *cupidity* never seemed to be satisfied; he was always looking for ways to increase his wealth.

   My definition _____

   Dictionary definition _____

5. Lard, vegetable oil, and certain moisturizers are *unctuous* substances.

   My definition _____

   Dictionary definition _____

6. With regard to their home countries, some people are indifferent, some show moderate loyalty, and some are *fervid* patriots.

   My definition _____

   Dictionary definition _____

7. One author wrote as if to obscure her meaning, but the other expressed even the most difficult subjects in *pellucid* prose.

   My definition _____

   Dictionary definition _____

8. Though the actor felt he was subjected to the most vicious *calumny*, he did not sue the person who had deliberately tried to damage his reputation.

   My definition _____

   Dictionary definition _____

Persuasion and Argument

WORD LIST

| axiomatic | definitive | dialectic | empirical | presuppose |
| rationalize | rebuttal | repudiate | tenuous | verifiable |

Lawyers, salespeople, and researchers use persuasion and argument in a professional capacity. But, of course, people also employ persuasion every day to support opinions or to try to get what they want. The words in this lesson relate to the many ways to make requests, support opinions, and clarify points of view.

1. **axiomatic** (ăk´sē-ə-măt´ĭk) *adjective* from Greek *axios,* "worthy"
   Self-evident; based on a universally accepted principle or rule
   • It is an **axiomatic** truth that people don't live forever.

   axiom *noun* The professor said, "The fact that ecosystems become more diverse as they mature is one of the **axioms** of modern ecology."

2. **definitive** (dĭ-fĭn´ĭ-tĭv) *adjective* from Latin *definire,* "to limit; to determine"
   a. Precisely described, defined, or characterized; explicit
   • **Definitive** descriptions of the human digestion system can be found in medical textbooks.
   b. Conclusive; decisive; providing a final settlement
   • The U.S. Supreme Court's decision is the **definitive** ruling on the subject.
   c. Authoritative and complete
   • Winston Churchill wrote a **definitive** biography of his ancestor John Churchill, a British general and the first Duke of Marlborough.

3. **dialectic** (dī´ə-lĕk´tĭk) *noun* from Greek *dialektos,* "speech; conversation"
   The practice of arriving at the truth by the exchange of opposing logical arguments
   • A debate is a form of **dialectic** that sharpens reasoning power and verbal skills.

   dialectical *adjective* One advantage of **dialectical** methods of searching for truth is that there are at least two minds at work.

   > *Dialectical* processes are central to certain methods in philosophy, including the Socratic method.

4. **empirical** (ĕm-pîr´ĭ-kəl) *adjective* from Greek *em-,* "in" + *peira,* "try; attempt"
   Relying on or derived from observation or experiment
   • The physicist gathered **empirical** data to support his hypothesis.

looking for empirical evidence

5. **presuppose** (prē´sə-pōz´) *verb* from Latin *pre-*, "in advance" + *supponere*, "to put under"
   a. To believe or assume in advance; to presume; to take for granted
      • **Presupposing** he would get permission to stay out late, Ted accepted the party invitation.
   b. To require or involve necessarily as a preexisting condition
      • Obviously, all theories about the origin of the universe **presuppose** the existence of a universe.

   presupposition *noun* Our **presuppositions** about artists requiring quiet work environments were shattered when we walked into the noisy, busy studio.

6. **rationalize** (răsh´ə-nə-līz´) *verb* from Latin *ration*, "reason"
   a. To devise self-satisfying but incorrect reasons for behavior
      • Sam **rationalized** his desire to avoid studying by telling himself that preparation wouldn't improve his test results.
   b. To make rational or to interpret from a logical, reasonable standpoint
      • The astronomer spent all night trying to **rationalize** the new data about the Andromeda galaxy.

   rationalization *noun* "I just can't do this" is often a **rationalization** for giving up.

   > Do not confuse *rationalization* with *rationale*, which means "the main reason or basis for something."

7. **rebuttal** (rĭ-bŭt´l) *noun* from Old French *re-*, "back" + *bouter*, "to push"
   Opposing evidence or arguments or the presentation of those arguments; a refutation
      • In her **rebuttal,** the mayor countered the assemblyman's objections to her new tax proposal.

   rebut *verb* In a press conference, the CEO **rebutted** the accusations.

8. **repudiate** (rĭ-pyōo´dē-āt´) *verb* from Latin *repudium*, "divorce"
   To reject the truth, the authority, or the validity of
      • The group **repudiated** the accusation that they had supported unfair labor restrictions.

   repudiation *noun* We were shocked by Roberto's sudden **repudiation** of his former beliefs.

9. **tenuous** (tĕn´yōo-əs) *adjective* from Latin *tenuis*, "thin"
   Having little strength or substance; flimsy
      • Your argument that people should never be compelled to obey laws is **tenuous** at best.

   > *Tenuous* also means "long and thin; slender," or "having a thin consistency; dilute."

10. **verifiable** (vĕr´ə-fī´ə-bəl) *adjective* from Latin *verus*, "true"
    Able to be proved true by presentation of evidence or testimony
       • Dr. Hong's detailed records made the results of his experiment easily **verifiable.**

    verification *noun* In accordance with store policy, his receipt was **verification** of his purchase.

    verify *verb* Please submit a copy of your transcript to **verify** that you graduated from college.

WRITE THE CORRECT WORD

Write the correct word in the space next to each definition. Use each word only once.

_____ **1.** conclusive; decisive

_____ **2.** self-evident

_____ **3.** flimsy; weak

_____ **4.** to interpret from a logical standpoint

_____ **5.** based on observation or experiment

_____ **6.** able to be proved

_____ **7.** a refutation

_____ **8.** to presume

_____ **9.** to reject the validity of

_____ **10.** the exchange of logical arguments to find the truth

COMPLETE THE SENTENCE

Write the letter for the word that best completes each sentence.

_____ **1.** To most endurance athletes, the phrase "no pain, no gain" is _____.
  a. dialectical   **b.** rationalized   **c.** axiomatic   **d.** rebutted

_____ **2.** _____ that she'd be able to leave work early, Jocelyn made a plan to visit her aunt.
  a. Presupposing   **b.** Rebutting   **c.** Repudiating   **d.** Rationalizing

_____ **3.** In his _____, Mr. Stegall pointed out the flaws in logic in his opponent's claim.
  a. empiricism   **b.** axiom   **c.** rebuttal   **d.** rationalization

_____ **4.** Charlotte thinks that she has the _____ answers to all the tough philosophical questions.
  a. tenuous   **b.** repudiated   **c.** dialectical   **d.** definitive

_____ **5.** The defense attorney brought in witnesses to _____ the testimony that had incriminated her client.
  a. verify   **b.** repudiate   **c.** rationalize   **d.** presuppose

_____ **6.** The refinement of many machines has been the result of _____ observation.
  a. axiomatic   **b.** tenuous   **c.** dialectic   **d.** empirical

_____ **7.** His _____ theories could not be proven.
  a. empirical   **b.** tenuous   **c.** definitive   **d.** verifiable

_____ **8.** If you want to learn from a(n) _____, you can't take the "arguments" personally.
  a. presupposition   **b.** axiom   **c.** dialectic   **d.** rationalization

_____ **9.** How can a person with so much to do _____ watching so much television?
  a. rationalize   **b.** presuppose   **c.** rebut   **d.** verify

_____ **10.** We hope that the stories presented on the news come from _____ sources.
  a. axiomatic   **b.** rationalized   **c.** rebutted   **d.** verifiable

Challenge: Frankie's rationalizations for buying the new car were _____, especially since she'd made the decision based on a groundless _____ that she'd get a raise.

_____   **a.** verifiable…dialectic   **b.** definitive…axiom   **c.** tenuous…presupposition

Jailed Journalists

In some countries, journalists can be sent to jail for publishing material that the government does not agree with, or for spreading information that the government does not want people to know. In fact, in 2003, more than 700 journalists around the world were imprisoned for various lengths of time because of what they wrote.

But in the United States, where freedom of the press is a basic, Constitutional right, can journalists be jailed? The answer is "no and yes." No, not for the content of their stories—but yes, possibly, if they refuse to reveal the identity of a source who is accused of criminal activity.

(1) Many people believe that the First Amendment, which guarantees freedom of the press, ensures that the identities of news sources may be kept secret—even if the sources committed a crime or can *verify* details of an illegal activity. In fact, most states have laws protecting the right of journalists to keep their sources secret under any circumstances.

(2) Journalists feel that the need to protect sources of information is *axiomatic*. Inside tips have helped reporters break news stories on important issues such as dangerous industrial practices, the Watergate scandal, and police corruption. **(3)** Often, for inside sources to feel safe enough to talk to reporters, the sources must be able to *presuppose* that their identities will remain secret. Journalists say that this is crucial for their profession and for society.

(4) Others *rebut* this claim, saying that upholding the rule of law is more important. **(5)** They would also argue that there is no *empirical* evidence that revealing sources harms the freedom of the press. **(6)** They *repudiate* the journalists' view, saying it is wrong for journalists to withhold information about crimes.

One example of how these issues play out is the case of Vanessa Leggett, a writer who was working on a book about a high-profile murder. Prosecutors in the case wanted her notes to help with their investigation.

(7) But Leggett could not *rationalize* revealing her sources, even if the alternative was a jail sentence. After all, for journalists and writers, a promise to keep a source anonymous is sacred. In 2002, after the case was brought to court, Leggett was ordered to serve a 168-day prison sentence for refusing to turn over her notes to the grand jury.

The lawyers and journalists who sided with Leggett argued that even though some sources may deserve punishment, the requirement to reveal sources would probably scare away even the ones who don't deserve punishment. Thus, many people say, all sources must be protected. **(8)** Otherwise, the future of journalism would be uncertain, and the democratic process, which relies on a well-informed public, might prove *tenuous*.

(9) The U.S. government, however, provides no *definitive* guarantee of the right of journalists to protect their sources. Because some sources may have committed crimes, reporters can face jail or fines for not revealing the identities of their sources to a federal judge.

The argument has even reached the U.S. Senate. As of this writing, a Republican and a Democrat have joined efforts to sponsor a bill that guarantees journalists the right to protect sources in federal court. **(10)** The *dialectic* that will follow, as Congress debates this proposal, will likely be heated. Both sides feel that matters of important principle are at stake.

Each sentence below refers to a numbered sentence in the passage. Write the letter of the choice that gives the sentence a meaning that is closest to the original sentence.

_____ **1.** Many people believe that journalists shouldn't reveal sources, even if they can _____ details of an illegal activity.

    a. assume   **b.** negate   **c.** debate   **d.** prove

_____ **2.** Journalists feel that the need to protect sources of information is _____.

    a. self-evident   **b.** self-defeating   **c.** self-satisfying   **d.** self-sufficient

_____ **3.** Sources must be able to _____ that their identities will remain secret.

    a. presume   **b.** define   **c.** disprove   **d.** theorize

_____ **4.** Others _____ this claim, saying that upholding the rule of law is more important.
   a. prove   **b.** assume   **c.** refute   **d.** explain

_____ **5.** They would argue that there is no _____ evidence that revealing sources harms the freedom of the press.
   a. flimsy   **b.** theoretical   **c.** contradictory   **d.** observable

_____ **6.** They _____ the journalists' view.
   a. define   **b.** prove   **c.** reject   **d.** excuse

_____ **7.** Leggett could not _____ revealing her sources.
   a. be weak about   **b.** justify to herself   **c.** go to jail for   **d.** require beforehand

_____ **8.** The democratic process would become _____.
   a. provable   **b.** weak   **c.** negated   **d.** conclusive

_____ **9.** The U.S. government provides no _____ guarantee of the right of journalists to protect their sources.
   a. explicit   **b.** flimsy   **c.** justified   **d.** observable

_____ **10.** The _____ that will follow will likely be heated.
   a. assumption   **b.** truth   **c.** law   **d.** debate

Indicate whether the statements below are TRUE or FALSE according to the passage.

_____ **1.** Vanessa Leggett was investigating a case of treason.

_____ **2.** Journalists have gone to jail for refusing to identify their sources.

_____ **3.** Sources who are involved in crimes are always protected from prosecution.

WRITING EXTENDED RESPONSES

What do you think about journalists protecting the identities of their sources? Does keeping them secret do more good than harm, or vice versa? In a persuasive essay with a minimum of three paragraphs, state your point of view and support it with at least two reasons or arguments. Be sure to address and refute potential opposing arguments. Use at least three lesson words in your essay and underline them.

WRITE THE DERIVATIVE

Complete the sentence by writing the correct form of the word shown in parentheses. You may not need to change the form that is given.

_____ **1.** _____ could be a good skill to have if you are planning to do something unethical. *(rationalize)*

_____ **2.** Because of her _____ about which character in the mystery novel was the culprit, Carlotta misinterpreted several key scenes. *(presuppose)*

3. After much pressure, the board of directors _____ agreed to oust the inept CEO. *(definitive)*

4. Geometry involves solving problems based on certain _____. *(axiomatic)*

5. If no _____ evidence for a theory has been discovered yet, does that mean the theory is wrong? *(empirical)*

6. The customer service representative asked me for my date of birth and my mother's maiden name in order to _____ my identity. *(verifiable)*

7. The stubborn man desperately clung to his _____ argument, just as a climber would cling to a fraying rope. *(tenuous)*

8. The Declaration of Independence was a _____ of Great Britain's control over the American colonies. *(repudiate)*

9. She began _____ her friend's argument with the simple phrase, "That would make sense, except that it's untrue." *(rebuttal)*

10. The philosophy students studied the _____ of Socrates and Plato. *(dialectic)*

FIND THE EXAMPLE

Choose the answer that best describes the action or situation.

1. The source of a *definitive* ruling on a lawsuit
  a. bailiff   **b.** defendant   **c.** judge   **d.** claimant

2. A discipline based on *empirical* data
  a. astrology   **b.** chemistry   **c.** philosophy   **d.** theater

3. Something modeled around *dialectics*
  a. a battle   **b.** a soccer game   **c.** a debate   **d.** a painful emotion

4. Something you would most likely *presuppose* about a veterinarian
  a. owns many animals   **b.** is a vegetarian   **c.** will save your pet   **d.** has a degree

5. Something you'd be most likely to *rationalize*
  a. buying a CD   **b.** doing homework   **c.** passing a test   **d.** cleaning the kitchen

6. Something *verifiable*
  a. meaning of life   **b.** truth of an opinion   **c.** size of Ohio   **d.** best ice-cream flavor

7. A word that describes a person with a *tenuous* grasp of a situation
  a. informed   **b.** authoritative   **c.** uninformed   **d.** knowledgeable

8. The most likely beginning of a *rebuttal*
  a. Who are you?   **b.** Hello!   **c.** I agree totally.   **d.** That's all wrong.

9. Statement most people consider *axiomatic*
  a. Music is bad.   **b.** Blue is best.   **c.** Pollution is fine.   **d.** People deserve respect.

10. How you might *repudiate* a claim
  a. explain it in detail   **b.** repeat it twice   **c.** prove it is false   **d.** ignore it completely

Words from Proper Names

WORD LIST

bedlam	bowdlerize	chauvinism	draconian	martinet
maudlin	mesmerize	silhouette	stentorian	titanic

You probably use eponymous words—words derived from the names of people or characters—every day. The next time you eat a *sandwich*, think about the Earl of Sandwich, who started the trend of eating meat between two pieces of bread. All the words in this lesson are similarly derived from names.

1. **bedlam** (běd´ləm) *noun* from Middle English *Bedlem*, after Hospital of Saint Mary of *Bethlehem*, an institution in London for the mentally ill
   A place or situation of noisy uproar and confusion
   • When the teacher walked in, the **bedlam** in the second-grade classroom immediately subsided.

> *Bedlam* is a shortened version of the word *Bethlehem*.

2. **bowdlerize** (bōd´lə-rīz´) *verb* after Thomas *Bowdler* (1754–1825), who published a censored edition of Shakespeare in 1818
   a. To censor prudishly
   • Popular movies based on fairy tales often **bowdlerize** the original stories.
   b. To modify or abridge, as by shortening, simplifying, or skewing content
   • Scientists generally hope that the media and other organizations that report on their work won't **bowdlerize** their findings.

   bowdlerization *noun* Calling it a "shameless **bowdlerization**," the author refused to approve the film script that was based on his novel.

3. **chauvinism** (shō´və-nĭz´əm) *noun* from French *chauvinisme*, after Nicolas *Chauvin*, a legendary French soldier known for his devotion to Napoleon
   a. A prejudiced belief in the superiority of one's own gender, group, or kind
   • Accused of male **chauvinism,** the athletic director was ordered to provide more sports opportunities for women.
   b. Fanatical patriotism; the glorification of one's country
   • His **chauvinism** was so extreme that he believed anyone who criticized the government was a traitor.

   chauvinist *noun* A good motto for a **chauvinist** would be "My country, right or wrong."

4. **draconian** (drā-kō´nē-ən) *adjective* after *Draco*, Athenian politician who codified the laws of Athens in or around 621 BC
   Exceedingly harsh; very severe
   • Boarding schools in Victorian England had the reputation of inflicting **draconian** punishments for even the most minor offenses.

5. **martinet** (mär´tn-ĕt´) *noun* after Jean *Martinet* (died 1672), a French army officer and drillmaster
   a. A rigid military disciplinarian
   • The drill sergeant was a **martinet** who demanded perfect posture and total uniformity of marching style.
   b. One who demands absolute adherence to forms and rules
   • The babysitter was such a **martinet** that she wouldn't let the hungry children eat anything, because their parents had said they disapproved of snacking.

6. **maudlin** (môd´lĭn) *adjective* alteration of (Mary) *Magdalene*, who was frequently depicted as a tearful penitent
   Effusively or tearfully sentimental; overly emotional
   • While some critics considered the novel "emotionally powerful," others called it **maudlin.**

7. **mesmerize** (mĕz´mə-rīz´) *verb* after Austrian physician Franz *Mesmer* (1734–1815), who unwittingly discovered hypnotism while trying to cure illnesses
   a. To spellbind; to enthrall
   • The daring feats of the trapeze artist **mesmerized** the audience.
   b. To hypnotize
   • The audience was amazed when the hypnotist **mesmerized** a man on stage.

8. **silhouette** (sĭl´ōō-ĕt´) from French, after Étienne de *Silhouette* (1709–1767), a French finance minister
   a. *noun* A drawing consisting of the outline of something, especially a human profile, filled in with a solid color
   • Instead of a detailed profile, the underexposed photo showed only a **silhouette** of the model's face.
   b. *noun* An outline that appears dark against a light background
   • The **silhouette** of the mountain range faded as the sky darkened.
   c. *verb* To cause to be seen as a silhouette; to outline
   • In the pale predawn light, the crows were **silhouetted** against the snowy field.

silhouette

9. **stentorian** (stĕn-tôr´ē-ən) *adjective* after *Stentor*, a Greek herald in Homer's *Iliad*, famous for his loud voice
   Extremely loud
   • The **stentorian** voice of the speaker could be heard from the back row of the enormous courtroom.

10. **titanic** (tī-tăn´ĭk) *adjective* from Greek *Titan*, after the *Titans*, a family of mythological giants
   Having enormous size, strength, power, or influence
   • The **titanic** waves destroyed much of the coastline.

You have probably heard of the *Titanic*, a gigantic luxury liner that sank on its maiden voyage in 1912.

WRITE THE CORRECT WORD

Write the correct word in the space next to each definition. Use each word only once.

_____ **1.** to enthrall

_____ **2.** noisy confusion

_____ **3.** enormous

_____ **4.** a rigid disciplinarian

_____ **5.** a prejudice in favor of one's own group

_____ **6.** extremely loud

_____ **7.** overly sentimental

_____ **8.** very severe; harsh

_____ **9.** to abridge

_____ **10.** an outline seen against a background

COMPLETE THE SENTENCE

Write the letter for the word that best completes each sentence.

_____ **1.** The rioters created utter _____ in the town square.
a. bedlam   **b.** chauvinism   **c.** bowdlerization   **d.** silhouettes

_____ **2.** Hundreds of feet in length, blue whales are truly _____ creatures.
a. chauvinistic   **b.** maudlin   **c.** titanic   **d.** silhouetted

_____ **3.** The photograph of the gnarled, bare branches _____ against the amber sky was breathtaking.
a. silhouetted   **b.** bowdlerized   **c.** mesmerized   **d.** titanic

_____ **4.** Her sweet, smooth voice had a _____ effect on the audience.
a. silhouetted   **b.** mesmerizing   **c.** bowdlerizing   **d.** draconian

_____ **5.** Jo made sure to _____ the violent Greek myth as she told it to her five-year-old child.
a. silhouette   **b.** mesmerize   **c.** martinet   **d.** bowdlerize

_____ **6.** The _____ blasts of the fireworks are still echoing in my ears.
a. chauvinistic   **b.** draconian   **c.** maudlin   **d.** stentorian

_____ **7.** The prison warden was known for employing _____ methods of discipline.
a. draconian   **b.** bowdlerized   **c.** maudlin   **d.** silhouetted

_____ **8.** The new principal was not the _____ he was rumored to be.
a. silhouette   **b.** martinet   **c.** bedlam   **d.** titanic

_____ **9.** Certain kinds of _____ are illegal when it comes to hiring practices.
a. bowdlerization   **b.** bedlam   **c.** chauvinism   **d.** mesmerism

_____ **10.** Rosie shed a tear every time she saw the _____ phone-company advertisement.
a. mesmerizing   **b.** maudlin   **c.** draconian   **d.** titanic

Challenge: Although many viewers adored the blockbuster movie about the sinking of the *Titanic*, others claimed that the plot _____ the true horrors of the shipwreck and focused too much on a _____ love story.

_____   **a.** silhouetted…draconian   **b.** bowdlerized…maudlin   **c.** mesmerized…chauvinistic

They Gave Their Names

People give their names to children, institutions, places, and, over time, to words. You might be surprised at the number of eponymous words in the English language. For example, picture a young man with sideburns in Washington, D.C., eating a Caesar salad. You probably know that "Washington" is named for George Washington. But did you know that "sideburns" originally referred to the unique whiskers worn by General Ambrose Burnside, or that the "Caesar salad" was named for its inventor, Caesar Cardini, an Italian chef who ran restaurants in Mexico?

The ten words in this lesson also have diverse and interesting etymologies. For example, in ancient Greek mythology, the Titans were giants who ruled the heavens for eons. **(1)** Although they were ultimately overthrown by the Olympians, the word *titanic* still refers to size, strength, and power.

Another lesson word originates from ancient Greek literature. Homer's epic *The Iliad* describes Stentor, a herald (an official announcer), as having a voice "as loud as the cry of fifty men." **(2)** Unfortunately, his ego and his *stentorian* voice got him into some trouble. When he challenged the god Hermes to a shouting match, Hermes enlisted outside aid and won.

Some English words also come from the names of the Greek people themselves. Roughly 2,600 years ago, the Athenians asked the politician Draco to record and systematize their laws. For better or worse, Draco's work included harsh and often outdated laws and sentencing customs. **(3)** He seemed to believe that severe *draconian* punishments should be meted out for minor offenses.

Other English words stem from biblical names or places. Mary Magdalene, whose surname has been shortened over time to *maudlin,* was a follower of Jesus. **(4)** She is often depicted in medieval art as a *maudlin* character, crying inconsolably at the crucifixion of Jesus. Also, during the Middle Ages, the Hospital of Saint Mary of Bethlehem (shortened to "Bedlam"), in London, became an asylum for the mentally ill. **(5)** This facility was undoubtedly the site of *bedlam.*

The French have also given their names to many English words. In the seventeenth century, Jean Martinet transformed the undisciplined troops of Louis XIV into the most powerful army in Europe. **(6)** As a result, a *martinet* is the one who demands absolute conformity to rules. Étienne de Silhouette (1709–1767), a stingy minister of finance, levied so many taxes that he was soon forced to resign. **(7)** The French began to call anything that was cheap "a la silhouette," including shoddy portraits that sometimes resembled what we now call *silhouettes.* Nicholas Chauvin was a soldier in Napoleon's army who was legendary for his devotion. **(8)** His unquestioning *chauvinism* toward the falling empire was irrational.

Austrian physician Franz Mesmer (1734–1815) believed that the "magnetic fluid" of the universe could be used to cure illness. **(9)** His use of dim lights and soft music had hypnotic *mesmerizing* effects on those he treated. Unsettled by the curious devotion of his patients, authorities exiled him from two countries.

In the early nineteenth century, the question arose whether Shakespearean literature should be read with all of its original—and sometimes controversial—language and subject matter. Englishman Thomas Bowdler (1754–1825) didn't think so. **(10)** In 1818, he censored and *bowdlerized* the bard's works so they would be suitable for family entertainment.

As you can see, many names enrich the English language. So, if you're in South Carolina (Charles I), in July (Julius Caesar), enjoying boysenberries (Rudolf Boysen), think about the people, characters, and places that have given us so many of our words.

a silhouette of a Titan

Each sentence below refers to a numbered sentence in the passage. Write the letter of the choice that gives the sentence a meaning that is closest to the original sentence.

_____ **1.** These _____ characters are still symbols of size, strength, and power.
    a. harsh   **b.** renowned   **c.** enormous   **d.** enthralling

_____ **2.** Unfortunately, his ego and his _____ voice got him into some trouble.
    a. influential   **b.** loud   **c.** prejudiced   **d.** severe

_____ **3.** He believed that _____ punishments should be meted out for minor offenses.
    a. harsh   **b.** sentimental   **c.** loud   **d.** prejudiced

_____ **4.** She is often depicted in medieval art as a(n) _____ character.
    a. loud   **b.** harsh   **c.** intensely strict   **d.** tearfully sentimental

_____ **5.** This facility was undoubtedly the site of _____.
    a. rioting   **b.** confusion   **c.** sentimentality   **d.** harsh punishments

_____ **6.** As a result, a _____ is one who demands absolute conformity to rules.
    a. noisy yeller   **b.** famous hypnotist   **c.** kind benefactor   **d.** rigid disciplinarian

_____ **7.** Shoddy portraits sometimes resembled _____.
    a. oil paintings   **b.** giant statues   **c.** outline drawings   **d.** censored art

_____ **8.** His _____ toward the falling empire was irrational.
    a. sentimental slop   **b.** valiant service   **c.** creative chaos   **d.** fanatic patriotism

_____ **9.** His use of dim lights and soft music had hypnotic _____ effects on patients.
    a. enthralling   **b.** gigantic   **c.** eerie   **d.** sentimental

_____ **10.** In 1818, he censored and _____ the bard's works.
    a. got weepy over   **b.** loudly announced   **c.** devoted himself to   **d.** prudishly edited

Indicate whether the statements below are TRUE or FALSE according to the passage.

_____ **1.** The *silhouette* was named for a master of the art form.

_____ **2.** Two French eponyms mentioned in the passage come from military personnel.

_____ **3.** A word based on someone's name can remain part of the language for centuries after that person's death.

FINISH THE THOUGHT

Complete each sentence so that it shows the meaning of the italicized word.

1. I think *bowdlerized* versions of the classics _____

_____

2. She showed her *chauvinism* by _____

_____

WRITE THE DERIVATIVE

Complete the sentence by writing the correct form of the word shown in parentheses. You may not need to change the form that is given.

_____ **1.** The air-traffic controller redirected flights around the _____ storm. *(titanic)*

_____ **2.** The _____ voice of the speaker held me in a trance. *(mesmerize)*

_____ 3. The artist was a master of freehand _____. (*silhouette*)

_____ 4. Sarah's weightlifting coach is a _____ who demands strict adherence to specialized diets and training schedules. (*martinet*)

_____ 5. His adaptation of the novel was an awful _____ of the original. (*bowdlerize*)

_____ 6. After we won the championship, there was complete _____ in the stadium. (*bedlam*)

_____ 7. The _____ assumed that someone with my background could not become a professor. (*chauvinism*)

_____ 8. The announcer's _____ voice boomed across the arena. (*stentorian*)

_____ 9. The candidates debated whether _____ penalties actually reduce crime. (*draconian*)

_____ 10. At the class reunion, the alumni sang a _____ song about "the good old days." (*maudlin*)

FIND THE EXAMPLE

Choose the answer that best describes the action or situation.

_____ 1. Something *stentorian*
    a. a poem   **b.** a punishment   **c.** a roar   **d.** a portrait

_____ 2. Someone most likely to be a *martinet*
    a. army captain   **b.** jazz musician   **c.** infant   **d.** abstract artist

_____ 3. A place in which you would most likely find *maudlin* writing
    a. news article   **b.** science book   **c.** greeting card   **d.** instruction manual

_____ 4. One type of *silhouette*
    a. shadow   **b.** lunch   **c.** aerial photo   **d.** text column

_____ 5. A *titanic* construction
    a. skyscraper   **b.** speedboat   **c.** cottage   **d.** mountain bike

_____ 6. Something most likely to bring about *bedlam* in a city
    a. limousine   **b.** earthquake   **c.** highway   **d.** museum

_____ 7. What a completely *bowdlerized* movie would be rated
    a. G   **b.** PG   **c.** PG-13   **d.** R

_____ 8. The type of music most often intended to have a *mesmerizing* effect
    a. funk   **b.** blues   **c.** lullabies   **d.** hip-hop

_____ 9. A *draconian* punishment for stealing a pen
    a. returning the pen   **b.** paying for the pen   **c.** writing an essay   **d.** serving jail time

_____ 10. A *chauvinist's* sentiment
    a. Go in peace.   **b.** I love you.   **c.** We're the best.   **d.** Sharing is caring.

Speaking and Expression

WORD LIST

exalt	exhort	garrulous	gist	histrionic
laconic	peremptory	polemic	vivacious	vociferous

The vocabulary in this lesson deals with the many ways in which we present ourselves—from the *laconic* person who uses few words, to the *garrulous* talker who rambles on and on, to the *histrionic* person who dramatizes everything.

1. **exalt** (ĭg-zôlt´) *verb* from Latin *ex-*, "up; away" + *altus*, "high"
   a. To raise in rank, character, or status; to elevate
   • According to the folktale, after the poor farm boy answered the riddle, he was **exalted** to the position of the king's advisor.
   b. To glorify, to praise, or to honor
   • Before we **exalt** a particular form of government, we must carefully observe it in action.

   exalted

   exalted *adjective* His **exalted** ideas about architecture were rejected as impractical by the building committee.

2. **exhort** (ĭg-zôrt´) *verb* from Latin *ex-*, "thoroughly" + *hortari*, "to encourage"
   To urge by strong, often stirring argument, advice, or appeal
   • The wartime broadcaster signed off every night by **exhorting** viewers to have courage.

   exhortation *noun* The union representative gave a riveting **exhortation** urging improvements in working conditions.

3. **garrulous** (găr´ə-ləs) *adjective* from Latin *garrire*, "to chatter"
   a. Given to excessive and often trivial talk
   • Della arrived late for her appointment because of the **garrulous** greeting she received from a friend she ran into on the way.
   b. Wordy and rambling
   • Maurice, obviously upset, left a **garrulous** message on my answering machine.

   garrulousness *noun* **Garrulousness** is not appreciated in a graduation speaker.

4. gist (jĭst) *noun*
The central idea; the essence
- The **gist** of my parents' message was "Do to others as you would have them do to you."

5. histrionic (hĭs´trē-ŏn´ĭk) *adjective* from Latin *histrio,* "actor"
Excessively dramatic or emotional; affected
- If the expressions and movements of silent-film stars often seem **histrionic,** remember that they could not express themselves in words.

histrionics *noun* The **histrionics** following an invitation mix-up for Trisha's sixteenth-birthday party caused the party to be canceled.

6. laconic (lə-kŏn´ĭk) *adjective* from Latin *Lakon,* "a Spartan"
Marked by the use of few words; terse or concise
- It is said that when Philip of Macedon threatened the city of Sparta by warning, "If I enter Laconia, I will raze Sparta to the ground," the Spartans' **laconic** reply was, "If."

Laconia was the district around Sparta, and the word *laconic* records the famed conciseness of these people.

7. peremptory (pə-rĕmp´tə-rē) *adjective* from Latin *perimere,* "to take away"
a. Putting an end to all debate or action; not allowing contradiction or refusal
- In a **peremptory** move, the judge simply announced a decision.
b. Offensively self-assured; dictatorial
- We could scarcely believe our eyes when the **peremptory** woman ordered the boy out of his seat so that she could take it.

Peremptory challenges during the jury selection process allow lawyers to eliminate jury members without having to give a reason.

8. polemic (pə-lĕm´ĭk) from Greek *polemikos,* "hostile"
a. *noun* A controversial argument, especially one refuting a specific opinion or doctrine
- The Roman orator Cicero was famous for his **polemic** against the politician Cataline.
b. *adjective* Relating to a controversy or argument
- The **polemic** argument surrounding the CEO's dismissal negatively affected the price of the company's stock.

polemicist *noun* The **polemicist** seemed to enjoy stirring up controversy.

Although *polemic* is preferred, the adjective form may also be expressed as *polemical.*

9. vivacious (vĭ-vā´shəs) *adjective* from Latin *vivere,* "to live"
Full of animation and spirit; lively
- The **vivacious** hostess circulated throughout the room, chatting with each guest at the large party.

vivacity or **vivaciousness** *noun* No picture could capture my grandmother's **vivacity.**

10. vociferous (vō-sĭf´ər-əs) *adjective* from Latin *vox,* "voice" + *ferre,* "to carry"
Marked by noisy, forceful, or intense outcries
- Residents' **vociferous** complaints about untethered dogs spurred a petition for a leash law in the community.

vociferousness *noun* The **vociferousness** of the shouting fans could be heard miles away from the stadium.

WRITE THE CORRECT WORD

Write the correct word in the space next to each definition. Use each word only once.

_____ **1.** to urge strongly

_____ **2.** lively

_____ **3.** using few words

_____ **4.** the essence

_____ **5.** a controversial argument

_____ **6.** wordy and rambling

_____ **7.** excessively dramatic

_____ **8.** to glorify or praise

_____ **9.** offensively self-assured

_____ **10.** marked by noisy outcries

COMPLETE THE SENTENCE

Write the letter for the word that best completes each sentence.

_____ **1.** I was amazed when he stated the _____ of my long argument in a few well-chosen words.
    a. histrionics   **b.** exaltation   **c.** vivacity   **d.** gist

_____ **2.** The _____ of the student musical production lifted the spirits of the audience.
    a. vivacity   **b.** garrulousness   **c.** vociferousness   **d.** polemics

_____ **3.** "Stop crying," said Dad, "_____ won't convince me to let you attend the party."
    a. exaltation   **b.** vivacity   **c.** histrionics   **d.** polemics

_____ **4.** At the award ceremony, the well-respected actor's achievements were _____.
    a. exalted   **b.** polemicized   **c.** garrulous   **d.** exhorted

_____ **5.** _____ protests disrupted the calm of the committee meeting.
    a. Exalted   **b.** Vociferous   **c.** Laconic   **d.** Vivacious

_____ **6.** My _____ grandfather spoke very little, but each word carried weight.
    a. histrionic   **b.** laconic   **c.** peremptory   **d.** garrulous

_____ **7.** The challenger launched into yet another _____ attacking the mayor's school policies.
    a. gist   **b.** vivacity   **c.** polemic   **d.** vociferousness

_____ **8.** No matter how hard we tried, we couldn't get our _____ friend to stop talking.
    a. peremptory   **b.** exhorted   **c.** laconic   **d.** garrulous

_____ **9.** Defense lawyers made a _____ challenge to the prospective juror.
    a. vivacious   **b.** laconic   **c.** peremptory   **d.** vociferous

_____ **10.** The animal-rights activist _____ her audience to protest the inhumane treatment of stray cats.
    a. exhorted   **b.** histrionical   **c.** polemicized   **d.** exalted

Challenge: After three hours of listening to one _____ presenter, the audience members were relieved when the next speaker gave the _____ of his argument and sat down.
_____   **a.** histrionic...polemic   **b.** vivacious...peremptory   **c.** garrulous...gist

Speaking Their Minds

Every Sunday morning in London, England, crowds gather at a place in Hyde Park known as Speakers' Corner. **(1)** *Exalted* as a symbol of democratic rights, Speakers' Corner is a place where anyone can publicly talk—or shout if need be—about politics, religion, or life in general.

The Speakers' Corner tradition goes back more than a century, and its origins may surprise you. **(2)** On the spot where people come today to deliver opinions and *polemics* for or against anything, there once stood a gallows. Called the Tyburn hanging tree, public executions were held there from 1196 to 1783.

By the 1500s, the Tyburn hangings had become almost carnival-like. Often, more than 100,000 people would line the streets to watch as the prisoners were brought in by horse-drawn carts. Grandstands were built to accommodate the spectators. But before the condemned were hanged, each had a chance to address the crowd.

Generally, prisoners would simply apologize for their crimes. **(3)** Some, however, *exhorted* the crowd to act on their behalf. **(4)** Other prisoners used the moments before their deaths to *vociferously* criticize the government.

Eventually, the public began to think of these gallows as the place to make protests and pleas. People from all walks of life began to gather in the park to demand such things as fair food prices.

In 1866, word spread that demonstrators should meet at the park to call for the government to let shops stay open on Sundays. **(5)** The prime minister gave the police a *peremptory* order to lock the park's entrances, but it made no difference. The crowd of over 150,000 protestors broke the gates down!

Afterward, fliers that were posted around the city declared that "The Parks are the People's and we hereby claim the right to the use of them for the purpose of discussing our political wrongs." A year-long debate followed. In 1872, the British Parliament created Speakers' Corner, declaring that the public could gather and give speeches there.

Over the years, the tides of British politics have ebbed and flowed at the Corner. Early on, both laborers seeking better working conditions and women fighting for the right to vote voiced their concerns there. **(6)** Today, the Corner draws a mix of the politically driven, the opinionated, and the simply *garrulous*.

On any given Sunday, speakers can be heard preaching about religion, taxes, human rights, soccer, and just about anything else. **(7)** Crowds gather around the presenters, who vary from calm to *vivacious* to combative. Sometimes, the talks provoke debates with the audience. **(8)** More *laconic* onlookers may simply utter a few words of comment.

The Corner also draws speakers with rather unusual opinions—such as the imminent threat of alien invasion. **(9)** Not surprisingly, the *histrionics* of such speakers tends to attract tourists simply looking for amusement. But the tradition of serious public debate made famous at Speakers' Corner continues there and elsewhere.

(10) Public debate, the *gist* of what goes on in many online forums, blogs, and Web sites, has followed in the tradition of the free expression found at London's Hyde Park. Many people are now making the Internet their own Speakers' Corner.

Each sentence below refers to a numbered sentence in the passage. Write the letter of the choice that gives the sentence a meaning that is closest to the original sentence.

_____ **1.** Speakers' Corner is _____ as a symbol of democratic rights.
   a. condemned   **b.** praised   **c.** preempted   **d.** dramatized

_____ **2.** People come today to deliver opinions and _____ for or against anything.
   a. performances   **b.** arguments   **c.** trivialities   **d.** warnings

_____ **3.** Some, however, _____ the crowd to act on their behalf.
   a. urged   **b.** praised   **c.** offended   **d.** dissuaded

_____ **4.** Other prisoners _____ criticized the government.
    a. unjustly   **b.** wordily   **c.** forcefully   **d.** honorably

_____ **5.** The prime minister gave the police a(n) _____ order to lock the park's entrances.
    a. temporary   **b.** urgent   **c.** impartial   **d.** dictatorial

_____ **6.** Today, the Corner still draws a mix of the politically driven, the opinionated, and the simply _____.
    a. rambling   **b.** honorable   **c.** dramatic   **d.** self-assured

_____ **7.** Crowds gather around the presenters, who vary from calm to _____ to combative.
    a. commanding   **b.** terse   **c.** appealing   **d.** animated

_____ **8.** More _____ onlookers may simply utter a few words of comment.
    a. honored   **b.** concise   **c.** essential   **d.** argumentative

_____ **9.** The _____ of such speakers tends to attract tourists simply looking for amusement.
    a. clever reasoning   **b.** subtle persuasion   **c.** excessive drama   **d.** glorification

_____ **10.** Public debate, the _____ of what goes on in many online forums, has followed in this tradition.
    a. controversy   **b.** essence   **c.** strength   **d.** waste

Indicate whether the statements below are TRUE or FALSE according to the passage.

_____ **1.** Public speaking enjoys a very long tradition in London.

_____ **2.** Speakers' Corner originally was created by a British king so that the common people would be able to make their opinions known.

_____ **3.** Some newer forms of communication follow the tradition of Speakers' Corner.

WRITING EXTENDED RESPONSES

Suppose that you were attending a Sunday morning session in London's Hyde Park at Speakers' Corner. In an essay of at least three paragraphs, describe the proceedings, including the topic, manner of presentation, and audience reaction. You may choose a serious or lighthearted topic but, either way, you should give specific descriptions of the event. Use at least three lesson words in your essay and underline them.

WRITE THE DERIVATIVE

Complete the sentence by writing the correct form of the word shown in parentheses. You may not need to change the form that is given.

_____ **1.** Sofia, known for her _____, hardly ever lets anyone else say a word. (*garrulous*)

_____ **2.** Senator Fogerty often presents _____ arguments to Congress. (*polemic*)

_____ 3. The party leader was seen in the conference room, _____ wavering party members to vote for the bill. *(exhort)*

_____ 4. The _____ of the impassioned speech was difficult to extract from the flowery verbiage. *(gist)*

_____ 5. The _____ of the argument startled the audience. *(vociferous)*

_____ 6. Jean's communication at family get-togethers usually consists of a few gestures and grunts, and an occasional _____ phrase. *(laconic)*

_____ 7. The graduate student found the _____ atmosphere at the theoretical physics symposium challenging and invigorating. *(exalt)*

_____ 8. Although the radio broadcast conveyed her message, it couldn't capture the _____ of her gestures and expressions. *(vivacious)*

_____ 9. Given to _____, the five-year-old screamed and cried when she didn't get her way. *(histrionic)*

_____ 10. The president issued a _____ decree offering immediate asylum to the endangered foreign nationals. *(peremptory)*

FIND THE EXAMPLE

Choose the answer that best describes the action or situation.

_____ 1. The most likely subject for a *vociferous* argument
   a. current politics   **b.** pastel colors   **c.** early literature   **d.** favorite food

_____ 2. Something that has a *gist*
   a. nothingness   **b.** complex idea   **c.** part of body   **d.** sum of money

_____ 3. Someone likely to be *exalted*
   a. school bully   **b.** average person   **c.** famous artist   **d.** convicted criminal

_____ 4. The most *laconic* response
   a. Well, certainly.   **b.** No, thank you.   **c.** Yes indeed.   **d.** Yep.

_____ 5. The purpose of a *peremptory* action on an issue
   a. extend the issue   **b.** open it to debate   **c.** close the issue   **d.** consider alternatives

_____ 6. Something an English teacher would NOT be likely to *exhort* her students to do
   a. read for fun   **b.** buy a new CD   **c.** write concisely   **d.** study for tests

_____ 7. A feature of *garrulous* talk
   a. triviality   **b.** essence   **c.** loudness   **d.** emotion

_____ 8. A likely descriptor of someone prone to *histrionics*
   a. stern   **b.** emotional   **c.** reserved   **d.** accurate

_____ 9. The most likely subject for a *polemic*
   a. a video rental   **b.** a proposed policy   **c.** a brand of car   **d.** a classic novel

_____ 10. A person who is LEAST likely to be *vivacious* at work
   a. salesperson   **b.** pop star   **c.** flight attendant   **d.** paramedic

Reading and Reasoning

Context Clues in Reading Literature

As you study literature, you are likely to encounter words you don't know. Some words may simply be difficult, while others may have meanings that have changed over time or may even be obsolete. You can often use context clues to help you understand the literature you read.

Strategies

1. *Consider the period of the work.* A work written two hundred years ago will probably have more unfamiliar words and meanings than one written twenty years ago. The meaning of the word *nice,* for example, has gone from "foolish" to "fastidious" to "pleasant."

2. *Consider the author and his or her style.* Some authors may use metaphors that will help you understand a difficult word. Others might use allusions to other works of literature. The context clues surrounding the allusion may help you understand the reference, even if you haven't read that work. Also, British usage often differs from that of the United States. In Britain, for example, *governor* can mean "warden of a penitentiary," and *warden* often refers to an official of a university or hospital.

3. *Consider the genre and the subject of the work.* If the work is fiction, for example, when and where is the story set? The setting and the subject of a work help to determine its vocabulary.

4. *Consult a dictionary.* If there aren't sufficient context clues, or if the word meaning is crucial to the understanding of the passage, find the definition. In some cases, a rare or obsolete word can only be found in an unabridged dictionary. Also, some works of literature may include an appendix or glossary that explains words and phrases that are now out of date.

Practice

The following passage is from *A Tale of Two Cities,* by Charles Dickens (1812–1870), a novel set in the French Revolution of the late eighteenth century. In the countryside, "four fierce figures" have set fire to the chateau of an oppressive marquis, or noble. Read the entire passage once to get a general idea of what it is about. Then slowly reread the passage, writing your own definition for each italicized word. Finally, look up each word in the dictionary and record the most suitable definitions on the lines that follow.

The (1) *chateau* was left to itself to flame and burn. In the roaring and raging of the (2) *conflagration,* a red-hot wind, driving straight from the infernal regions, seemed to be blowing the edifice away. With the rising and falling of the blaze, the stone faces showed as if they were in torment. When great masses of stone and timber fell, the face with the two (3) *dints* in the nose became obscured: (4) *anon* struggled out of the smoke again, as if it were the face of the cruel Marquis, burning at the stake and contending with the fire.

The chateau burned; the nearest trees, laid hold of by the fire, scorched and shriveled; trees at a distance, fired by the four fierce figures, (5) *begirt* the blazing edifice with a new forest of smoke. Molten lead and iron boiled in the marble basin of the fountain; the water ran dry; the extinguisher tops of the towers vanished like ice before the heat, and trickled down into four rugged wells of flame. Great (6) *rents* and splits branched out in the solid walls, like crystallization; stupefied birds wheeled about and dropped into the furnace; four fierce figures trudged away, East, West, North, and South along the (7) night-*enshrouded* roads, guided by the beacon they had lighted, towards their destination. The illuminated village had seized hold of the (8) *tocsin*, and, abolishing the lawful ringer, rang for joy.

1. chateau

My definition _____

Dictionary definition _____

2. conflagration

My definition _____

Dictionary definition _____

3. dints

My definition _____

Dictionary definition _____

4. anon

My definition _____

Dictionary definition _____

5. begirt

My definition _____

Dictionary definition _____

6. rents

My definition _____

Dictionary definition _____

7. enshrouded

My definition _____

Dictionary definition _____

8. toscin

My definition _____

Dictionary definition _____

Health and Illness

WORD LIST

| atrophy | debilitate | livid | moribund | noxious |
| pestilence | prostrate | salubrious | scourge | unscathed |

Much effort goes into maintaining our health. Public policy on medical care is constantly being debated. We are advised to eat healthy food, to exercise, and to visit physicians regularly. The words in this lesson will expand the ways you understand and express the concepts involved with health

atrophy

1. **atrophy** (ăt´rə-fē) from Greek *a-*, "without" + *trophe*, "food"
   a. *verb* To waste away; to wither or deteriorate
   • Sam's leg muscles **atrophied** during his long recovery from surgery.
   b. *noun* Wasting away or deterioration, often due to disease, injury, or lack of use
   • Not practicing a foreign language usually results in the **atrophy** of your ability to speak it.

2. **debilitate** (dĭ-bĭl´ĭ-tāt´) *verb* from Latin *debilis*, "weak"
   To sap the strength or the energy of; to weaken
   • Because they were **debilitated** by lack of food and water, the lost hikers could barely move by the time they were rescued.

   debilitation *noun* People who have multiple sclerosis may experience **debilitation** due to muscle weakness and fatigue.

3. **livid** (lĭv´ĭd) *adjective* from Latin *livere*, "to be bluish"
   a. Discolored, as from a bruise; black-and-blue
   • The **livid** spot on my leg formed right after I fell on the sidewalk.
   b. Pale or ashen
   • When she heard the news, her face was **livid** with shock.
   c. Furious with anger
   • Dad was **livid** that I missed the school bus, after he warned me to be on time.

> The idea that *livid* means "furious" comes from the pallor of an extremely angry person's face.

4. **moribund** (môr´ə-bŭnd´) *adjective* from Latin *mori*, "to die"
   a. About to die
   • Our **moribund** dog gazed at us with sad eyes.
   b. On the verge of becoming obsolete or outdated
   • This manual typewriter is so **moribund** that I can't find anyone to repair it.

5. **noxious** (nŏk´shəs) *adjective* from Latin *noxa*, "damage"
   a. Poisonous or harmful to living things; injurious to health
   • Carbon monoxide is **noxious**, even in very small quantities.
   b. Corrupting; harmful to the mind or morals
   • Many parents feel that violent movies are **noxious** to their children.

6. **pestilence** (pĕs´tə-ləns) *noun* from Latin *pestis*, "a plague" A usually fatal epidemic disease; anything regarded as harmful or dangerous
   • At its worst during the Middle Ages, the bubonic plague was a **pestilence** that killed approximately two million Europeans each year.

   pestilent *adjective* The **pestilent** locust invasion destroyed African crops.

7. **prostrate** (prŏs´trāt´) from Latin *pro-*, "forward" + *sternere*, "to spread; to cast down"
   a. *verb* To reduce to extreme weakness; to overcome
      • The disease **prostrated** him to the point that he couldn't get out of bed.
   b. *verb* To lie flat or at full length
      • The peasant **prostrated** himself before the king.
   c. *adjective* Reduced to extreme weakness; overcome
      • **Prostrate** from a flu epidemic, half of our class was absent.
   d. *adjective* Lying flat, face down, at full length
      • The physician asked her patient to lie **prostrate** on the examination table.

   > *Prostrating* one's self usually implies submission.

8. **salubrious** (sə-lōō´brē-əs) *adjective* from Latin *salus*, "health" Conducive or favorable to health or well-being
   • The polluted neighborhood near the factory is not a **salubrious** place to live.

9. **scourge** (skûrj) from Old French *escorgier*, "to whip"
   a. *noun* A cause of great harm, affliction, or devastation, such as war
      • The Nazi invasions were the **scourge** of Europe in the 1930s and 1940s.
   b. *verb* To afflict with severe suffering; to ravage
      • The Central American nation was **scourged** by civil war.

10. **unscathed** (ŭn-skā*th*d´) *adjective* from Old Norse *skadha*, "to harm" Not harmed; uninjured
    • Astonishingly, the pilot walked away from the plane crash **unscathed**.

WORD ENRICHMENT

Colorful words

The word *livid* has its origin in color, originally suggesting something "bluish" or something "pale." Like *livid*, many color words' meanings have expanded. To be *blue* can mean to be "depressed or sad." In slang, to describe someone as *yellow* connotes "cowardice." *Black* deeds are "dishonorable." *In the pink of health* means "in very good health."

In ancient times, purple dyes were expensive and difficult to obtain. Perhaps for this reason, purple was the color traditionally favored by those of high rank. In fact, at times, only royalty was allowed to wear it. From this custom, *born to the purple* has come to mean "born to royalty or nobility."

WRITE THE CORRECT WORD

Write the correct word in the space next to each definition. Use each word only once.

_____ **1.** an epidemic disease

_____ **2.** about to die

_____ **3.** to wither away

_____ **4.** poisonous

_____ **5.** favorable to health

_____ **6.** black-and-blue

_____ **7.** completely uninjured

_____ **8.** to sap the energy of

_____ **9.** lying flat, face down

_____ **10.** a cause of great devastation

COMPLETE THE SENTENCE

Write the letter for the word that best completes each sentence.

_____ **1.** Make sure to lock that cabinet so that the baby cannot access the _____ cleaning products.
    a. moribund   **b.** prostrate   **c.** noxious   **d.** salubrious

_____ **2.** Are health officials worried that avian flu might turn into a global _____?
    a. pestilence   **b.** atrophy   **c.** debilitation   **d.** moribund

_____ **3.** He fell off his skateboard and crashed into the pavement, but somehow remained _____.
    a. debilitated   **b.** livid   **c.** salubrious   **d.** unscathed

_____ **4.** A rising crime rate is the _____ of some American cities.
    a. atrophy   **b.** lividity   **c.** scourge   **d.** debilitation

_____ **5.** _____ from running for miles without water, the runner collapsed.
    a. Scourged   **b.** Prostrate   **c.** Unscathed   **d.** Salubrious

_____ **6.** A regular exercise routine paired with healthy eating is _____.
    a. noxious   **b.** pestilent   **c.** prostrate   **d.** salubrious

_____ **7.** As soon as Celia saw the nurse holding a needle, her face became _____.
    a. livid   **b.** unscathed   **c.** moribund   **d.** debilitated

_____ **8.** The dentist still keeps that old, _____ X-ray machine on display.
    a. pestilent   **b.** moribund   **c.** salubrious   **d.** atrophied

_____ **9.** The disease caused her entire body to _____.
    a. pestilent   **b.** livid   **c.** atrophy   **d.** scourge

_____ **10.** Without medication, Helen's condition completely _____ her.
    a. debilitates   **b.** scourges   **c.** pestilent   **d.** unscathed

Challenge: Although Nicholas and Alan both fell off the scooter, Alan's shoulder was left _____ and bloodied, while Nicholas was completely _____.

_____   **a.** scourged...atrophied   **b.** livid...unscathed   **c.** salubrious...moribund

Yellow Fever

During the Spanish-American War (1898), U.S. soldiers sent to Cuba soon learned to fear one thing more than enemy fire: yellow fever. **(1)** In fact, during the war, 968 U.S. soldiers were killed in combat, while over 5,000 died from the *scourge* of disease. In order to combat the disease, an army doctor, Walter Reed, established the U.S. Army Yellow Fever Commission (now often called the Reed Commission).

At the time, no one knew how the infection was spread. In 1881, Cuban physician Carlos Juan Finlay had suggested that, like malaria, yellow fever was carried by mosquitoes. Other doctors found this idea unlikely and ridiculed Finlay. But Reed thought Finlay might be right. The Reed Commission was set up to test the mosquito theory.

(2) First, the commission had to prove that the *pestilence* was not spread simply by contact. To do this, Dr. Robert P. Cooke, a member of the commission, and two volunteer soldiers were each paid $100 to be shut

QUARANTINE

ENTRANCE TO THIS AREA IS PROHIBITED

into a shack for twenty days. The cabin's temperature was kept at 90 degrees, and the building was filled with the soiled, bloody clothing and bedding of those who had recently died of yellow fever. **(3)** If yellow fever was spread by germs, the "infected" clothing would be *noxious*.

Once inside the cabin, Cooke and the other men shook the stained sheets, beat the dirty pillows, and flapped the dead men's pajamas and towels about the room, doing their best to spread the "yellow-fever poison." And so it went for twenty days. **(4)** The men wondered whether the disease would *prostrate* or kill them as it had so many others.

(5) However, the volunteers all emerged *unscathed*, so more tests were planned. The next group of volunteers took deadly risks as well. **(6)** Several doctors worked among *moribund* patients to see whether they would catch the disease. Again, they did not. It seemed as if yellow fever germs did not travel through the air or by contact.

Next, Doctor James Carroll and Private William Dean allowed mosquitoes that had bitten sick people to bite their own arms. Carroll and Dean both became ill, but survived. Soon, other doctors and soldiers volunteered to be bitten. **(7)** Nearly all caught the disease, and, sadly, a few died, their livers having *atrophied* as a result of the disease.

At that point, however, the experiments were subjected to public pressure. News reporters frowned on the doctors' use of humans as experimental subjects. **(8)** Reports of the research-induced deaths made the public *livid*. The experiments were halted, but by then the doctors had their answer: Mosquitoes were indeed the culprit.

As a result, massive efforts were undertaken to eliminate mosquitoes in yellow-fever areas. Marshes and standing water were drained to destroy mosquito eggs. **(9)** These *salubrious* measures decreased the disease dramatically.

In 1937, when a vaccine was discovered, soldiers once again played a heroic role, as several volunteered to test its safety. A few of these brave soldiers died from impurities in the injections.

Since then, the purified vaccine has saved thousands. Yellow fever was nearly wiped out in most countries between the 1950s and 1980s. Unfortunately, though, other countries cannot afford the vaccine. **(10)** This *debilitating* disease is on the rise in Africa. More than 200,000 people become ill each year, and about 30,000 die. The next tool in the fight against yellow fever will not be bravery, but financial resources.

Each sentence below refers to a numbered sentence in the passage. Write the letter of the choice that gives the sentence a meaning that is closest to the original sentence.

_____ **1.** Over 5,000 soldiers died from the _____ of disease.
  a. infection   **b.** mystery   **c.** experiment   **d.** affliction

_____ **2.** First, the commission had to prove that the _____ was not spread simply by contact.
  a. epidemic disease   **b.** paralysis   **c.** discoloration   **d.** cause of weakness

_____ **3.** If yellow fever was spread by germs, the "infected" clothing would be _____.
  a. bleached   **b.** poisonous   **c.** burned   **d.** harmless

_____ **4.** They wondered whether the disease would _____ or kill them as it had so many others.

    a. frustrate   **b.** infect   **c.** overcome   **d.** heal

_____ **5.** However, the volunteers all emerged _____.

    a. unharmed   **b.** victorious   **c.** stretched out flat   **d.** weakened

_____ **6.** Doctors worked among _____ patients to see whether they would catch the disease.

    a. poisoned   **b.** ill   **c.** dying   **d.** infected

_____ **7.** Nearly all caught the disease, and, sadly, a few died, their livers having _____ as a result of the disease.

    a. been poisoned   **b.** wasted away   **c.** suddenly grown   **d.** bled internally

_____ **8.** Reports of the research-induced deaths made the public _____.

    a. suspicious   **b.** rejoice   **c.** healthy   **d.** furious

_____ **9.** These _____ measures decreased the disease dramatically.

    a. favorable   **b.** mixed   **c.** devastating   **d.** stifling

_____ **10.** This _____ disease is on the rise in Africa.

    a. unknown   **b.** always fatal   **c.** nonthreatening   **d.** energy-sapping

Indicate whether the statements below are TRUE or FALSE according to the passage.

_____ **1.** After animal experiments were unsuccessful in finding the cause of yellow fever, human subjects were used.

_____ **2.** Experiments in the early twentieth century proved that yellow fever was spread through soiled clothing and fabric.

_____ **3.** Yellow fever remains a problem today.

FINISH THE THOUGHT

Complete each sentence so that it shows the meaning of the italicized word.

1. After his *debilitating* illness, _____

_____

2. She was *livid* when _____

_____

WRITE THE DERIVATIVE

Complete the sentence by writing the correct form of the word shown in parentheses. You may not need to change the form that is given.

_____ **1.** The tsunami _____ the coastal area of the island nation. *(prostrate)*

_____ **2.** Sadly, many of the patients in this ward of the hospital are _____. *(moribund)*

_____ 3. The muscle tissue of people afflicted with Lou Gehrig's disease slowly _____. (*atrophy*)

_____ 4. Some nutritionists suggest that this vitamin isn't as _____ as once believed. (*salubrious*)

_____ 5. My great-grandfather's _____ can be traced to the malaria he contracted when he fought in jungles during World War II. (*debilitate*)

_____ 6. Serious injury is the _____ of professional boxers. (*scourge*)

_____ 7. Frostbitten fingers and toes often have a _____ appearance. (*livid*)

_____ 8. The chemical can be _____ harmful if released into a stream. (*noxious*)

_____ 9. Few people escape psychologically _____ from severe criticism. (*unscathed*)

_____ 10. At one time, diseases such as the bubonic plague and malaria were thought to be caused by _____ air. (*pestilence*)

FIND THE EXAMPLE

Choose the answer that best describes the action or situation.

_____ 1. A *noxious* thing to drink
    a. ginger ale   **b.** bleach   **c.** fruit punch   **d.** spring water

_____ 2. Something that would cause muscles to *atrophy*
    a. disease   **b.** stretching   **c.** lifting weights   **d.** drinking water

_____ 3. The best example of a *salubrious* activity
    a. chewing gum   **b.** swimming laps   **c.** getting sick   **d.** watching television

_____ 4. Someplace where a person would most likely be *prostrate*
    a. at a track meet   **b.** on an airplane   **c.** in a classroom   **d.** in a bed

_____ 5. Behavior of a person who is *livid*
    a. giving a present   **b.** laughing scornfully   **c.** shaking hands   **d.** screaming and shouting

_____ 6. An event from which one would be LEAST likely to walk away *unscathed*
    a. auto accident   **b.** hospital visit   **c.** county fair   **d.** lesson on self-defense

_____ 7. A *moribund* technology
    a. DVD   **b.** CD player   **c.** phonograph   **d.** laser printer

_____ 8. Something that a person who is *debilitated* might have difficulty doing
    a. lying down   **b.** resting   **c.** telling the truth   **d.** climbing stairs

_____ 9. An example of a *scourge*
    a. clean water   **b.** poverty   **c.** public garden   **d.** employment

_____ 10. A *pestilence*
    a. malaria   **b.** headaches   **c.** deafness   **d.** paralysis

Willingness and Unwillingness

WORD LIST

audacious	contumacy	dour	éclat	indefatigable
irresolute	obdurate	obsequious	pertinacity	stoic

"Where the willingness is great, the difficulties cannot be great."
—*Niccolo Machiavelli, Italian statesman and author (1459–1527)*

Approaching tasks with a positive attitude can bring about success, whereas a negative attitude often leads to failure. The words in this lesson relate to willingness, unwillingness, and their results.

1. **audacious** (ô-dā′shəs) *adjective* from Latin *audere,* "to dare"
   a. Fearlessly daring; bold
      • The **audacious** civilian ran into the burning building to save the child.
   b. Not held back by what others consider acceptable; showing willingness to offend others
      • The **audacious** teen said to his tennis instructor, "You should let *me* teach the class."

   audacity *noun* The man had the **audacity** to publicly accuse the mayor of awarding contracts only to those who campaigned for him.

2. **contumacy** (kŏn′tōō-mə-sē) *noun* from Latin *contumax,* "insolent"
   A scornful resistance to authority; a stubborn rebelliousness
      • In a display of **contumacy,** the administrative assistant told his boss that her suggestions were silly and he would not follow them.

   contumacious *adjective* The **contumacious** lieutenant was demoted after she repeatedly disobeyed her commanding officer.

3. **dour** (dŏor, dour) *adjective* from Latin *durus,* "hard"
   a. Marked by sternness, harshness, ill temper, or gloom
      • The **dour** professor almost never gives high grades.
   b. Sternly unyielding or stubborn
      • Her **dour** determination to ignore her tormentors was admirable.

   dourness *noun* Known for his **dourness,** our neighbor had few visitors.

4. **éclat** (ā-klä′) *noun* from Old French *esclater,* "to burst out; to splinter"
   Brilliance in performance and achievement; dazzling display
      • Determined to celebrate the symphony's hundredth anniversary with **éclat,** the directors planned several gala events.

dour

Éclat connotes an element of high style in achieving success.

5. **indefatigable** (ĭn´dĭ-făt´ĭ-gə-bəl) *adjective* from Latin *in-*, "not" + *de-*, "from" + *fatigare*, "to weary"
Tireless, incapable of wearing out or becoming fatigued
  • Although Rhonda hated to do even an hour's worth of writing, she was **indefatigable** when it came to working on math.

6. **irresolute** (ĭ-rĕz´ə-lo͞ot´) *adjective* from Latin *ir-*, "not" + *resolvere*, "to relax; to untie"
Undecided or uncertain about what to do; wavering
  • When the music suddenly stopped, the dancers stood **irresolute,** waiting for direction from the choreographer.

  resolute *adjective* Certain; having great determination
  • Kim was **resolute** in her decision to go to the best college that she could afford.

  resolve *noun* Once he had made his decision, the strength of Angelo's **resolve** was impressive.

7. **obdurate** (ŏb´do͝o-rĭt) *adjective* from Latin *ob-*, "to turn toward" + *durus*, "hard"
  a. Hardhearted; stubbornly persistent in wrongdoing
    • In the fairy tale, the **obdurate** giant remained determined to steal the town's gold despite the people's pleas for mercy.
  b. Not giving in to persuasion
    • Martin's **obdurate** refusal to cooperate made it difficult for the committee to complete the project.

8. **obsequious** (ŏb-sē´kwē-əs) *adjective* from Latin *ob-*, "to turn toward" + *sequi*, "to follow"
Excessively eager to serve, obey, or win the favor of another; fawning
  • We were disgusted by the **obsequious** employee who complied unquestioningly with all of his boss's ridiculous requests.

  obsequiousness *noun* His **obsequiousness** resembled the behavior of a lapdog.

9. **pertinacity** (pûr´tn-ăs´ĭ-tē) *noun* from Latin *per-*, "completely" + *tenere*, "to hold"
The quality of holding firmly or stubbornly to a purpose, an intention, or a belief; stubborness
  • Police Superintendent LeRoy Martin's **pertinacity** made the Chicago Police Department the last one in the area to abandon the requirement of wearing hats.

  pertinacious *adjective* Jonathan was extremely **pertinacious** when it came to completing tasks on time.

10. **stoic** (stō´ĭk) from Greek *stoa*, "porch"
  a. *adjective* Seemingly indifferent to or unaffected by joy, grief, pleasure, or pain; determined not to complain or show feeling
    • The **stoic** child bore the pain without flinching.
  b. *noun* A person who is seemingly indifferent to or unaffected by joy, grief, pleasure, or pain
    • A **stoic** by nature, Adam found it difficult to express his grief when his golden retriever died.

  stoicism *noun* The workers accepted the harsh working conditions with their usual **stoicism.**

Capitalized, *Stoic* refers to followers of the ancient Greek philosopher Zeno, who believed that God had already determined destiny, and that virtue was all that was required for a good life. Zeno taught his followers from a podium, known as the "Painted Porch." The Roman version of Stoicism later advocated the calm acceptance of all things.

WRITE THE CORRECT WORD

Write the correct word in the space next to each definition. Use each word only once.

_____ **1.** uncomplaining

_____ **2.** excessively eager to serve

_____ **3.** daring; fearless

_____ **4.** undecided

_____ **5.** brilliance in performance

_____ **6.** tireless

_____ **7.** stern; harsh

_____ **8.** rebelliousness

_____ **9.** hardhearted

_____ **10.** stubbornness

COMPLETE THE SENTENCE

Write the letter for the word that best completes each sentence.

_____ **1.** The _____ of the rebels frustrated government efforts to reach a compromise.
   a. éclat   **b.** contumacy   **c.** obsequiousness   **d.** stoicism

_____ **2.** With impressive _____, Mel listened to his sister rehearse her speech five times.
   a. stoicism   **b.** obdurateness   **c.** éclat   **d.** contumacy

_____ **3.** Our _____ supervisor seems irritable and unfriendly most of the time.
   a. audacious   **b.** indefatigable   **c.** pertinacious   **d.** dour

_____ **4.** People who lack self-confidence may welcome _____ flattery.
   a. audacious   **b.** obsequious   **c.** obdurate   **d.** irresolute

_____ **5.** The brilliant pianist performed the Beethoven sonata with great _____.
   a. pertinacity   **b.** dourness   **c.** éclat   **d.** stoicism

_____ **6.** The saying "If at first you don't succeed, try, try again" is all about _____.
   a. audacity   **b.** obsequiousness   **c.** pertinacity   **d.** stoicism

_____ **7.** Mazal was unable to persuade the _____ police officer to waive her speeding ticket, even though it was clear she had a medical emergency.
   a. obsequious   **b.** irresolute   **c.** audacious   **d.** obdurate

_____ **8.** The _____ student changed his college major several times.
   a. obdurate   **b.** irresolute   **c.** indefatigable   **d.** dour

_____ **9.** The crowd applauded the _____ feats of the tightrope walker.
   a. audacious   **b.** obsequious   **c.** obdurate   **d.** irresolute

_____ **10.** Brian, seemingly _____ on the dance floor, didn't take a break for hours.
   a. dour   **b.** obdurate   **c.** stoic   **d.** indefatigable

Challenge: While one child remained _____ about whether to brave the deep water of the pool, the other _____ dove right in.

_____   **a.** irresolute…audaciously   **b.** dour…indefatigably   **c.** obdurate…obsequiously

A Slave Girl's Rags to Riches

Of all the rags-to-riches stories that have happened in the United States, Mary Ellen Pleasant's is one of the most spectacular. Although born a slave, she managed to amass millions of dollars, using much of her money to help the less fortunate and to fight for civil rights. Her success brought fame but, unfortunately, also invited rumors. Eventually, Pleasant would be accused of many crimes, though no evidence of these crimes has ever been produced. Hers is one of the great stories of the Old West.

(1) Although Pleasant *obdurately* refused to reveal facts about her past, historians believe that she was born a slave in Georgia in 1817. As a child, she was bought and sold twice, and then placed into indentured servitude with a Quaker family in Massachusetts.

The Quakers were strong believers in equal rights. **(2)** Rather than insisting that Pleasant be an *obsequious* servant, her bosses taught her business skills in their general store. They also shared with her their abolitionist beliefs that all slaves should be freed. When her nine-year service ended, they got Pleasant a job with a tailor in Boston. It would prove a life-changing move.

In Boston, Pleasant married a wealthy man named James W. Smith. **(3)** He was secretly a rescuer on the Underground Railroad, and the ever *audacious* Pleasant joined the effort. But when Smith died, Pleasant became a wanted woman because she helped slaves, so she fled west with a sheriff in pursuit.

Pleasant settled in San Francisco, a dirty, dangerous Gold Rush town, where there were six men to every woman, 700 saloons, and nearly a murder per day. **(4)** Here, Pleasant became *pertinacious* in her pursuit of both success and civil rights. She had a genius for investing and turned her inheritance of roughly $15,000 into a fortune. She opened laundries, restaurants, boarding houses, and a dairy farm.

(5) She also used her riches to become an *indefatigable* advocate for her race. After paying for scores of fugitive and freed slaves to come to San Francisco, she fed and clothed them, found them jobs, and helped them start businesses. **(6)** Her *éclat* in performing these deeds led people to call her "the black City Hall."

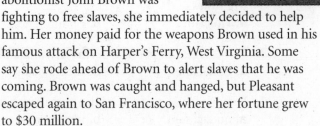

Pleasant also took her battle for civil rights to the courts. **(7)** Although some found her actions *contumacious,* she fought to change the law that prevented blacks from testifying in court—and she won. Later, she sued for the right for blacks to ride on streetcars. Again, she won. For this, she earned another nickname: "the mother of civil rights in California."

(8) Never one to be *irresolute,* when Pleasant heard that white abolitionist John Brown was fighting to free slaves, she immediately decided to help him. Her money paid for the weapons Brown used in his famous attack on Harper's Ferry, West Virginia. Some say she rode ahead of Brown to alert slaves that he was coming. Brown was caught and hanged, but Pleasant escaped again to San Francisco, where her fortune grew to $30 million.

Her success made many uneasy, though. Unfounded rumors spread that she used voodoo or blackmail to build her wealth. Bizarre stories of murder and sacrifices circulated, although no evidence was ever produced. Nonetheless, the absurd accusations made front-page news.

(9) Perhaps tiring of constant rumors, Pleasant grew *dour* in her old age, frightening off news reporters with her sternness. She also lost much of her fortune. **(10)** To the end, though, she *stoically* accepted her fate, and when she died, mourners by the hundreds paid tribute to her with flowers.

Each sentence below refers to a numbered sentence in the passage. Write the letter of the choice that gives the sentence a meaning that is closest to the original sentence.

_____ **1.** Pleasant _____ refused to reveal facts about her past.
    a. undecidedly   **b.** stubbornly   **c.** annoyingly   **d.** boldly

_____ **2.** Her bosses did not insist that Pleasant be a(n) _____ servant.
    a. fawning   **b.** annoying   **c.** pleasant   **d.** uncertain

_____ **3.** The ever _____ Pleasant joined the effort.
    a. energetic   **b.** stubborn   **c.** harsh   **d.** bold

_____ **4.** Here, Pleasant became _____ in her pursuit of both success and civil rights.
   a. uncertain   **b.** secretive   **c.** vacillating   **d.** unwavering

_____ **5.** She used her riches to become a(n) _____ advocate for her race.
   a. tireless   **b.** hardened   **c.** impatient   **d.** powerful

_____ **6.** Her _____ in performing these deeds led people to call her "the black City Hall."
   a. immense daring   **b.** modest efficiency   **c.** great success   **d.** harshness

_____ **7.** Although some found her actions _____, she fought to change the law that prevented blacks from testifying in court.
   a. fearless   **b.** rebellious   **c.** uncertain   **d.** hardhearted

_____ **8.** Never one to be _____, when Pleasant heard that white abolitionist John Brown was fighting to free slaves, she immediately decided to help him.
   a. uncertain   **b.** apologetic   **c.** idle   **d.** stubborn

_____ **9.** Pleasant grew _____ in her old age, frightening off news reporters.
   a. silent   **b.** fawning   **c.** ill-humored   **d.** certain

_____ **10.** To the end, though, she _____ accepted her fate.
   a. with anger   **b.** without complaint   **c.** with harshness   **d.** without friends

Indicate whether the statements below are TRUE or FALSE according to the passage.

_____ **1.** When she was young, Mary Ellen Pleasant was an indentured servant.

_____ **2.** Mary Ellen Pleasant's philosophy was probably "take the money and run."

_____ **3.** In old age, Mary Ellen Pleasant reflected happily on her accomplishments.

WRITING EXTENDED RESPONSES

Mary Ellen Pleasant's story is one of astonishing success in the face of seemingly overwhelming obstacles. What kind of character traits must such a person have in order to succeed? In an expository essay, describe the character traits required to overcome obstacles, explaining why they are necessary. Your essay should be at least three paragraphs long and contain a minimum of two well-supported reasons for your choices. Use at least three lesson words in your essay and underline them.

WRITE THE DERIVATIVE

Complete the sentence by writing the correct form of the word shown in parentheses. You may not need to change the form that is given.

_____ **1.** During the debate, both opponents held to their positions, equally resolute _____. (*irresolute*)

_____ **2.** _____ is usually not regarded as an admirable trait. (*obsequious*)

_____ **3.** In the 1700s, American colonists _____ protested British taxes by dumping tea into Boston Harbor. *(contumacy)*

_____ **4.** The _____ of the expression on my boss's face suggested the meeting would not be pleasant. *(dour)*

_____ **5.** The teenage chess player defeated her older opponent with _____. *(éclat)*

_____ **6.** Mark is known to be _____ when confronted with obstacles. *(pertinacity)*

_____ **7.** While some people face life's challenges _____, others are more timid. *(audacious)*

_____ **8.** Once Christina embarks on a project, she works _____. *(indefatigable)*

_____ **9.** Despite mitigating circumstances, the judge _____ refused to consider a shorter jail sentence. *(obdurate)*

_____ **10.** Pioneers who traveled west in covered wagons often showed remarkable _____ in the face of many hardships. *(stoic)*

FIND THE EXAMPLE

Choose the answer that best describes the action or situation.

_____ **1.** A nickname for someone *dour*
    a. Old Frownface   **b.** Mary Sunshine   **c.** Happy Jack   **d.** Steady Freddie

_____ **2.** Something an *obdurate* person is most likely to do
    a. accept defeat   **b.** take advice   **c.** reject advice   **d.** listen intently

_____ **3.** NOT a good situation in which to be *stoic* about discomfort
    a. hiding from danger   **b.** taking an exam   **c.** visiting a doctor   **d.** competing in an event

_____ **4.** Usually the most *audacious* professional
    a. story writer   **b.** lion tamer   **c.** opera singer   **d.** reference librarian

_____ **5.** The most likely description of an *indefatigable* person
    a. energetic   **b.** lethargic   **c.** lazy   **d.** unmotivated

_____ **6.** An example of *contumacy*
    a. quiet respect   **b.** questioning unfairness   **c.** following orders   **d.** political rebellion

_____ **7.** The person most likely to demonstrate *éclat*
    a. novice   **b.** incompetent clown   **c.** experienced pro   **d.** scared toddler

_____ **8.** The person most likely to behave *obsequiously*
    a. customs agent   **b.** personal valet   **c.** superintendent   **d.** firefighter

_____ **9.** An *irresolute* response
    a. I'm not sure.   **b.** Absolutely!   **c.** No way.   **d.** Stop it now.

_____ **10.** A key feature of *pertinacity*
    a. clear conscience   **b.** frequent bad luck   **c.** regret   **d.** determination

Plenty and Excess

WORD LIST

austere	avarice	florid	insatiable	inundate
myriad	parsimony	prodigal	replete	voluminous

Throughout history, sages have cautioned against excess. The ancient Chinese philosopher Lao-Tse advised people to "embrace simplicity." Aristotle is credited with saying, "Moderation in all things." Sister Elizabeth Ann Seton, founder of the Daughters of Charity, once remarked, "Live simply, so that others may simply live."

1. **austere** (ô-stîr´) *adjective* from Greek *austeros,* "severe"
   a. Severe or stern in personality or appearance; somber and grave
      • Our **austere** algebra teacher never laughed during class.
   b. Bare, without adornment
      • His office was very **austere,** with bare walls, and nothing but an old desk, a chair, and a filing cabinet for furniture.

   austerity *noun* The mayor won the election by promising **austerity** in government spending.

2. **avarice** (ăv´ə-rĭs) *noun* from Latin *avarus,* "greedy"
   Greed, or an extreme desire for wealth
      • By inflating the importance of gifts and money, adults may fuel the **avarice** of their children.

   avaricious *adjective* The press labeled the athlete **avaricious** when he refused to sign the contract unless he received more money.

austere

3. **florid** (flôr´ĭd) *adjective* from Latin *flor,* "flower"
   a. Flushed with rosy color
      • The cheeks of the children were **florid** from running so quickly.
   b. Very ornate; flowery
      • The author used **florid** language in her romantic story.

   floridity *noun* Sandra wore a gaudy hat that reflected the **floridity** of her style.

> The word *florid* often refers to overblown, fancy language.

4. **insatiable** (ĭn-sā´shə-bəl, ĭn-sā´-shē-ə-bəl) *adjective* from Latin *in-,* "not" + *satiare,* "to fill"
   Not capable of being fully satisfied
      • The two tiny puppies had **insatiable** appetites, and we soon ran out of pet food.

5. **inundate** (ĭn´ŭn-dāt´) *verb* from Latin *in-,* "in" + *unda,* "wave"
   a. To flood or cover over with water
      • The engineers warned that if the dam burst, water would **inundate** the small village.
   b. To overwhelm as if with a flood
      • The children's rooms were **inundated** with stuffed toys.

6. **myriad** (mĭr´ē-əd) from Greek *murios*, "countless"
   a. *adjective* Referring to a large but undetermined number
   • **Myriad** choices lay before them in the dollar store.
   b. *adjective* Made up of many diverse elements or facets
   • The children were fascinated by the **myriad** sea life in the enormous aquarium.
   c. *noun* A huge number
   • We couldn't count the **myriads** of crabs running along the ocean shore.

Myriad meant "ten thousand" in ancient Greece.

7. **parsimony** (pär´sə-mō´nē) *noun* from Latin *parcere*, "to spare"
   Displaying extreme stinginess or cheapness
   • Famous for his **parsimony,** Mr. MacDougal has never bought a present for a friend.

   parsimonious She was so **parsimonious** that she refused to leave a tip, even though the waitress did a great job.

8. **prodigal** (prŏd´ĭ-gəl) *adjective* from Latin *prodigere*, "to drive away; to squander"
   a. Carelessly or wastefully extravagant; lavish
   • Within a year, the **prodigal** man had wasted his inheritance on expensive cars and vacations.
   b. Giving or given in abundance
   • The **prodigal** praise heaped on the play resulted in a year of sold-out performances.

   prodigality *noun* The hostess became famous for the **prodigality** of her parties.

9. **replete** (rĭ-plēt´) *adjective* from Latin *re-*, "again" + *plere*, "to fill"
   Plentifully supplied; abounding
   • The garden was **replete** with the aromas of spring.

10. **voluminous** (və-lōō´mə-nəs) *adjective* from Latin *volumen*, "a roll of writing"
    a. Having great fullness, size, or number
    • French noblewomen in the 1700s had such **voluminous** hairstyles that they sometimes had trouble getting through doorways.
    b. Ample or lengthy in speech or writing
    • The **voluminous** documents relating to the court case filled three offices.

WORD ENRICHMENT

Rolls of writing

The parchment rolls that held ancient writings took up much more room than today's books do. The Latin word *volumen*, meaning "roll of writing," gave rise to the word *volume*, which is now used to refer to a single book.

The Latin verb *volvere*, which is related to *volumen*, means "to roll." It is the basis of the modern word *voluble*, which means "talkative" or "fluent."

WRITE THE CORRECT WORD

Write the correct word in the space next to each definition. Use each word only once.

_____ **1.** impossible to satisfy

_____ **2.** a huge number

_____ **3.** stern or somber

_____ **4.** to flood with water

_____ **5.** having great size or number

_____ **6.** extreme greed

_____ **7.** flowery; ornate

_____ **8.** stinginess

_____ **9.** plentiful; abounding

_____ **10.** wastefully extravagant

COMPLETE THE SENTENCE

Write the letter for the word that best completes each sentence.

_____ **1.** Many students avoided the class when they saw the _____ list of articles and books that the syllabus included as required reading.
a. insatiable   **b.** voluminous   **c.** florid   **d.** austere

_____ **2.** Dickens's miserly character Ebenezer Scrooge was a model of _____.
a. floridity   **b.** prodigality   **c.** myriad   **d.** parsimony

_____ **3.** There are _____ reasons why it pays to be polite to others.
a. myriad   **b.** avaricious   **c.** parsimonious   **d.** austere

_____ **4.** His _____ desire to understand other cultures made him a tireless traveler.
a. replete   **b.** austere   **c.** insatiable   **d.** parsimonious

_____ **5.** Demonstrating incredible _____, the manager attempted to keep all of his workers' year-end bonuses for himself.
a. floridity   **b.** myriad   **c.** avarice   **d.** prodigality

_____ **6.** After the pipes burst, our basement was quickly _____ with water.
a. repleted   **b.** florid   **c.** prodigal   **d.** inundated

_____ **7.** The _____ lifestyle required of monks forbids them any luxuries.
a. austere   **b.** replete   **c.** voluminous   **d.** myriad

_____ **8.** Taking some of the unnecessary adjectives out of your writing would make it less _____.
a. insatiable   **b.** florid   **c.** austere   **d.** prodigal

_____ **9.** After trick-or-treating, the child's sack was _____ with candy, gum, and other treats.
a. florid   **b.** replete   **c.** austere   **d.** parsimony

_____ **10.** _____ expenditures will soon exhaust your savings.
a. Parsimonious   **b.** Austere   **c.** Inundated   **d.** Prodigal

Challenge: _____ with choices from the buffet table, my apparently _____ brother kept going back to fill up his plate.
_____   **a.** Florid…replete   **b.** Avaricious…parsimonious   **c.** Inundated…insatiable

Freedom Ship

Plans are currently underway to build the biggest ship in history. **(1)** At over a mile long and 350 feet high, *Freedom Ship* would be the most *voluminous* vessel to ever travel the sea. It is being designed as a flat-bottomed barge with a twenty-five-story-high building on top. Weighing about 3 million tons, it would be like setting ten blocks of New York City afloat.

Builders of the ship say that their goal is to create the first floating community. **(2)** It will come *replete* with homes for 40,000 people and living space for 20,000 crewmembers. **(3)** *Myriad* onboard facilities will include a library, a hospital, schools, and shopping malls. Banks, movie theaters, pools, and parks will also be provided. The ship will feature an airstrip where small planes can land. In effect, *Freedom Ship* will be a city at sea.

(4) Residents with an *insatiable* desire to travel will certainly feel at home. The boat will circle the globe every three years, stopping at major ports. This will allow children living on the ship to make firsthand contact with cultures they have studied in school.

(5) The ship will likely be *inundated* by tourists at each port. Plans allow for 30,000 per day, and hotels on *Freedom Ship* will be able to accommodate 10,000 guests. Visitors can shop, visit conventions held in the trade center, or simply take in this engineering wonder.

The ship is expected to take three years to build and to cost around $10 billion. **(6)** *Parsimony* has not governed the planning process. **(7)** No expense is to be spared for luxuries like public artwork, fountains, and *florid* interiors.

The project does have its critics, though. **(8)** Some of the more *austere*-minded object to what they consider needless luxury. **(9)** For others, the amount of money needed to build it seems *prodigal*. These people doubt that the construction funds will ever be raised. However, a good number of the ship's homes, ranging in price from $180,000 to $44 million, have already been sold.

(10) Some accuse the buyers of *avarice*. The ship will collect no sales, property, or income taxes. So wealthy passengers could potentially avoid paying taxes by living on *Freedom Ship*. Yet, project planners point out that most residents will likely hail from countries that will still require them to pay taxes.

Critics also voice concerns about safety. They point out that *Freedom Ship* has no plans to carry lifeboats because designers claim it will be unsinkable. This claim was also made about the *Titanic*, which sank on its maiden voyage in 1912. But project engineers boast that the hull will be composed of 600 huge airtight steel boxes. A significant number of these would have to be damaged before the ship would be in any danger of sinking. Likewise, due to *Freedom Ship*'s great size, a normally deadly 100-foot wave would move the vessel only about one inch.

For now, the ship is still a dream. Once it is built, though, it will provide a unique maritime experience.

Each sentence below refers to a numbered sentence in the passage. Write the letter of the choice that gives the sentence a meaning that is closest to the original sentence.

_____ **1.** At over a mile long and 350 feet high, *Freedom Ship* would be the most _____ vessel to ever travel the sea.
    a. destructive   **b.** colorful   **c.** massive   **d.** well-armed

_____ **2.** It will come _____ with homes for 40,000 people and living space for 20,000 crewmembers.
    a. sailing   **b.** overloaded   **c.** protected   **d.** well-supplied

_____ **3.** _____ onboard facilities will include a library, a hospital, schools, and malls.
    a. Numerous   **b.** Mysterious   **c.** Strict   **d.** Haphazard

_____ 4. Residents with a(n) _____ desire to travel will certainly feel at home.
     a. small   **b.** unlimited   **c.** large   **d.** uncertain

_____ 5. The ship will likely be _____ by tourists at each stop.
     a. flooded   **b.** impeded   **c.** made ornate   **d.** heckled

_____ 6. _____ has not governed the planning process.
     a. Guilt   **b.** Politics   **c.** Stinginess   **d.** Awe

_____ 7. No expense is to be spared for luxuries like public artwork, fountains, and _____ interiors.
     a. high-tech   **b.** ornate   **c.** beautiful   **d.** hazardous

_____ 8. Some of the more _____-minded object to what they consider needless luxury.
     a. somber   **b.** lavish   **c.** greedy   **d.** public

_____ 9. For others, the amount of money needed to build it seems _____.
     a. ornate   **b.** endangered   **c.** unrealistic   **d.** wasteful

_____ 10. Some accuse the buyers of _____.
     a. stinginess   **b.** greed   **c.** somberness   **d.** never being satisfied

Indicate whether the statements below are TRUE or FALSE according to the passage.

_____ 1. At the time the reading passage was written, *Freedom Ship* had already sailed on its maiden voyage.

_____ 2. It will be possible to live for long periods of time on the *Freedom Ship*.

_____ 3. Designers of *Freedom Ship* plan to equip it with thousands of lifeboats.

FINISH THE THOUGHT

Complete each sentence so that it shows the meaning of the italicized word.

1. She was *replete* with happiness when _____

_____

2. My *austere* piano teacher _____

_____

WRITE THE DERIVATIVE

Complete the sentence by writing the correct form of the word shown in parentheses. You may not need to change the form that is given.

_____ **1.** Our town's zoo is _____ with animals from all over the world. (*replete*)

_____ **2.** The _____ of the play's set design helped to show the difficult financial situation of the characters. (*austere*)

3. You're _____ me with facts and figures, but I will only be able to remember a few of them. (*inundate*)

4. Nick thought about donating money to the charity, but his _____ attitude prevented him from doing so. (*parsimony*)

5. Students accustomed to the terse, spare styles of modern prose may complain of the _____ of such nineteenth-century writers as Herman Melville. (*florid*)

6. We found _____ of luscious, ripe fruits and vegetables at the farmer's market. (*myriad*)

7. After being asleep for twenty years, Rip Van Winkle's beard had grown _____. (*voluminous*)

8. Laura has an _____ desire to help others, so she volunteers at several homeless shelters. (*insatiable*)

9. After winning the lottery, Sue's spending habits became so _____ that she eventually eventually went into debt. (*prodigal*)

10. The _____ of the board of directors, who spent company money on personal luxuries, bankrupted the business. (*avarice*)

FIND THE EXAMPLE

Choose the answer that best describes the action or situation.

_____ **1.** The place most likely to be *replete* with musical instruments
a. golf course   **b.** funeral parlor   **c.** concert hall   **d.** monastery

_____ **2.** What an *insatiable* person would be most likely to say
a. That's enough.   **b.** No, thank you.   **c.** Give it to her.   **d.** I want more.

_____ **3.** An example of a *voluminous* text
a. an epic novel   **b.** a pamphlet   **c.** a horoscope   **d.** driving directions

_____ **4.** Something that might cause a person to become *florid*
a. sleeping soundly   **b.** hiking a steep hill   **c.** whistling   **d.** talking on the phone

_____ **5.** What a *parsimonious* person would be LEAST likely to give freely
a. advice   **b.** money   **c.** effort   **d.** time

_____ **6.** The thing MOST likely to cause an *inundation*
a. tornado   **b.** snowfall   **c.** hurricane   **d.** hailstorm

_____ **7.** The place most likely to be *austere*
a. prison cell   **b.** dorm room   **c.** hotel ballroom   **d.** room in a castle

_____ **8.** Something an *avaricious* person might say
a. Let's share.   **b.** May I help you?   **c.** It's all mine!   **d.** It's only money.

_____ **9.** Where *myriad* food choices would most likely be found
a. hot-dog stand   **b.** supermarket   **c.** family dinner   **d.** airplane

_____ **10.** Where people might be expected to spend *prodigal* amounts of money
a. discount store   **b.** park   **c.** grocery store   **d.** fancy restaurant

Taking Tests

SAT Writing Tests

The new SAT, first administered in 2005, has a Writing section that includes an essay question and a set of multiple-choice questions on grammar, usage, and composition. There are three different kinds of multiple-choice questions. Each kind is described below.

Strategies

1. The **identification of sentence error** questions require you to look at four underlined parts of a sentence and determine whether one of them is faulty. First, read the entire sentence. Then reread the sentence and choose the part that has an error in grammar, usage, or syntax. (No more than one part can be incorrect.) If you find no errors, choose E.

2. **Sentence correction** items also present a sentence with underlined words. Here, your task is to choose the correct version of the underlined part in order to improve the sentence. Note that choice A is the same as the underlined version.

3. **Paragraph improvement** items present a paragraph with several sentences. Each item asks how a specific sentence or part of the paragraph can be improved. Your task is to choose the change that will improve the paragraph. To answer these kinds of questions, read through the paragraph and all of the answer choices first. The key is to choose the answer that combines the sentences—or makes another kind of change—without changing the meaning of the sentences. Decide what the sentences mean, and then choose the answer that is best written and retains the same meaning.

Practice

In questions 1–3, choose the underlined part of the sentence that contains an error in grammar, usage, or word choice. If there is no error, choose answer E.

_____ 1. Ms. Fletcher <u>appointed</u> Clarissa and <u>myself</u> <u>to serve on</u>
                                   A   B   C
the <u>committee.</u> <u>No error</u>
           D   E

_____ 2. Richard <u>seems</u> <u>more capable</u> than Franny, but Franny is clearly
                        A   B
<u>most conscientious</u> <u>than he.</u> <u>No error</u>
           C   D   E

_____ 3. The increase <u>in the price</u> of sugar <u>can't hardly</u> <u>be attributed</u> to
                              A   B   C
<u>last year's</u> hurricane season. <u>No error</u>
        D   E

In questions 4–6, the underlined part of the sentence may need to be corrected. Choice A is the same as the original underlined part; the other choices are different. Choose the answer that best expresses the meaning of the original sentence.

_____ 4. <u>Trying to order our meals in French</u>, the waiter just stared at me.
    a. Trying to order our meals in French,
    b. After trying to order our French meals,
    c. As I tried to order our meals in French,
    d. Trying to order our meals in French, but
    e. In French trying to order our meals,

_____ 5. Aunt Margaret, <u>which is in Kansas</u>, called just after midnight.
    a. which is in Kansas
    b. that is in Kansas
    c. which was in Kansas
    d. who are in Kansas
    e. who is in Kansas

_____ 6. <u>Considered a great writer now, and</u> Edgar Allan Poe was not as popular in his day.
    a. Considered a great writer now, and
    b. Considered a great writer now, but
    c. Since being considered a great writer now,
    d. Although he is considered a great writer now,
    e. Considered a great writer now, however

For questions 7–8, read the paragraph. Some parts of it need to be improved. Choose the best answer to each question about the way the paragraph is written.

(1) The United States currently has 57 national parks and numerous protected areas, such as historic sites, battlefields, and memorials. (2) The first official national park was established in 1872. (3) That was Yellowstone National Park. (4) Yosemite and Sequoia national parks were both established in 1890. (5) Grand Canyon National Park joined the list in 1893. (6) President Theodore Roosevelt added between 1901 and 1909 five new national parks. (7) He contributed greatly to the expansion of the national park system.

_____ 7. Which is the best way to combine sentences 2 and 3?
    a. The first official national park was established in 1872, but that was Yellowstone National Park.
    b. The first official national park was Yellowstone, and it was established in 1872.
    c. The first official national park established in 1872 was Yellowstone.
    d. Yellowstone, the first official national park, established in 1872.
    e. The first official national park was Yellowstone, established in 1872.

_____ 8. Which is the best version of sentence 6?
    a. President Theodore Roosevelt added between 1901 and 1909 five new national parks.
    b. Between 1901 and 1909, President Theodore Roosevelt added five new national parks.
    c. Five new national parks, added by president Theodore Roosevelt between 1901 and 1909.
    d. Between President Theodore Roosevelt and national parks, five were added from 1901 to 1909.
    e. President Theodore Roosevelt added five new national parks in 1901 and 1909.

Wrongdoing and Justice

WORD LIST

abscond	bilk	clemency	contrite	impute
iniquity	redress	reprehensible	restitution	vindicate

"Disgrace does not consist in the punishment, but in the crime," wrote the Italian dramatist Vittorio Alferi. The words in this lesson will help you communicate about wrongdoing and justice.

1. **abscond** (ăb-skŏnd´) *verb* from Latin *ab-*, "away" + *condere*, "to put"
   To leave quickly and secretly and hide oneself, often to avoid arrest or prosecution
   • The thief **absconded** to another state after he was released on bail.

   absconder *noun* Pursuing leads given by neighbors, the police captured the **absconder.**

   > The phrase *abscond with* is common, as in "to *abscond with* the money."

2. **bilk** (bĭlk) *verb*
   To cheat or swindle out of money
   • The art dealer **bilked** wealthy clients out of millions of dollars by selling them fake masterpieces.

3. **clemency** (klĕm´ən-sē) *noun* from Latin *clemens*, "mild; merciful"
   a. Mercy, especially toward a criminal or an enemy
   • The judge tended to show **clemency** toward young offenders.
   b. Mildness, especially of weather
   • The parks were crowded with walkers and ball players enjoying the unexpected **clemency** of the March day.

   clement *adjective* Enjoy the **clement** weather; we are expecting a storm tomorrow.

4. **contrite** (kən-trīt´) *adjective* from *com-*, "thoroughly" + *terere*, "to grind"
   Feeling regret and sorrow for things one has done wrong
   • Isabel was **contrite** about not cleaning up the spilled juice after her mother slipped on it.

   contrition or **contriteness** *noun* In a public display of **contrition,** the criminal apologized to the victim's family.

contrite

5. **impute** (ĭm-pyo͞ot´) *verb* from Latin *in-*, "in" + *putare*, "to settle an account"
   a. To attribute the fault or responsibility to; to relate to a particular cause or source
   • The coach **imputed** the loss of the game to an unfair penalty.
   b. To assign as a characteristic
   • The gracefulness we **impute** to swans disappears when we see them move on land.

   imputation *noun* I resent your **imputation** that I lost the equipment, when it was not my responsibility to keep track of it.

6. **iniquity** (ĭ-nĭk´wĭ-tē) *noun* from Latin *in-,* "not" + *aequus,* "equal"
Wickedness; immorality; a wicked or an immoral act; a sin
   • The superhero fought to save the world from the **iniquities** of villains.

   iniquitous *adjective* It is **iniquitous** to attack defenseless people.

7. **redress** from Latin *re-,* "back" + Old French *drecier,* "to arrange"
   a. *verb* (rĭ-drĕs´) To right a wrong; to make up for
   • Although nothing can ever fully **redress** the wrongs done to
   Japanese Americans interned during World War II, they have
   been offered financial compensation.
   b. *noun* (rē´drĕs) Satisfaction for a wrong or injury; a correction
   • The union sought **redress** for the employee who had been unfairly
   treated when he requested time off to recover from his injury.

8. **reprehensible** (rĕp´rĭ-hĕn´sə-bəl) *adjective* from Latin *re-,* "back"
   + *prehendere,* "to seize"
   Deserving of blame or criticism
   • The company engaged in the **reprehensible** practice of inflating the
   price of medicine it sold to elderly patients.

   reprehend *verb* The social worker **reprehended** the intern for her lack
   of sensitivity to the young child's feelings.

9. **restitution** (rĕs´tĭ-tōo´shən) *noun* from Latin *re-,* "back" + *statvere,*
   "to set up"
   a. The act of restoring something to its proper owner or to its original,
   undamaged state
   • The policemen were commended for the apprehension of the thieves
   and the **restitution** of the priceless painting to the museum.
   b. The act of compensating for loss, damage, or injury
   • The boy's parents told him that he would have to use the money he
   had saved to make full **restitution** for the window he broke.

10. **vindicate** (vĭn´dĭ-kāt´) *verb* from Latin *vindic,* "avenger"
    a. To clear of blame, suspicion, or doubt with supporting arguments
    or proof
    • The woman was **vindicated** when surveillance videos showed that
    she did not commit the robbery.
    b. To justify or prove the worth of something
    • After making several mistakes in his first week at work, Jasper
    vindicated himself by doing an excellent job.

    vindication *noun* The team's winning season proved to be a
    welcome **vindication** of the coach's draft choices.

> *Vindicate* has several other
> meanings, including "to
> provide support for (a claim),"
> "to defend," and "to exact
> revenge for."

WORD ENRICHMENT

Dressing

The common word *dress,* which is the root of the word *redress,* originally
meant "to arrange" rather than "to put on clothes." Although it is most
commonly used in relation to clothes, *dress* continues to have many other
meanings. Among these are "to decorate," as in *to dress a store window for the
holidays.* It can also mean "to garnish," as in *to dress the turkey.* We are said *to
dress a wound* when we apply medication. These are only a few of the eleven
meanings of *dress* given in the unabridged *American Heritage Dictionary.*

WRITE THE CORRECT WORD

Write the correct word in the space next to each definition. Use each word only once.

_____ **1.** to right a wrong

_____ **2.** mercy

_____ **3.** compensation

_____ **4.** to clear of blame

_____ **5.** wickedness

_____ **6.** to swindle or cheat

_____ **7.** to attribute fault

_____ **8.** to leave to avoid arrest

_____ **9.** deserving of criticism

_____ **10.** regretful

COMPLETE THE SENTENCE

Write the letter for the word that best completes each sentence.

_____ **1.** Many groups have been fighting hard to rid the world of the _____ of child labor.
a. iniquity   **b.** clemency   **c.** contrition   **d.** imputation

_____ **2.** The _____ driver apologized profusely for causing the accident.
a. clement   **b.** vindicated   **c.** bilked   **d.** contrite

_____ **3.** I hope that swindler gets what he deserves, after _____ my grandmother out of her life savings.
a. bilking   **b.** absconding   **c.** imputing   **d.** vindicating

_____ **4.** Carelessness while driving is a _____ habit that can have serious consequences.
a. vindicated   **b.** clement   **c.** reprehensible   **d.** contrite

_____ **5.** The thief _____ with the proceeds from the charity fundraiser.
a. imputed   **b.** absconded   **c.** vindicated   **d.** redressed

_____ **6.** Emphasizing the defendant's obligation to care for his children, the attorney pleaded for _____ from the judge.
a. iniquity   **b.** clemency   **c.** redress   **d.** contrition

_____ **7.** When my sister confessed to breaking the lamp, our cat was _____.
a. bilked   **b.** absconded   **c.** redressed   **d.** vindicated

_____ **8.** After overbooking the flight, the airline _____ its error by providing free tickets for several travelers.
a. redressed   **b.** bilked   **c.** absconded   **d.** imputed

_____ **9.** When tomatoes were brought to Europe from the Americas, many Europeans _____ harmful effects to them.
a. absconded   **b.** redressed   **c.** imputed   **d.** vindicated

_____ **10.** The vandals were ordered to make _____ for the damage they had done.
a. vindication   **b.** contrition   **c.** restitution   **d.** iniquity

Challenge: Our softball team succeeded in _____ our disappointment from the previous season's playoff loss and _____ ourselves in the eyes of our die-hard fans.

_____ **a.** redressing…vindicating   **b.** imputing…bilking   **c.** absconding…reprehending

Guilty Until Proven Innocent

In May 1997, while waiting for a bus, Stephan Cowans was arrested and later charged with a crime. A police officer had been shot while trying to arrest a suspect, and supposedly Cowans's fingerprint was found at the scene.

Two eyewitnesses and the victim claimed that they had seen Cowans at the crime scene. The jury believed the evidence and convicted Cowans of shooting the officer, even though Cowans maintained his innocence. **(1)** The judge showed no *clemency,* and the twenty-seven-year-old Cowans was sentenced to thirty-five to fifty years in prison. He would not be eligible for parole until the age of sixty-two.

(2) Six years later, with the help of the New England Innocence Project, Cowans was *vindicated* and released. As it turned out, the fingerprint used to help convict him was not a match; it belonged to a resident of the house where the shooting took place. DNA testing, which had not been performed at the time of the trial, also showed that the shooter had been someone else. The eyewitness accounts were a case of mistaken identity.

Cowans is not alone in suffering a wrongful conviction. **(3)** Innocence Projects across the nation report that serious crimes are frequently *imputed* to people who are not guilty. In about 25 percent of the cases processed by the FBI lab during the past ten years, DNA found at the crime scenes did not match the DNA of the suspect. DNA test results have helped prove hundreds of defendants innocent each year, before their cases even go to trial.

But DNA testing, which uses biological evidence such as hair or blood to identify a person's unique genetic marker, has only become common in recent years. For this reason, the nonprofit groups known as Innocence Projects, run by lawyers and law students, are pushing to reconsider old cases in which DNA evidence might establish the innocence of a person convicted of a crime. **(4)** In this way, they hope to *redress* wrongful convictions.

Since 1989, over 300 false convictions have been overturned in the United States. Thousands more such cases await reconsideration. **(5)** These are generally not white-collar crimes where, for example, a con artist *bilks* his investors. **(6)** Usually, these cases involve *reprehensible* acts of violence, like murder. Thus, innocent people may be sentenced to decades, or even life, in jail.

(7) They often suffer harsh sentences, in part because they do not appear *contrite* about their alleged offenses. It is, after all, hard to appear sorry for something you did not do. **(8)** Others, worried they will not receive a fair trial, *abscond*—but doing so can lead to a stiffer sentence if you are found.

The Innocence Projects point to a combination of factors for wrongful convictions, with mistaken witnesses being the most common problem. Sloppy lab work, questionable clues, and corrupt officials who fake or conceal evidence are also factors.

The impact, though, is clear. While most of the time the right perpetrator is convicted, sometimes mistakes are made, and the wrong person goes to jail. When this happens, an innocent person may spend years in a dangerous prison, missing out on births, weddings, funerals, and all other aspects of a normal life.

(9) Thus, many advocates argue that the falsely imprisoned should receive financial *restitution.* **(10)** They view a lack of compensation of the wrongfully convicted as an *iniquitous* policy. Currently, only nineteen states pay those cleared of crimes for their lost earnings and suffering due to incarceration.

Innocence Project workers also point out that the miscarriage of justice hurts us all. When the innocent are imprisoned, the guilty go unpunished and remain free to commit more crimes.

Each sentence below refers to a numbered sentence in the passage. Write the letter of the choice that gives the sentence a meaning that is closest to the original sentence.

_____ **1.** The judge showed no _____.
   a. regret   **b.** morality   **c.** mercy   **d.** blame

_____ **2.** Six years later Cowans was _____ and released.
   a. arrested   **b.** examined   **c.** convicted   **d.** cleared

_____ **3.** Innocence Projects across the nation report that serious crimes are frequently _____ people who are not guilty.
   a. deserving of   **b.** attributed to   **c.** restored to   **d.** legalized by

_____ 4. In this way, they hope to _____ wrongful convictions.
  a. eliminate   **b.** cover up   **c.** make up for   **d.** explain away

_____ 5. These are generally not white-collar crimes where, for example, a con artist
  _____ his investors.
  a. swindles   **b.** hides from   **c.** confuses   **d.** compensates

_____ 6. Usually, these cases involve _____ acts of violence, like murder.
  a. unusual   **b.** sorrowful   **c.** blameworthy   **d.** suspicious

_____ 7. They often suffer harsh sentences, in part because they do not appear _____
  about their alleged offenses.
  a. humble   **b.** regretful   **c.** merciful   **d.** guilty

_____ 8. Others, worried they will not receive a fair trial, _____.
  a. right a wrong   **b.** confess their guilt   **c.** hire a lawyer   **d.** flee to avoid arrest

_____ 9. Many advocates argue that the falsely imprisoned should receive financial _____.
  a. blame   **b.** advice   **c.** mercy   **d.** compensation

_____ 10. They view a lack of compensation of the wrongfully convicted as a(n)
  _____ policy.
  a. immoral   **b.** old-fashioned   **c.** fair-minded   **d.** suspicious

Indicate whether the statements below are TRUE or FALSE according to the passage.

_____ 1. The most common cause of wrongful conviction is that witnesses identify the
  wrong person as the culprit.

_____ 2. DNA testing is accepted as a very accurate way of identifying people.

_____ 3. False convictions are, fortunately, very rare.

WRITING EXTENDED RESPONSES

The passage discusses the issue of payment to those who have been
wrongfully convicted. Do you think that such restitution should be
granted? In a persuasive essay of at least three paragraphs, defend your
point of view with a minimum of two supporting points. Use at least
three lesson words in your essay and underline them.

WRITE THE DERIVATIVE

Complete the sentence by writing the correct form of the word shown in
parentheses. You may not need to change the form that is given.

_____ 1. Sir Isaac Newton's experiments with physics were _____ for Galileo's early
  theories of motion. (*vindicate*)

_____ 2. Intentionally harming another person is clearly an _____ act. (*iniquity*)

_____ 3. The merchant _____ his customers by overcharging them on credit card purchases. (*bilk*)

_____ 4. The politician was severely _____ for her role in the bribery scandal. (*reprehensible*)

_____ 5. Some people are required to do community-service work as _____ for their crimes. (*restitution*)

_____ 6. The _____ fled to a small country that had no extradition agreement with the United States. (*abscond*)

_____ 7. Marcy denied the _____ of her low grades to her afterschool job. (*impute*)

_____ 8. After the hearing, the company _____ employee grievances. (*redress*)

_____ 9. After days of gray skies and dismal cold, we hoped for more _____ weather. (*clemency*)

_____ 10. Billy's face showed his _____ as he stood beside the scraped front fender of his parents' car. (*contrite*)

FIND THE EXAMPLE

Choose the answer that best describes the action or situation.

_____ 1. Something generally thought to be *iniquitous*
   a. slavery   **b.** speeding   **c.** rudeness   **d.** bad grammar

_____ 2. Something a jury may *impute*
   a. money   **b.** innocence   **c.** guilt   **d.** doubt

_____ 3. Something to *redress*
   a. a right   **b.** a claim   **c.** a mannequin   **d.** a wrong

_____ 4. What a judge would do to demonstrate *clemency*
   a. exact revenge   **b.** sentence lightly   **c.** apologize   **d.** attribute blame

_____ 5. Something often *absconded* with
   a. awards   **b.** valuables   **c.** references   **d.** ideas

_____ 6. The essence of *contrition*
   a. regret   **b.** pride   **c.** dishonesty   **d.** justice

_____ 7. Something a *reprehensible* act would most likely lead to
   a. mercy   **b.** reverence   **c.** popularity   **d.** punishment

_____ 8. The usual object of *bilking*
   a. reputation   **b.** awards   **c.** money   **d.** food

_____ 9. Something a *vindicated* person would most likely say
   a. Prove it.   **b.** Maybe I did it.   **c.** I confess.   **d.** I told you so.

_____ 10. One common source of *restitution*
   a. victim   **b.** insurance   **c.** bank   **d.** family

Problems and Solutions

WORD LIST

adduce	confound	construe	conundrum	cryptic
equivocate	paradox	patent	perspicacity	rudimentary

The ways we come up with solutions to our problems have a direct effect on the quality of our lives. The words in this lesson relate to problems and solutions. As you learn the words, consider how they apply to problems you have faced.

1. **adduce** (ə-dōōs´) *verb* from Latin *ad-*, "toward; to" + *ducere,* "to lead"
   To cite as an example or a means of proof in an argument
   • Good persuasive writers **adduce** convincing evidence to support their arguments.

2. **confound** (kən-found´) *verb* from Latin *con-*, "together" + *fundere,* "to pour"
   a. To cause to become confused or perplexed
   • The unexpected results of the experiment **confounded** the scientist.
   b. To fail to distinguish; to mix up
   • Without realizing it, Terry was **confounding** fiction and fact.
   c. To make something bad even worse
   • Don't **confound** the mess by cleaning it up with an oily rag.

confound

3. **construe** (kən-strōō´) *verb* from Latin *con-*, "together" + *struere,* "to pile up"
   a. To interpret; to explain the meaning of
   • Allison **construed** her brother's silence as proof that he was guilty.
   b. To translate, especially to do so aloud
   • Together, the students **construed** the ancient Hebrew sentence.

Misconstrue means "to interpret incorrectly."

4. **conundrum** (kə-nŭn´drəm) *noun*
   a. A difficult, unsolvable, or self-contradictory problem; a dilemma
   • The question "Which came first, the chicken or the egg?" is a **conundrum.**
   b. A riddle which is answered by a pun
   • Here's a corny old **conundrum:** "What did the rug say to the floor? 'I've got you *covered.*'"

5. **cryptic** (krĭp´tĭk) *adjective* from Greek *kruptos*, "hidden"
   a. Having hidden meaning; mysterious
   • When Dad laughed at the **cryptic** note Mom had left, we suspected that it referred to a private joke.
   b. Using or based on code
   • Frequent **cryptic** radio messages raised the suspicions of federal agents and the local police.

6. equivocate (ĭ-kwĭv´ə-kāt´) *verb* from Latin *equi-*, "equal" + *vocare*, "to call"
To use language that is evasive or ambiguous, often in an attempt to mislead; to avoid making an explicit or a straightforward statement
• "I might have been around," the defendant **equivocated,** when asked whether he was in the area at the time of the robbery.

equivocal *adjective* Jeremy was frustrated with his boss's **equivocal** response to his request for a raise.

Equivocal also means "of uncertain significance or nature."

7. paradox (păr´ə-dŏks´) *noun* from Greek *para-*, "beyond" + *doxa,* "opinion"
a. A seemingly contradictory statement that may nonetheless be true
• The fact that standing is almost always more tiring than walking is something of a **paradox.**
b. Something exhibiting inexplicable or contradictory aspects
• A boxer campaigning for world peace is something of a **paradox.**

paradoxical *adjective* Humans have been described as **paradoxical** because we are capable of both incredible kindness and extreme cruelty.

8. patent (păt´nt) from Latin *patere,* "to be open"
a. *adjective* Obvious; plain; apparent
• The teacher chuckled at the child's **patent** lie about three ostriches destroying her homework.
b. *noun* A grant made by a government that confers upon the creator of an invention the sole right to make, use, and sell that invention for a set period of time
• The first person to obtain a **patent** on new technology is usually credited with having invented it, even if someone else designed and built it first.

The adjective form of *patent* can also be pronounced pāt´nt.

9. perspicacity (pûr´spĭ-kăs´ĭ-tē) *noun* from Latin *per-*, "thoroughly" + *specere,* "to look"
An acuteness of perception, observation, or understanding; a sharpness
• Unfortunately for the salesman, Mr. Yin had the **perspicacity** to know the difference between a well-built machine and a piece of junk.

perspicacious *adjective* Young Rafaela's **perspicacious** understanding of human motivation amazed us all.

10. rudimentary (rōō´də-mĕn´tə-rē) *adjective* from Latin *rudis*, "rough; unformed"
a. Of or relating to basic facts or principles; elementary
• Duing his first visit to Mexico, Jon wished he'd had more than a **rudimentary** grasp of the Spanish language.
b. In the earliest stages of development
• The instrument found at the archaeological dig was identified as a **rudimentary** flute.

rudiment *noun* Professor Altman often needs to review the **rudiments** of grammar with her freshman English classes.

WRITE THE CORRECT WORD

Write the correct word in the space next to each definition. Use each word only once.

_____ 1. a sharpness; an astuteness

_____ 2. obvious; apparent

_____ 3. to cite as an example

_____ 4. having hidden meaning

_____ 5. a difficult problem

_____ 6. basic; elementary

_____ 7. to make confused

_____ 8. to interpret

_____ 9. to use evasive language

_____ 10. a contradictory statement that may be true

COMPLETE THE SENTENCE

Write the letter for the word that best completes each sentence.

_____ 1. Clearly created by someone with a wry sense of humor, the _____ sign read, "Please ignore this sign."
   a. patented   **b.** adduced   **c.** construed   **d.** paradoxical

_____ 2. Jim _____ so often that his friends no longer expect a straight answer from him.
   a. equivocates   **b.** patents   **c.** construes   **d.** adduces

_____ 3. Rita's error was so _____ that we couldn't believe no one else noticed it.
   a. paradoxical   **b.** cryptic   **c.** patent   **d.** perspicacious

_____ 4. Considering that poetry is generally intended to have multiple layers of meaning, it is not surprising that people often _____ the same poem differently.
   a. equivocate   **b.** construe   **c.** adduce   **d.** confound

_____ 5. _____ experience with a potter's wheel is a prerequisite for this ceramics class.
   a. Patent   **b.** Rudimentary   **c.** Cryptic   **d.** Perspicacious

_____ 6. Marie complained that the play's convoluted plot _____ her completely.
   a. confounded   **b.** adduced   **c.** construed   **d.** equivocated

_____ 7. In his helpful talk, the treasurer clearly _____ the relevant economic realities.
   a. confounded   **b.** equivocated   **c.** patented   **d.** adduced

_____ 8. The clues for the treasure hunt were so _____ that no one found the treasure.
   a. rudimentary   **b.** cryptic   **c.** patent   **d.** construed

_____ 9. The exact method of the transmission of hereditary characteristics remained a _____ until the discovery of DNA.
   a. perspicacity   **b.** patent   **c.** conundrum   **d.** rudiment

_____ 10. Only a few investors had the _____ to foresee the stock's growth potential.
   a. equivocation   **b.** paradox   **c.** perspicacity   **d.** patent

Challenge: The _____ philosopher solved the conundrum, but none of his peers could understand his _____ explanation.
_____   **a.** rudimentary...patent   **b.** perspicacious...cryptic   **c.** equivocating...patent

A Code of Honor

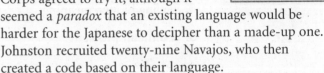

(1) As U.S. forces fought in the Pacific during World War II, the Japanese were *confounded* by unrecognizable words being used by American radio operators. Unknown to the Japanese, what they had been hearing came from specially trained Native Americans from the Navajo Nation, who created a code using their own language.

During the war, the United States and Japan eavesdropped on each other's radio messages constantly, trying to decipher the other side's coded messages. **(2)** These *cryptic* communications usually worked for a while, but eventually the codes on both sides were broken—that is, until the Navajo code talkers joined the battle. **(3)** The Japanese never solved the *conundrum* of their mysterious code. It is believed that without the Navajos' contribution, the war might have ended differently.

Almost a century earlier, in the 1860s, white settlers began taking Navajo lands in the southwestern United States. Violence erupted between the newcomers and the native Navajos. **(4)** In 1864, in an act of *patent* cruelty the U.S. Army destroyed Navajo crops and livestock, and marched tribe members 300 miles to a prison camp, where 2,000 of them eventually died. In 1888, the remaining 8,000 Navajos were granted reservation lands to live on, but the government insisted that only English be taught and spoken in the Navajo schools. However, the Navajo continued to teach their children their native language at home, so it survived.

By the spring of 1942, Japan was achieving significant victories in the Pacific. **(5)** Military leaders did not *equivocate*—U.S. forces needed an unbreakable code, if they were to have any chance to defeat the Japanese.

A civilian named Philip Johnston came up with the solution. Having lived on a Navajo reservation as a child, he knew that the complex language spoken there would seem indecipherable to those unfamiliar with it. And because the language had never been written down, the Japanese could not learn it from books. **(6)** His idea to use it as the basis for a code showed considerable *perspicacity*.

(7) Johnston *adduced* a few Navajo phrases in order to illustrate the intricacy of the language to military officials. **(8)** The Marine Corps agreed to try it, although it seemed a *paradox* that an existing language would be harder for the Japanese to decipher than a made-up one. Johnston recruited twenty-nine Navajos, who then created a code based on their language.

Much of the code was logical and straightforward. Dive bombers behaved like sparrow hawks, so the Navajo called them *gini*, their word for these hawks. Bombs, which had an oval shape, were dubbed *a-ye-shi*, which meant "eggs." The code talkers also designed an alphabet with a different Navajo word for each letter. The letter *a*, for example, was represented by the Navajo word for *ant*, which is *wol-la-chee*. **(9)** Later, to make the code even harder to crack, this *rudimentary* alphabet was expanded to include several Navajo words for each letter. In tests, the code stumped the best U.S. code breakers. **(10)** Navajo speakers who did not know the code were also unable to *construe* the meaning of the seemingly random groupings of words. The code talkers soon joined U.S. troops in the Pacific.

As soldiers advanced through the thick jungles and waist-deep mud of the islands occupied by the Japanese, the code talkers were there, coordinating activities, reporting enemy positions, and calling in air and sea support when needed.

During the critical battle of Iwo Jima, six code talkers sent more than 800 messages, working for two days without sleep. After the United States finally conquered the island, Major Howard Connor, a marine signal officer, said, "Were it not for the Navajos, the marines would have never taken Iwo Jima." The language once banned from Navajo schools had helped the United States take Iwo Jima and ultimately win the war.

Each sentence below refers to a numbered sentence in the passage. Write the letter of the choice that gives the sentence a meaning that is closest to the original sentence.

_____ **1.** The Japanese were _____ by unrecognizable words being used by American radio operators.

    a. fooled   **b.** confused   **c.** frightened   **d.** contradicted

_____ **2.** These _____ communications usually worked for a while.

    a. coded   **b.** imaginative   **c.** obvious   **d.** perceptive

_____ **3.** The Japanese never solved the _____ of this mysterious code.
     a. basics   **b.** contradiction   **c.** obviousness   **d.** problem

_____ **4.** In 1864, in an act of _____ cruelty, the U.S. Army destroyed crops and
livestock, and marched the Navajos 300 miles to a prison camp.
     a. confusing   **b.** mysterious   **c.** elementary   **d.** obvious

_____ **5.** Military's leaders did not _____—U. S. forces needed an unbreakable code.
     a. explain the need   **b.** bolster their ideas   **c.** become confused   **d.** use evasive language

_____ **6.** His idea to use it as the basis for a code showed considerable _____.
     a. perceptiveness   **b.** ambiguity   **c.** contradiction   **d.** obviousness

_____ **7.** Johnston _____ a few Navajo phrases to illustrate the intricacy of the language.
     a. camouflaged   **b.** evaded   **c.** cited   **d.** interpreted

_____ **8.** It seemed to be a(n) _____.
     a. riddle and pun   **b.** insoluble problem   **c.** sharp perception   **d.** apparent contradiction

_____ **9.** Later, this _____ alphabet was expanded.
     a. basic   **b.** mysterious   **c.** hidden   **d.** evasive

_____ **10.** Navajo speakers who did not know the code were also unable to _____ the words.
     a. contradict   **b.** interpret   **c.** evade   **d.** mix up

Indicate whether the statements below are TRUE or FALSE according to the passage.

_____ **1.** The Navajo have always had a cooperative relationship with the U.S. military.

_____ **2.** The Navajo language was particularly suitable for creating a coding system.

_____ **3.** The Navajo code talkers contributed to American successes in World War II.

FINISH THE THOUGHT

Complete each sentence so that it shows the meaning of the italicized word.

1. A question that *confounds* me is _____

_____

2. If you *equivocate* _____

_____

WRITE THE DERIVATIVE

Complete the sentence by writing the correct form of the word shown in parentheses. You may not need to change the form that is given.

_____ **1.** Some people think that wearing a baseball cap sideways is _____ silly. *(patent)*

_____ **2.** The crossword puzzle completely _____ Ira. *(confound)*

3. The fortuneteller described my future so _____ that I wondered if he was just trying to avoid saying anything definite at all. *(cryptic)*

4. A _____ interviewer draws illuminating responses from his or her subject. *(perspicacity)*

5. Deciding which kitten to adopt was a _____ for Sue. *(conundrum)*

6. To safely navigate the course of a boat in unfamiliar waters, you must know at least the _____ of reading nautical charts. *(rudimentary)*

7. Because the candidate did not want to offend anyone before the election, she answered most questions _____ . *(equivocate)*

8. The clues were so strange and _____ that the detective could only scratch his head in bewilderment. *(paradox)*

9. The phrase "nice job" can be _____ in totally different ways, depending on the speaker's tone of voice and the situation. *(construe)*

10. The councilwoman will _____ what happened recently in nearby Smallville, when she makes her case for the recycling proposal. *(adduce)*

FIND THE EXAMPLE

Choose the answer that best describes the action or situation.

1. An example of a *paradox*
a. fit athlete   b. lawyer in nice car   c. small baby   d. pacifist in the army

2. How you would likely feel if you were facing a *conundrum*
a. facts   b. satisfied   c. confident   d. puzzled

3. Something *adduced* to support an argument
a. facts   b. stone columns   c. questions   d. science fiction

4. An expression defined as *to equivocate*
a. run circles around you   b. beat around the bush   c. walk a country mile   d. chill like ice cream

5. Something that can be *confounded*
a. perfect solution   b. rocks   c. bad situation   d. dictionary

6. Something musically *rudimentary*
a. Mozart symphony   b. conductor's score   c. simple scale   d. live jazz performance

7. Something that you *construe*
a. building   b. symbol   c. future event   d. autobiography

8. Something that may be clear to you but *cryptic* to others
a. your class notes   b. your speaking voice   c. your eyes   d. your species

9. Someone NOT expected to be *perspicacious*
a. professor   b. expert   c. infant   d. doctor

10. Something you might receive a *patent* for
a. ice sculpture   b. oil painting   c. opinion   d. invention

Normality and Abnormality

WORD LIST

aberrant	anomaly	eccentricity	endemic	incongruous
mundane	outlandish	paragon	ubiquitous	unwonted

Normality and abnormality are somewhat fleeting ideas; what is normal in one time and place may be wildly abnormal in another. Just as we tend to see certain things as normal if we are accustomed to them, we may perceive other things as abnormal if they are unfamiliar to us. The words in this lesson are used to describe varying degrees of these concepts.

1. aberrant (ăb´ər-ənt) *adjective* from Latin *ab-*, "away from" + *errare*, "to stray"
Deviating from the proper or expected course; abnormal
• His volatile temper and **aberrant** mood swings were signs that he was experiencing unusual stress at work.

aberration *noun* Economists didn't know whether recent rising prices signaled an inflationary trend, or were just a short-term **aberration**.

2. anomaly (ə-nŏm´ə-lē) *noun* from Greek *an-*, "not" + *homos*, "same"
A departure from the normal or ordinary form, order, or rule
• Three-leaf clovers are the norm, and four-leaf clovers are **anomalies.**

anomalous *adjective* The mayor assured the public that the sewage spill was an isolated, **anomalous** event.

an anomaly

3. eccentricity (ĕk´sĕn-trĭs´ĭ-tē) *noun* from Greek *ex-*, "out of" + *kentron*, "center"
The quality of straying from what is conventional or customary; a deviation from the normal, expected, or established
• One of my uncle's **eccentricities** is his refusal to stay in any hotel room that is on an even-numbered floor.

eccentric *adjective* The singer's **eccentric** behavior was legendary, so no one was surprised when she arrived at the outdoor concert in a hot-air balloon, wearing a python around her neck.

4. endemic (ĕn-dĕm´ĭk) *adjective* from Greek *en-*, "in" + *demos*, "people"
Common in or unique to a certain location or population
• Though almost entirely eliminated in the United States, polio remains **endemic** in some Asian and African countries.

> Do not confuse *endemic* with *epidemic*, which means "spreading rapidly and widely through infection."

5. incongruous (ĭn-kŏng´grōō-əs) *adjective* from Latin *in-*, "not" + *congruere*, "to agree"
a. Lacking in harmony; incompatible
• The modern furniture seemed **incongruous** with the stone walls of the ancient castle.

> *Congruous*, the opposite of *incongruous*, means "appropriate" or "harmonious."

b. Not in agreement; inconsistent
  • Many agree that not exercising one's right to vote is **incongruous** with patriotism.
c. Not in keeping with what is proper, logical, or correct
  • It is **incongruous** to yell when attending a dignified, formal gathering.

incongruity *noun* There was an **incongruity** between her excellent education and the menial jobs listed on her resume.

6. mundane (mŭn-dān´) *adjective* from Latin *mundus*, "world"
Commonplace; ordinary
  • In a famous story by James Thurber, mild-mannered Walter Mitty escapes his **mundane** job and nagging family by daydreaming about heroic deeds.

7. outlandish (out-lăn´dĭsh) *adjective* from Old English *utland*, "foreign land"
Strikingly bizarre or unfamiliar
  • When she first wore a Japanese kimono to work, people considered it **outlandish,** but now they admire the grace of her outfits.

outlandishness *noun* Amusing us with his **outlandishness,** the team mascot did flips and somersaults in the aisles and juggled spectators' hats.

8. paragon (păr´ə-gŏn´) *noun* from Old Italian *paragone*, "a touchstone"
A model of perfection or excellence of a kind; an unparalleled example
  • Mother Teresa is considered by many to have been a **paragon** of virtue for dedicating her life to the sick and poor of India.

9. ubiquitous (yōō-bĭk´wĭ-təs) *adjective* from Latin *ubique*, "everywhere"
Being or seeming to be everywhere at the same time
  • You can always find a bite to eat in the **ubiquitous** cafes of Paris.

ubiquity *noun* Neighborhood residents complained about the **ubiquity** of the campaign posters taped to every lamp post.

10. unwonted (ŭn-wôn´tĭd) *adjective* from Old English *un-*, "not" + *wurian*, "to be used to"
Not habitual or ordinary; unusual
  • Seattle residents, who are accustomed to wet weather, are usually delighted by an **unwonted** dry spell.

> As an adjective, *wont* means "accustomed," or "likely." As a noun, it means "customary practice or habit."

WORD ENRICHMENT

Words of the people

The root *dem*, from the Greek word *demos*, meaning "people," is the root of many words besides *endemic*. The word *democracy* means "government by the people." *Pandemic* and *epidemic* both mean "widespread," and are often used to refer to rapidly spreading diseases; a *pandemic* is a worldwide *epidemic*. The word *demography* means "the study of a population." A *demagogue* is a leader who gains power by appealing to the emotions and prejudices of the people.

WRITE THE CORRECT WORD

Write the correct word in the space next to each definition. Use each word only once.

_____ **1.** strikingly bizarre

_____ **2.** uncustomary

_____ **3.** the quality of being unconventional

_____ **4.** a departure from the norm

_____ **5.** a model of excellence

_____ **6.** commonplace

_____ **7.** incompatible or inconsistent

_____ **8.** deviating from the expected course

_____ **9.** common in a certain location

_____ **10.** seeming to be everywhere

COMPLETE THE SENTENCE

Write the letter for the word that best completes each sentence.

_____ **1.** The _____ fog of San Francisco seemed to follow us around the city.
    a. ubiquitous   **b.** mundane   **c.** outlandish   **d.** incongruous

_____ **2.** Her very conventional neighbors felt that Mrs. Laurent's _____ had gotten out of control when she painted murals on each side of her house.
    a. paragon   **b.** ubiquity   **c.** eccentricity   **d.** endemic

_____ **3.** Tired of _____ food, Jared decided to go to the most exotic restaurant in town.
    a. aberrant   **b.** eccentric   **c.** anomalous   **d.** mundane

_____ **4.** The _____ green tuxedo was one oddity at the bizarre wedding.
    a. mundane   **b.** endemic   **c.** outlandish   **d.** ubiquitous

_____ **5.** This type of berry is _____ to the northern coast of California.
    a. aberrant   **b.** endemic   **c.** anomalous   **d.** unwonted

_____ **6.** The politician's negative ad is _____ with her promise to run a positive campaign.
    a. incongruous   **b.** eccentric   **c.** paragon   **d.** mundane

_____ **7.** Getting struck by lightning on two occasions would be a statistical _____ .
    a. anomaly   **b.** paragon   **c.** ubiquity   **d.** endemic

_____ **8.** "I will not tolerate _____ behavior," snapped the man known as "Sarge."
    a. ubiquitous   **b.** mundane   **c.** endemic   **d.** aberrant

_____ **9.** A(n) _____ of wisdom, she was constantly sought out for advice.
    a. ubiquity   **b.** paragon   **c.** eccentricity   **d.** anomaly

_____ **10.** The usually stern father gave his son a(n) _____ hug.
    a. mundane   **b.** outlandish   **c.** unwonted   **d.** endemic

Challenge: My aunt's blunt remarks were a shocking _____ , considering she is normally a(n) _____ of politeness and diplomacy.
_____   **a.** endemic…aberrant   **b.** aberration…paragon   **c.** ubiquity…anomaly

An Incongruous Pair

In a nature preserve in Kenya, a one-year-old hippopotamus and a 129-year-old Aldabran tortoise have become the best of friends. **(1)** The two may look like an *incongruous* pair, but Mzee (the tortoise) and Owen (the hippo) act like mother and son. **(2)** Their unusual arrangement seems even more *eccentric* because "mom" is a male.

The story began when Owen became separated from his herd, probably due to the heavy flooding that followed the catastrophic 2004 tsunami. Owen was helplessly struggling in saltwater when he was rescued. Hippos are freshwater animals, and the saltwater had dehydrated him.

To help Owen recover, local officials took him to Haller Wildlife Park, a 185-acre wildlife preserve near Mombasa, Kenya. There, he was placed in an enclosure with two large tortoises. When Owen, a one-year-old hippo still needing a mother's protection, spotted Mzee, who is the same color as a grown hippo, he must have thought that the ancient tortoise looked maternal, for Owen went right up to him.

Instantly, Owen became Mzee's faithful companion. **(3)** Living in close contact, they share life's *mundane* activities. Owen walks behind the tortoise and sleeps beside him. If he wants to play in the water, he touches Mzee to announce his intentions, and then proceeds to walk away. After a few steps, Owen looks back to make certain Mzee is following.

They also play together. **(4)** Owen licks Mzee and, in a rather *outlandish* display of affection, puts his mouth around Mzee's head. To relax, Owen rests his head on the giant tortoise.

But life is not all play. **(5)** When danger threatens, Owen is a *paragon* of filial loyalty. When unfamiliar humans approach Mzee, his 650-pound hippo bodyguard chases them away.

Mzee's presence has proven critical to Owen's survival. **(6)** Wild hippos eat grasses that are *ubiquitous* in their habitat. Unfortunately, these grasses are not prevalent in Haller Park. But, by watching Mzee, Owen learned that the brown food given to tortoises was edible, and he began to eat it, too. This enabled Owen to gain weight and assume a healthy, pinkish-gray color.

How does the tortoise feel about this arrangement? Mzee, whose name means "old man" in Swahili, seems to accept his role in the peaceful fashion of an elderly gentleman (although he isn't quite elderly yet; tortoises can live to be 200 years old). In fact, Mzee is quite sociable—for a tortoise. When wildlife manager Sabine Baer enters his enclosure, he ambles up to her and stretches out his neck. **(7)** Mzee then invites Sabine to pick off the ticks that are *endemic* to so many kinds of animals.

(8) It is not *aberrant* for living things to form bonds with other species, as illustrated by people and their pets. **(9)** However, this close relationship between mammal and reptile is particularly *unwonted*. **(10)** Although their friendship may be an *anomaly,* the pair lives together contentedly.

But children must grow up sometime. Owen's keepers are planning to introduce him to a lonely twelve-year-old hippo named Cleo. Hopefully, Owen will adjust to life with hippo friends, but he will still be able to spend time with Mzee if he likes.

Each sentence below refers to a numbered sentence in the passage. Write the letter of the choice that gives the sentence a meaning that is closest to the original sentence.

_____ 1. The two look like a(n) _____ pair.
   a. perfect   **b.** incompatible   **c.** common   **d.** inseparable

_____ 2. Their arrangement seems even more _____ because "mom" is a male.
   a. perfect   **b.** commonplace   **c.** unconventional   **d.** widespread

_____ 3. Living in close contact, they share life's _____ activities.
   a. frustrating   **b.** unconventional   **c.** bizarre   **d.** commonplace

_____ 4. In a rather _____ display of affection, Owen puts his mouth around Mzee's head.
   a. dangerous   **b.** bizarre   **c.** proper   **d.** aggressive

_____ **5.** When danger threatens, Owen is a(n) _____ of filial loyalty.
    a. custom   **b.** animal   **c.** model   **d.** harmony

_____ **6.** Wild hippos eat grasses that are _____ in their habitat.
    a. everywhere   **b.** bizarre   **c.** harmonious   **d.** irregular

_____ **7.** Mzee invites Sabine to pick off the ticks that are _____ to so many kinds of animals.
    a. bizarre   **b.** distasteful   **c.** common   **d.** cruel

_____ **8.** It is not _____ for living things to form bonds with other species.
    a. abnormal   **b.** devious   **c.** harmonious   **d.** commonplace

_____ **9.** However, this close relationship between mammal and reptile is particularly _____.
    a. excellent   **b.** commonplace   **c.** problematic   **d.** unusual

_____ **10.** Although their friendship may be a(n) _____, the pair lives together contentedly.
    a. institution   **b.** irregularity   **c.** impossibility   **d.** model

Indicate whether the statements below are TRUE or FALSE according to the passage.

_____ **1.** Mzee is extremely old for an Aldabran tortoise.

_____ **2.** Owen will chase humans away if he feels they're threatening Mzee.

_____ **3.** Owen probably got separated from his herd because he followed a tortoise into the sea.

WRITING EXTENDED RESPONSES

This passage describes an unusual bond between two animals. Think of another unusual bond between two animals (one of which may be a human). In a descriptive essay of at least three paragraphs, explain the features that make this relationship unique. Draw on a real-life example or use your imagination. You may also write about a bond that is familiar to you from television, movies, or books. Use at least three lesson words in your essay and underline them.

WRITE THE DERIVATIVE

Complete the sentence by writing the correct form of the word shown in parentheses. You may not need to change the form that is given.

_____ **1.** It is _____ for Ramone to get sick, but when he does, he becomes very ill. *(unwonted)*

_____ **2.** The _____ radar reading that had puzzled the pilots turned out to be a flock of geese. *(anomaly)*

_____ 3. Some found it an _____ that the hard-punching boxer was so mild-mannered and kind when out of the ring. *(incongruous)*

_____ 4. Washing the dishes is a _____ but important task that must be done regularly. *(mundane)*

_____ 5. The _____ man slept in his backyard each night while his pets slept indoors. *(eccentricity)*

_____ 6. The _____ of Sam's comedy act shocked some members of the audience. *(outlandish)*

_____ 7. When my hard-working brother earned a scholarship, my mother called him "a _____ of perseverance and achievement." *(paragon)*

_____ 8. The security personnel who work at airports are taught to look for _____ in passenger behavior or appearance. *(aberrant)*

_____ 9. The _____ of cell phones is both convenient and irritating. *(ubiquitous)*

_____ 10. Lack of sufficient funds is _____ in many urban school systems. *(endemic)*

FIND THE EXAMPLE

Choose the answer that best describes the action or situation.

_____ 1. An example of a *mundane* activity
  a. flying a plane   **b.** drinking water   **c.** deep-sea diving   **d.** appearing on TV

_____ 2. An *aberrant* behavior
  a. a kitten playing   **b.** a baby crying   **c.** a child driving   **d.** a politician speaking

_____ 3. Something that would be *incongruous* in a mechanic's garage
  a. a wrench   **b.** a tuxedo   **c.** safety glasses   **d.** a hammer

_____ 4. Something that is *ubiquitous* in rural areas in summertime
  a. traffic   **b.** snow   **c.** falling leaves   **d.** insects

_____ 5. An example of an animal that is *endemic* to some deserts
  a. parrot   **b.** dolphin   **c.** frog   **d.** rattlesnake

_____ 6. A situation when *outlandish* behavior would be most frowned upon
  a. at a lively party   **b.** at a ball game   **c.** at a security check   **d.** hanging out with friends

_____ 7. An *eccentric* color to paint a car
  a. black   **b.** brown   **c.** solid blue   **d.** zebra-striped

_____ 8. An *unwonted* time to brush your teeth
  a. in the morning   **b.** at the dentist   **c.** during class   **d.** right before bed

_____ 9. A *paragon* of scientific achievement
  a. Nobel Prize winner   **b.** lab assistant   **c.** biotech secretary   **d.** C-student

_____ 10. An example of a medical *anomaly*
  a. broken hand   **b.** allergy to pollen   **c.** Type A blood   **d.** Siamese twins

Taking Tests

Sentence Completion with Two Blanks

Standardized tests, including the new SAT, may contain sentence-completion items with either one or two blanks. You practice answering two-blank items in this book when you do the Challenge that is found in each lesson. You can apply what you have already learned about context clues to sentence-completion test items. Following these steps will also help you to choose the correct answers.

Strategies

1. *Read the directions carefully.* You can lose credit if you don't follow the directions.

2. *Read the sentence completely.* Because two-blank items involve different parts of the sentence, it is wise to get an overview by carefully reading the entire sentence. Substitute the word *blank* for the empty spaces as you read.

3. *Look for words that fit the first blank.* To start, try to narrow your choices down to words that fit the first empty space. Make sure the word is the correct part of speech and fits in the context. Eliminate the other choices. Here is an example:

    When the governor realized that he had _____ made an extremely _____ remark, he was extremely embarrassed.
    a. fortuitously...premeditated   d. coincidental...insoluble
    b. prophetic...notoriety   e. vehemently...protracted
    c. unwittingly...impolitic

    By focusing on the first blank, you can eliminate choices (B) and (D); neither *prophetic* nor *coincidental* will fit. They are both adjectives, and an adverb is called for.

4. *From the remaining choices, look for words that fit into the second blank.* Eliminate any remaining choices in which the second word doesn't fit in the second blank. In the example above, try the second word for choices (A), (C), and (E) in the second blank. The second portion of the sentence provides a hint that something embarrassed the governor, so the second word will be something the governor would not want to have done. You can now eliminate choice (A)—for not only is the governor's remark unlikely to be *fortuitous,* but it is unlikely that a *premeditated* remark would be embarrassing. (E) is also an unlikely choice, for a *protracted* remark would be much less likely to embarrass the governor than an *impolitic* one. The answer is (C).

5. *Reread the sentence with your choices inserted.* Two-item tests are difficult. Make certain to check your choices. At times, a few choices may fit, and you must choose the one that fits best.

At times, the two missing words are related. Words such as *although* signal that the first blank and the second blank are opposites. Words like *in addition to* indicate that the answer choices are probably similar. Some other key words that might indicate a relationship include:

   not, but, never, hardly, and *in spite of* (signaling opposites)
   and, as well as, and *in addition to* (signaling agreement)

Practice

Each sentence below has two blanks, each blank indicating that something has been omitted. Beneath the sentence are five sets of words labeled A through E. Choose the word or set of words that, when inserted in the sentence, *best* fits the meaning of the sentence as a whole.

_____ 1. A history of unbridled _____ contributed to the woman's _____ reputation.
  a. avarice . . . nefarious
  b. perfidy . . . empirical
  c. austerity . . . replete
  d. arcane . . . jocularity
  e. garrulousness . . . stoicism

_____ 2. Summoning all of his _____ skills, the lawyer delivered a _____ of the prosecution's argument that convinced the entire jury of the defendant's innocence.
  a. verifiable . . . conclave
  b. vociferous . . . lampoon
  c. tenuous . . . contumacy
  d. rhetorical . . . rebuttal
  e. diffuse . . . parody

_____ 3. _____ his reputation for _____, the CEO donated generously to a foundation that helps indigent families.
  a. Mesmerizing . . . empiricism
  b. Belying . . . parsimony
  c. Debilitating . . . bedlam
  d. Regaling . . . buffoonery
  e. Adumbrating . . . audaciousness

_____ 4. The scientists' _____ finding was so unexpected that it ultimately resulted in an entirely new _____ in the field of physics.
  a. succinct . . . polemic
  b. irrevocable . . . hiatus
  c. pertinacious . . . rebuttal
  d. arcane . . . martinet
  e. empirical . . . paradigm

_____ 5. It is simply _____ of you to deny any knowledge of the _____ at which the plot was hatched, for we know you were in attendance.
  a. verifiable . . . clandestine
  b. irresolute . . . compatriot
  c. disingenuous . . . conclave
  d. garrulous . . . bedlam
  e. noxious . . . hiatus

_____ 6. Try as we might to _____ the meaning of the poem, it was a work that remained _____ to our efforts.
  a. repudiate . . . diffuse
  b. scourge . . . impervious
  c. parody . . . spurious
  d. fathom . . . impenetrable
  e. educe . . . contiguous

_____ 7. After the _____ air near the factory had compromised his health, the unspoiled environment of the rural campsite had a(n) _____ effect.
  a. livid . . . unscathed
  b. noxious . . . salubrious
  c. inundated . . . voluminous
  d. pestilent . . . myriad
  e. arcane . . . limpid

_____ 8. The couple had complementary verbal styles; his _____ nature contrasted with her _____ approach to conversation.
  a. vociferous . . . vivacious
  b. dour . . . obduracy
  c. florid . . . prodigal
  d. garrulous . . . laconic
  e. dialectic . . . repudiated

Building and Destroying

WORD LIST

caustic	deleterious	despoil	effectual	obviate
pinnacle	raze	stultify	surmount	wrest

The words in this lesson deal with strengthening and building, or the opposite—destruction. Learning these words will increase your ability to understand and describe many kinds of real-world situations involving building and destroying.

1. **caustic** (kô´stĭk) *adjective* from Greek *kaiein,* "to burn"
   a. Capable of burning, corroding, dissolving, or eating away by chemical action
   • The **caustic** hydrochloric acid damaged the laboratory floor.
   b. Cruelly cutting and sarcastic
   • The standup comedian made some **caustic** jokes about the new government policy.

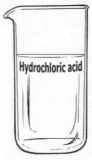
Hydrochloric acid

caustic chemical

> *Caustic* may also be used as a noun, as in "Lye is a harmful *caustic.*"

   causticity *noun* The **causticity** of his remarks offended his friends.

2. **deleterious** (dĕl´ĭ-tîr´ē-əs) *adjective* from Greek *deleisthai,* "to harm"
   Harmful; injurious
   • The pesticide DDT had **deleterious** effects on birds of prey in the United States, including the national bird, the bald eagle.

   deleteriousness *noun* Nutritionists now agree on the **deleteriousness** of a high-fat diet.

3. **despoil** (dĭ-spoil´) *verb* from Latin *de-,* "out of" + *spoliare,* "to plunder"
   a. To thoroughly rob and destroy a place; to plunder; to loot
   • The barbarian hordes swept down on horseback, **despoiling** the village and burning the fields.
   b. To deprive of something valuable by force
   • The forest fire **despoiled** the hillsides of their lush vegetation.

   despoliation *noun* The poachers' **despoliation** of the national park infuriated wildlife advocates.

4. **effectual** (ĭ-fĕk´choo-əl) *adjective* from Latin *ex-,* "out" + *facere,* "to make; to do"
   Producing or able to produce a desired effect; fully adequate; effective
   • Several antidotes are **effectual** against poisonous snake bites.

5. **obviate** (ŏb´vē-āt´) *verb* from Latin *ob-,* "against" + *via,* "way"
   To anticipate and prevent a difficulty; to make unnecessary
   • The careful building up of reserve funds in the state treasury **obviated** the need to raise taxes.

6. **pinnacle** (pĭnʹə-kəl) *noun* from Latin *pinna*, "feather"
   a. A tall, pointed formation, such as a mountain peak
      • The **pinnacle** of the building formed a dramatic triangle against the sky.
   b. The highest, most successful point
      • The **pinnacle** of the actor's career was when he played Hamlet at the Royal Shakespeare Theater.

7. **raze** (rāz) *verb* from Latin *rodere*, "to scrape off; scratch"
   To level to the ground; to demolish
   • When the ancient Romans defeated Carthage, they **razed** the city.

8. **stultify** (stŭlʹtə-fīʹ) *verb* from Latin *stultus*, "foolish" + *facere*, "to make; do"
   To make useless or ineffective; to negate
   • Forcing reluctant piano students to practice may **stultify** their interest in music.

   stultification *noun* Years of mismanagement by the Soviet Union led to the **stultification** of many Eastern European economies.

   > In law, *stultify* means "to allege or prove a person insane and therefore not legally responsible."

9. **surmount** (sər-mountʹ) *verb* from Old French *sur-*, "over; above" + *monter*, "to mount"
   a. To overcome a difficulty or an obstacle
      • Wilma Rudolph **surmounted** the crippling effects of polio to win three Olympic gold medals.
   b. To be placed on top
      • A beautifully crafted steeple **surmounts** the church.

   surmountable *adjective* Many problems become **surmountable** when approached with energy and courage.

10. **wrest** (rĕst) *verb* from Middle English *wresten*, "to twist"
    a. To obtain through a violent, twisting motion
       • I had to **wrest** the ball from my dog's mouth before I could throw it again.
    b. To obtain by force or great effort
       • The rebels seized the capital and **wrested** control of the government.

    > *Wrestle* is a common word that is closely related to *wrest*.

WORD ENRICHMENT

Winged words

The word *pinnacle* comes from the Latin word *pinna*, meaning "feather," or "wing point." Many English idioms are formed from the word *wing*. *To take under one's wing* means "to protect." *Waiting in the wings* means "available on short notice." *To wing it*, a slang usage, means "to do something without preparation."

The Latin word for "feather" also gives us the word *pen*. For thousands of years, the hollow stems of feathers, or quills, were used as pens.

WRITE THE CORRECT WORD

Write the correct word in the space next to each definition. Use each word only once.

_____ **1.** harmful

_____ **2.** the peak

_____ **3.** to make unnecessary

_____ **4.** to overcome

_____ **5.** to level to the ground

_____ **6.** to negate

_____ **7.** to obtain by force

_____ **8.** effective; adequate

_____ **9.** corrosive

_____ **10.** to plunder

COMPLETE THE SENTENCE

Write the letter for the word that best completes each sentence.

_____ **1.** Sydney devised an unconventional yet _____ method for solving the problem.
a. effectual **b.** obviated **c.** caustic **d.** deleterious

_____ **2.** In the last seconds of the game, our team managed to _____ the championship from our rivals.
a. stultify **b.** wrest **c.** surmount **d.** obviate

_____ **3.** After the powerful tsunami in Southeast Asia, images of _____ buildings and hotels appeared in newspapers all over the world.
a. deleterious **b.** caustic **c.** razed **d.** obviated

_____ **4.** Corrective surgery performed during infancy can _____ the need for more dangerous procedures later in life.
a. surmount **b.** raze **c.** despoil **d.** obviate

_____ **5.** For centuries, infamous pirates _____ ships on the high seas.
a. effected **b.** obviated **c.** stultified **d.** despoiled

_____ **6.** The director tried to make suggestions without _____ the actors' spontaneity.
a. stultifying **b.** wresting **c.** surmounting **d.** despoiling

_____ **7.** The _____ chemical ate right through the metal wires.
a. obviated **b.** wrested **c.** caustic **d.** effectual

_____ **8.** Winning the award was the _____ of the writer's career.
a. stultification **b.** obviation **c.** pinnacle **d.** despoliation

_____ **9.** _____ the obstacles of poverty and a lack of education, the woman became a successful entrepreneur.
a. Wresting **b.** Despoiling **c.** Surmounting **d.** Obviating

_____ **10.** Secondhand smoke is _____ to one's health.
a. despoiling **b.** deleterious **c.** effectual **d.** razing

Challenge: The army was sent in to _____ control from the lawless forces who had _____ homes and shops after the dictator was expelled.
_____ **a.** wrest…despoiled **b.** despoil…wrested **c.** raze…surmounted

The Prince's Architecture

As befits one of the world's greatest cities, bold new buildings are continually constructed in London. **(1)** In fact, since World War II, the London skyline has grown to include the *pinnacles* of several skyscrapers. But modern architecture has encountered a royal critic.

Prince Charles, current heir to the British throne, is an outspoken critic of contemporary architecture in his home city. He believes that buildings should be viewed as part of a "living language" that reflects the people's culture and traditions. **(2)** In 1984, he disapproved of a plan to erect a sleek new tower beside some older buildings, *caustically* calling the proposed development "a glass stump." **(3)** Criticism from the monarchy is often *effectual*, and this was no exception: the structure was never built.

Meanwhile, professional architects fiercely oppose the prince's efforts to block other modern structures from being built. **(4)** Many feel that the Prince, who has no architectural training, is trying to *wrest* control from highly qualified professionals. **(5)** They argue that to oppose new forms of architecture is to *stultify* the city's great tradition of growth and change.

Others, however, feel that Prince Charles has a point. **(6)** They agree with the Prince that impersonal modern architecture may have a *deleterious* effect on the human psyche. They also cite problems with many new buildings. **(7)** For example, to keep the modern Lloyds of London building from being *razed,*

$350 million had to be spent to correct structural flaws. Many also sympathize with the Prince's fight to maintain the space and sense of ambiance around such prized structures such as St. Paul's Cathedral, designed by the famous London architect Christopher Wren in the late 1600s. His supporters admire him for his courage to voice what many feel but are afraid to express.

The Prince, however, has done more than just complain. He donated some of his own land to a visionary housing project. In the community built on this land, the homes of the wealthy cannot be distinguished from those of the unemployed. **(8)** In building this village, Prince Charles showed that today's architects can design affordable yet beautiful structures that suit a wide range of people, potentially *obviating* the existence of "poor neighborhoods" and "rich neighborhoods."

To share his ideas, Prince Charles wrote the book *A Vision of Britain*. **(9)** In its pages, he articulately argues that new construction need not *despoil* its surroundings. He also discusses how constructed environments can affect the human spirit. For those who want to learn even more, he founded a school, *The Prince of Wales's Institute of Architecture,* where students are comprehensively trained in architectural form as well as philosophy.

Some decry the school as a conservative, rather backward institution. **(10)** But this criticism has been easily *surmounted* by the graduates of the school. Many of them work in prestigious firms and are fully educated in modernist architecture. One of their main concerns, however, is preserving the humanity of architecture.

The debate continues, with some lauding the Prince and others ridiculing him. One thing is for certain: in modern democratic Britain, architecture is a subject of lively debate.

Each sentence below refers to a numbered sentence in the passage. Write the letter of the choice that gives the sentence a meaning that is closest to the original sentence.

_____ **1.** London's skyline has grown to include the _____ of several skyscrapers.
    a. success   **b.** foundations   **c.** causticity   **d.** peaks

_____ **2.** He _____ called the proposed development "a glass stump."
    a. cuttingly   **b.** surmountably   **c.** unnecessarily   **d.** truly

_____ **3.** Criticism from the monarchy is often _____.
    a. overcome   **b.** effective   **c.** negated   **d.** lauded

_____ **4.** Many feel that the Prince is trying to _____ control from professionals.
    a. harm   **b.** destroy   **c.** forcibly take   **d.** overcome

_____ **5.** They argue that to oppose new forms of architecture is to _____ the city's great tradition of growth and change.
   a. cause   **b.** negate   **c.** plunder   **d.** force

_____ **6.** They agree with the prince that impersonal modern architecture may have a(n) _____ effect on the human psyche.
   a. effective   **b.** pointed   **c.** numbing   **d.** harmful

_____ **7.** To keep the modern Lloyds of London building from being _____, $350 million had to be spent to correct structural flaws.
   a. demolished   **b.** rebuilt   **c.** condemned   **d.** reappraised

_____ **8.** Prince Charles showed that today's architects can design structures that suit a wide range of people, potentially _____ the existence of "poor neighborhoods."
   a. plundering   **b.** obtaining by force   **c.** reinforcing   **d.** making unnecessary

_____ **9.** He articulately argues that new construction need not _____ its surroundings.
   a. make unnecessary   **b.** destroy   **c.** make ineffective   **d.** glorify

_____ **10.** But this criticism has been easily _____ by the graduates of the school.
   a. effected   **b.** injured   **c.** overcome   **d.** obtained

Indicate whether the statements below are TRUE or FALSE according to the passage.

_____ **1.** Prince Charles admires most forms of modern architecture.

_____ **2.** According to the Prince, architecture has a psychological effect on people.

_____ **3.** Many professional architects oppose Prince Charles's views.

FINISH THE THOUGHT

Complete each sentence so that it shows the meaning of the italicized word.

1. One thing that has a *deleterious* effect on grades _____

_____

2. The need for a special meeting of the legislature was *obviated* _____

_____

WRITE THE DERIVATIVE

Complete the sentence by writing the correct form of the word shown in parentheses. You may not need to change the form that is given.

_____ **1.** Aggressive logging was responsible for _____ this once-lush forest. (*raze*)

_____ **2.** The _____ of her career was serving as CEO of the corporation. (*pinnacle*)

_____ **3.** Enid's excellent and creative suggestion has _____ resolved our dilemma. *(effectual)*

_____ **4.** _____ even a small harvest from the rocky soil was a challenging task for the settlers. *(wrest)*

_____ **5.** Some say that memorizing is a good way to learn, while others maintain that it leads to the _____ of creativity. *(stultify)*

_____ **6.** The obstacles to peace are _____ if we direct our efforts to reaching a compromise. *(surmount)*

_____ **7.** Listening to loud music for extended periods of time is known to affect one's hearing _____. *(deleterious)*

_____ **8.** Substances known for their _____ should not be handled without special gloves. *(caustic)*

_____ **9.** Fatima decided to use the new computer program to analyze her data, _____ her original plan to hire a statistician. *(obviate)*

_____ **10.** Army leaders wanted, at all cost, to avoid any _____ of the area by renegade soldiers. *(despoil)*

FIND THE EXAMPLE

Choose the answer that best describes the action or situation.

_____ **1.** The thing most likely to have a *deleterious* effect on your health
     a. natural flavors   **b.** organic produce   **c.** varied diet   **d.** artificial additives

_____ **2.** A *caustic* remark
     a. Excuse me, please.   **b.** Is that true?   **c.** That's just stupid.   **d.** I disagree.

_____ **3.** A word that describes a child who *wrests* a toy away from another
     a. kind   **b.** shy   **c.** possessive   **d.** sleepy

_____ **4.** Something *surmounted*
     a. advantages   **b.** perks   **c.** friends   **d.** difficulties

_____ **5.** A reason why a home would be *razed*
     a. chipped paint   **b.** unsound structure   **c.** clogged pipe   **d.** angry tenant

_____ **6.** The most likely *pinnacle* of a successful musician's career
     a. humming a tune   **b.** making a painting   **c.** winning a Grammy   **d.** winning a talent show

_____ **7.** Something that would *despoil* a shopping mall
     a. earthquake   **b.** renovation   **c.** rain   **d.** restaurants

_____ **8.** Something most likely to *obviate* a tough financial decision
     a. buying a house   **b.** taking a class   **c.** working late   **d.** receiving an inheritance

_____ **9.** An *effectual* way to prevent the spread of many diseases
     a. pain relievers   **b.** vaccinations   **c.** traveling   **d.** increasing stress levels

_____ **10.** Something that would be most likely to *stultify* motivation
     a. disapproval   **b.** praise   **c.** award   **d.** opportunity

Emotions

WORD LIST

deplore	disconsolate	domineering	halcyon	lachrymose
mercurial	revel	sanguine	tirade	vex

Emotions can be powerful, subtle, complex, and changeable. They provide links between us and everyone we know, as well as the motivation for most of what we do. Understanding emotional states and the words that describe them can help us appreciate human nature.

1. deplore (dĭ-plôr´) *verb* from Latin *de-*, "from" + *plorare*, "to wail; to cry loudly"
  a. To express strong disapproval of; to condemn
   • I **deplore** my neighbor's cruel treatment of his dog.
  b. To express grief over; to regret
   • He **deplored** the life mistakes that had led him to joblessness and alienation from family and friends.

  deplorable *adjective* Human rights activists condemned the **deplorable** living conditions of the refugees.

2. disconsolate (dĭs-kŏn´sə-lĭt) *adjective* from Latin *dis-*, "not" + *consolari*, "to console"
  Incapable of being comforted; hopelessly dejected or sad
  • Mrs. Harrison was **disconsolate** after hearing of her sister's sudden death.

3. domineering (dŏm´ə-nîr´ĭng) *adjective* from Latin *dominari*, "to rule"
  Ruling or controlling arrogantly; overbearing; tyrannical
  • Sylvie's **domineering** father demanded that he know his daughter's whereabouts at all times.

  domineer *verb* A tyrant **domineers** a country with little concern for the lives of citizens.

4. halcyon (hăl´sē-ən) *adjective* from Greek *halkuon*, "a mythical bird; kingfisher"
  a. Calm and peaceful; tranquil
   • The **halcyon** days of our vacation in the Caribbean islands provided a much needed break from the stress and hectic pace at work.
  b. Prosperous; golden
   • During the Great Depression, people looked back longingly to the **halcyon** days of the early 1920s.

5. lachrymose (lăk´rə-mōs´) *adjective* from Latin *lacrima*, "tear"
  Tending to produce tears; tearful; inclined to weep
  • The critic found the **lachrymose** movie silly and sentimental.

Deplore and *disconsolate* are extremely strong words.

halcyon

In Greek mythology, the mythical *halcyon* nested on the calm seas for fourteen days during the winter solstice.

6. mercurial (mər-kyŏŏr´ē-əl) *adjective* from Latin *Mercurius,* the mythological Roman god Mercury
   a. Quick and changeable in temperament; volatile
   • His **mercurial** nature often displayed itself in temper tantrums.
   b. Having characteristics similar to those of the god Mercury
   • The package arrived with **mercurial** speed.

Mercury, the Roman messenger god, was shrewd, swift, and mischievous. (In Greek mythology, he was called Hermes.)

7. revel (rěv´əl) *verb* from Latin *rebellare,* "to rebel"
   a. To take great pleasure or delight in something
   • She **reveled** in the warm ocean waters.
   b. To make merry; to celebrate
   • They **reveled** through the night to celebrate the victory.

revelry *noun* The **revelry** at the party included jokes and games.

reveler *noun* The **revelers** enjoyed themselves at the Mardi Gras party.

8. sanguine (săng´gwĭn) *adjective* from Latin *sanguis,* "blood"
   a. Of the color of blood; red; ruddy
   • Her **sanguine** complexion made her look very healthy.
   b. Cheerfully confident and optimistic
   • Those with **sanguine** temperaments often make good salespeople.

9. tirade (tī´-rād, tī-rād´) *noun* from Old French *tirer,* "to draw out; endure"
   A long, angry or violent speech
   • The advertising executive flew into a **tirade** when she learned that her company had lost its best client to a competitor.

The expressions *fly into a tirade* and *go on a tirade* are commonly used.

10. vex (věks) *verb* from Latin *vexare,* "to agitate"
   a. To irk, irritate, annoy, or bother
   • Abe was **vexed** by the constant whispering of the people sitting next to him at the symphony.
   b. To bring distress or suffering to; to plague or affect
   • Mrs. Raul was so **vexed** by her arthritis during the long, cold winters that she finally moved to Arizona.
   c. To puzzle or baffle
   • The difficult math problem completely **vexed** me.

vexation *noun* When his car wouldn't start after many tries, Jerome pounded the dashboard in **vexation.**

vexatious *adjective* The **vexatious** problem stumped us.

WORD ENRICHMENT

Red as blood

The word *sanguine* was originally one of the four *humors,* or fluids, that medieval people thought made up the human body. In order for a person to have an ideal temperament, the four humors had to be in balance. Each had a different quality. *Sanguine* referred to blood, and a *sanguine* temperament was confident and optimistic. The other humors were *phlegm,* which made one peaceful and self-possessed; *choler,* which made one angry and irritable; and *melancholy* (or black bile), which made one sad. The words *sanguine, phlegmatic, choleric,* and *melancholy* are still used today to refer to moods that correspond to the now-outdated humors.

WRITE THE CORRECT WORD

Write the correct word in the space next to each definition. Use each word only once.

_____ 1. tearful

_____ 2. to condemn

_____ 3. changeable

_____ 4. to celebrate

_____ 5. hopelessly sad

_____ 6. an angry speech

_____ 7. peaceful

_____ 8. to baffle or puzzle

_____ 9. optimistic

_____ 10. tyrannical

COMPLETE THE SENTENCE

Write the letter for the word that best completes each sentence.

_____ 1. The child's behavior in the theater was _____ and his parents had to take him outside before the movie was over.
a. mercurial   **b.** sanguine   **c.** halcyon   **d.** deplorable

_____ 2. Jenna was _____ when her friend called to cancel their plans at the last minute.
a. deplorable   **b.** vexed   **c.** mercurial   **d.** sanguine

_____ 3. The diva loves attention and _____ in the praises of her admirers.
a. revels   **b.** vexes   **c.** deplores   **d.** domineers

_____ 4. The little girl was _____ when her gerbil died.
a. sanguine   **b.** disconsolate   **c.** halcyon   **d.** reveling

_____ 5. So _____ was he that no one on the staff was willing to disagree with him.
a. reveling   **b.** lachrymose   **c.** domineering   **d.** sanguine

_____ 6. The singer is known for his tragic, _____ ballads.
a. sanguine   **b.** mercurial   **c.** domineering   **d.** lachrymose

_____ 7. Nora found that practicing yoga each morning helped her control her _____ mood swings.
a. mercurial   **b.** lachrymose   **c.** reveling   **d.** disconsolate

_____ 8. The foreign minister was _____ about the new peace agreement, confident that it would succeed.
a. mercurial   **b.** halcyon   **c.** sanguine   **d.** deplored

_____ 9. My grandfather nostalgically reflected on the _____ days of his youth.
a. lachrymose   **b.** halcyon   **c.** vexatious   **d.** disconsolate

_____ 10. Justine launched into a _____ about the way the company was cutting benefits for regular employees while executives were getting huge bonuses.
a. tirade   **b.** vexation   **c.** revelry   **d.** halcyon

Challenge: Our halcyon morning was disrupted when Aunt Jean went into an unprovoked _____ about the _____ manners of today's youth.
_____   **a.** tirade...deplorable   **b.** vexation...domineering   **c.** revelry...vexatious

Persephone Kidnapped

The rhythms of life fascinated the ancient Greeks, who created stories, or myths, to explain natural phenomena. The ancient Greek myth that follows explains the cycle of the seasons.

Demeter, the goddess of grain, was believed to rule over all the crops that sustained human life. **(1)** With her aid, human beings were able to grow crops all year round, and *halcyon* days reigned on Earth. **(2)** With constant abundance surrounding them, people were *sanguine.*

But things were about to change. **(3)** Demeter had a beautiful daughter, Persephone, who caught the eye of Hades, the *domineering* god of the underworld and the brother of Zeus, the king of the gods. Hades plotted to kidnap Persephone and make her his wife.

(4) One day, Persephone was *reveling* in the beauty of the flowers, when she became enchanted with a blooming narcissus that Hades had planted to tempt her. As Persephone bent to pick the blossom, the earth opened up and Hades jumped out, seized her, and carried her off to the underworld, where he made the unwilling Persephone his queen.

(5) Soon Demeter went looking for her daughter, *vexed* that she had wandered off. **(6)** When Demeter discovered that Persephone had been kidnapped by Hades, she was *disconsolate.* **(7)** The once-joyful goddess became a *lachrymose* mother mourning the loss of her child. In her terrible anguish, she withheld the gifts of warmth, light, and sun from Earth. The planet turned into a frozen wasteland.

A year went by, and Zeus grew angry with this situation. **(8)** He *deplored* the evil act of his brother. Should the entire human race starve because of Hades' selfishness? **(9)** Of course, Zeus had shown his own share of disregard for humankind, but known for his *mercurial* temperament, he resolved to restore justice. **(10)** As king of the gods, Zeus felt it would detract from his own dignity to descend into the underworld to deliver a *tirade.* Instead, he sent Hermes to demand Persephone's release.

Hades could not refuse the order of Zeus. Nevertheless, he plotted one final trick. Begging Persephone to remember him kindly, he asked her to eat some pomegranate seeds. Persephone consented to consume six, not realizing that anyone who ate in the underworld was required to remain there. Unwittingly, by accepting those seeds, she bound herself to return to her husband for six months every year.

And so, from then on, Persephone lived half of the year with her mother on Earth, and half with Hades in the underworld. Just as her life was divided, so was her character. In the summer, Persephone was a beautiful, joyful, childlike girl under the protection of her mother. In the winter months, she was the stern queen of the underworld.

Each year when Persephone arrived to live with her mother, Demeter's pleasure caused the earth to flower and produce crops. But her daughter's departure to the underworld signaled the coming of winter, when Demeter's sadness would cause plant life to wither and die.

This Greek myth not only provides an explanation for the changing of the seasons, but also shows how the rhythms of life are bound with those of nature.

Each sentence below refers to a numbered sentence in the passage. Write the letter of the choice that gives the sentence a meaning that is closest to the original sentence.

_____ **1.** Human beings were able to grow crops all year round, and _____ days reigned on Earth.
    a. optimistic   **b.** hopeless   **c.** tumultuous   **d.** prosperous

_____ **2.** People on Earth were _____.
    a. peaceful   **b.** comforted   **c.** optimistic   **d.** temperamental

_____ **3.** Persephone caught the eye of Hades, the _____ god of the underworld.
    a. irksome   **b.** delightful   **c.** tyrannical   **d.** prosperous

_____ **4.** One day, Persephone was _____ the beauty of the flowers.
    a. delighting in   **b.** questioning   **c.** pondering   **d.** ruling over

_____ **5.** Soon Demeter went looking for her daughter, _____ that she had wandered off.
    a. tearful   **b.** delighted   **c.** annoyed   **d.** optimistic

_____ **6.** When Demeter discovered that her daughter was missing, she was _____.
    a. tranquil   **b.** hopelessly sad   **c.** violently angry   **d.** blood red

_____ **7.** The once-joyful goddess became a(n) _____ mother mourning the loss of a child.
    a. moody   **b.** tearful   **c.** overbearing   **d.** incompetent

_____ **8.** He _____ the evil act of his brother.
    a. condoned   **b.** condemned   **c.** changed   **d.** plotted

_____ **9.** Zeus, known for his _____ temperament, resolved to restore justice.
    a. changeable   **b.** swift   **c.** even   **d.** overbearing

_____ **10.** Zeus felt it would detract from his own dignity to descend into the underworld to deliver a(n) _____.
    a. divine gift   **b.** eloquent message   **c.** angry speech   **d.** destructive thunderbolt

Indicate whether the statements below are TRUE or FALSE according to the passage.

_____ **1.** Ancient myths often attempt to explain natural occurrences.

_____ **2.** For the most part, the Greek gods were kind and even-tempered.

_____ **3.** The ancient Greeks believed that Demeter controlled the growth of crops.

WRITING EXTENDED RESPONSES

The myth you have just read is generally told from the point of view of Demeter. Choose another character in this myth, such as Hades, Zeus, or Persephone, and, in a narrative piece of three or more paragraphs, tell the story from his or her point of view. Use at least three lesson words in your piece and underline them.

WRITE THE DERIVATIVE

Complete the sentence by writing the correct form of the word shown in parentheses. You may not need to change the form that is given.

_____ **1.** Hayyim stared _____ at the empty parking space from which his new car had been stolen. (*disconsolate*)

_____ **2.** To his urban cousins, Jonah's _____ life on the farm seemed idyllic. (*halcyon*)

_____ 3. The Persian king was known more as a _____ than as an astute politician. *(revel)*

_____ 4. The mere mention of his estranged brother's name is enough to send Jorge into a _____. *(tirade)*

_____ 5. Viviane apologized _____ for breaking her aunt's valuable vase. *(lachrymose)*

_____ 6. She is known to react _____, crying one minute and laughing the next. *(mercurial)*

_____ 7. Although at first glance the secret code seemed simple, it turned out to be _____. *(vex)*

_____ 8. Alison grew tired of her _____ friend's attempts to order her around. *(domineering)*

_____ 9. The principal was notified of the _____ behavior of the vandals. *(deplore)*

_____ 10. In a process known as blushing, strong emotion imparts a _____ color to a person's cheeks. *(sanguine)*

FIND THE EXAMPLE

Choose the answer that best describes the action or situation.

_____ 1. Something that would *vex* you
  a. a present   **b.** a comic strip   **c.** a pet peeve   **d.** an easy puzzle

_____ 2. A type of television show that is most likely to have a *lachrymose* plot
  a. reality show   **b.** documentary   **c.** soap opera   **d.** situation comedy

_____ 3. An occasion for *revelry*
  a. math exam   **b.** graduation   **c.** job interview   **d.** doctor visit

_____ 4. A characteristic of a *halcyon* time
  a. turmoil   **b.** excitement   **c.** depression   **d.** peace

_____ 5. The person most likely to *deplore* working conditions at a company
  a. laborer   **b.** customer   **c.** CEO   **d.** shareholder

_____ 6. A topic about which someone would most likely go on a *tirade*
  a. the weather   **b.** fashion   **c.** unfair grade   **d.** party decorations

_____ 7. The way that someone with a *mercurial* temperament might be described
  a. optimistic   **b.** moody   **c.** healthy   **d.** depressed

_____ 8. The most *domineering* political leader
  a. dictator   **b.** senator   **c.** mayor   **d.** school board member

_____ 9. An activity that requires a *sanguine* personality
  a. playing chess   **b.** writing   **c.** painting   **d.** cheerleading

_____ 10. Something that an athlete would most likely be *disconsolate* about
  a. a victory   **b.** improved skill   **c.** permanent injury   **d.** a missed shot

Size and Amount

WORD LIST

commodious	finite	gamut	incalculable	iota
lofty	minuscule	picayune	vestige	wane

We talk about size and amount many times each day. This lesson presents precise options for describing sizes and amounts.

1. **commodious** (kə-mō′dē-əs) *adjective* from Latin *com-*, "with" + *modus*, "measure"
   Spacious and roomy
   • We were disappointed to find that the hotel room we reserved was not as attractive or **commodious** as it had appeared in the brochure.

2. **finite** (fī′nīt′) *adjective* from Latin *finis*, "end"
   Limited; having an ending or a boundary
   • Joy's parents had only a **finite** amount of money to spend on her college education.

3. **gamut** (găm′ət) *noun* from Medieval Latin *gamma ut*, the lowest note in a scale
   The complete range or extent of something
   • Her amazing stage performance ran the **gamut** of human emotions, from joy to despair.

4. **incalculable** (ĭn-kăl′kyə-lə-bəl) *adjective* from Latin *in-*, "not" + *calculus*, "small stone used in counting"
   Very great; beyond measurement
   • The value of clean air is **incalculable.**

5. **iota** (ī-ō′tə) *noun* from Greek *iota*, the ninth and smallest letter in the Greek alphabet
   A tiny bit; an extremely small amount
   • Saadia's allergy to peanuts is so severe that an **iota** of peanut oil could cause him to have a fatal reaction.

6. **lofty** (lôf′tē) *adjective* from Old Norse *lopt*, "upstairs room; sky; air"
   a. Of great height; towering
   • We skied and explored the **lofty** peaks of the Rockies.
   b. Elevated and noble in character
   • His **lofty** ideals led him to dedicate his life to helping poverty-stricken children.
   c. Arrogant; haughty; pompous
   • In **lofty** tones, the count explained that his title made him superior to "common folk."

   loftiness *noun* The **loftiness** of his manner and his self-righteous statements alienated those around him.

TRAVEL
We offer commodious rooms and suites

commodious

To *run the gamut* is a commonly used expression.

Calculable is the opposite of *incalculable.*

7. **minuscule** (mĭn´ə-skyōōl´) *adjective* from Latin *minus*, "less; smaller"
Very small; tiny
• Using an eyedropper, Samantha fed the abandoned kitten **minuscule** amounts of milk.

Minuscule is sometimes spelled *miniscule*.

8. **picayune** (pĭk´ə-yōōn´) *adjective* from Louisiana French *picaillon*, "small coin"
Of little value or importance; paltry; trivial
• The thorough seamstress made me stand in my dress for an hour while she fussed over **picayune** details.

9. **vestige** (vĕs´tĭj) *noun* from Latin *vestigium*, "footprint"
A visible trace, evidence, or sign of something that no longer exists
• Searching for **vestiges** of the Anasazi civilization, the anthropologists came across the ruins of a cliff dwelling.

vestigial *adjective* The fear of the number thirteen is a **vestigial** superstition left over from ancient times.

10. **wane** (wān) from Old English *wanian*, "to lessen"
a. *verb* To decrease; to diminish in power or size; to near an end
• The full moon is **waning** and will reflect less light tonight.
b. *noun* The act or process of declining or diminishing
• By 1950, French influence in the Middle East was on the **wane**.

On the wane is a common phrase.

ANALOGIES

On the answer line, write the letter of the answer that best completes each analogy. Refer to Lessons 16–18 if you need help with any of the lesson words.

_____ 1. *Caustic* is to *polite* as _____.
    a. *effectual* is to *operational*   **c.** *finite* is to *limited*
    b. *sanguine* is to *confident*   **d.** *domineering* is to *submissive*

_____ 2. *Raze* is to *destroy* as _____.
    a. *wane* is to *strengthen*   **c.** *deplore* is to *approve*
    b. *surmount* is to *overcome*   **d.** *revel* is to *vex*

_____ 3. *Sanguine* is to *pessimistic* as _____.
    a. *minuscule* is to *huge*   **c.** *deleterious* is to *harmful*
    b. *disconsolate* is to *sad*   **d.** *commodious* is to *spacious*

_____ 4. *Mercurial* is to *constant* as _____.
    a. *halcyon* is to *chaotic*   **c.** *lofty* is to *height*
    b. *gamut* is to *range*   **d.** *lachrymose* is to *tearful*

WRITE THE CORRECT WORD

Write the correct word in the space next to each definition. Use each word only once.

_____ 1. the complete range

_____ 2. a trace

_____ 3. paltry; unimportant

_____ 4. spacious

_____ 5. to diminish

_____ 6. a tiny bit

_____ 7. elevated

_____ 8. having boundaries

_____ 9. very small

_____ 10. beyond measurement

COMPLETE THE SENTENCE

Write the letter for the word that best completes each sentence.

_____ 1. Interior designers sometimes use a mirrored wall to make a small room appear more _____.
   a. commodious   b. incalculable   c. minuscule   d. picayune

_____ 2. The last _____ of the roast turkey was devoured by the dog.
   a. wane   b. finite   c. vestige   d. gamut

_____ 3. In one day, the price of the stock ran the _____ from its all-time high to its all-time low.
   a. wane   b. gamut   c. commodity   d. vestige

_____ 4. The sorrow she suffered after the death of her mother was _____.
   a. picayune   b. finite   c. incalculable   d. lofty

_____ 5. "Don't come to me with _____ details—just get the job done!" barked the boss.
   a. commodious   b. waning   c. lofty   d. picayune

_____ 6. Mr. Wu wouldn't budge one _____ when I asked for an extension on my paper.
   a. iota   b. wane   c. gamut   d. minuscule

_____ 7. Many knights in the Middle Ages held firm to the _____ ideals of chivalry.
   a. commodious   b. picayune   c. finite   d. lofty

_____ 8. The band was on the _____ when the singer left to go out on her own.
   a. gamut   b. vestige   c. wane   d. picayune

_____ 9. There is much debate over whether the universe is _____ or infinite.
   a. lofty   b. finite   c. commodious   d. incalculable

_____ 10. The spider's _____ eggs were barely visible to the unaided eye.
   a. commodious   b. finite   c. waning   d. minuscule

Challenge: Never one to make _____ points, Grandma said wisely that _____ ideas don't matter one iota if you don't put them into action.
   _____   a. lofty…finite   b. picayune…lofty   c. finite…minuscule

The Iceman

(1) On a fall day in 1991, two German tourists hiking among the *lofty* peaks of the Alps stumbled upon a body poking out of the ice. Assuming it was that of a hiker who had recently died on the mountain, they alerted the authorities and went home. Later, they were surprised to hear that they had, in fact, discovered the oldest naturally preserved mummy ever found. The "Iceman" was 5,300 years old.

Like the German couple, the officials who first went to retrieve the corpse thought it was from modern times. **(2)** Just three weeks earlier, the bodies of two hikers missing since 1934 had been found in an area where the ice cover was *waning*. The Iceman's body was so well preserved that it, too, seemed more likely to be relatively recent.

Soon, though, it became clear this was a man from another time. The mummy wore clothes made of fur, hand-sewn shoes padded with grass, and a cloak woven out of straw. He carried a bow and arrows. **(3)** Other *vestiges* of the Neolithic era were also preserved near him. These included containers made from birch bark, a leather pouch, and an ancient dagger and ax.

The Iceman was found in the Ötzal Alps region, which straddles Italy and Austria. **(4)** Both countries claimed him, perhaps because experts realized that the find was of *incalculable* value. **(5)** Neither side budged one *iota* until geographers determined that the Iceman, who had since been named Ötzi, was found on Italian soil. Now Ötzi is on display in Italy, where millions flock to see him each year. **(6)** His confines, however, are far from *commodious*. To keep him from decaying further, he remains in a cold, climate-controlled room. Viewers peek through a window to observe him.

Scientists have pondered about who Ötzi was and how he died. **(7)** Theories about his death run the *gamut* from accident to human sacrifice. An arrowhead was found deep in Ötzi's shoulder, and his hand was cut, so it is likely he was assaulted in some way. **(8)** Tests found that *minuscule* amounts of blood on his clothing belonged to another person—perhaps his attacker.

(9) No details relevant to Ötzi or his life have been too *picayune* for curious minds. Researchers have studied the contents of his colon and determined that his last meal consisted of ibex meat, grains, and pollen. They have analyzed his shoes and discovered that fat from animal brains and livers was used to tan the leather. Tests on his teeth and bones have revealed that he originally came from a nearby Italian valley.

Ötzi has also changed our understanding of the past. For instance, his copper ax dates from before the time that experts had believed that people had started using copper. Ötzi also bore fifty-nine tattoos and an earring, but scientists do not believe that the tattoos were a fashion statement. Instead, they think that the lines burned into his skin were to treat arthritis. The marks were found at points on the body that are used in Chinese acupuncture treatments. But, curiously, Ötzi lived far from China and 500 years before the earliest known use of this medicinal art.

(10) Like most human beings, Ötzi likely imagined that his influence on the world would be *finite*, lasting only as long as his life. Instead, he still sheds light on human history for those of us living 5,300 years after he died.

Each sentence below refers to a numbered sentence in the passage. Write the letter of the choice that gives the sentence a meaning that is closest to the original sentence.

_____ **1.** Two German tourists hiking among the _____ peaks of the Alps stumbled upon a body poking out from some ice.
    a. spacious   **b.** towering   **c.** diminishing   **d.** trivial

_____ **2.** The bodies of two hikers had been found in an area where the ice cover was _____ .
    a. limited   **b.** insignificant   **c.** diminishing   **d.** very great

_____ **3.** Other _____ of the Neolithic era were also preserved near him.
    a. traces   **b.** tools   **c.** boundaries   **d.** peaks

_____ **4.** Experts realized that the find was of _____ value.
     a. modest   **b.** very great   **c.** insignificant   **d.** spacious

_____ **5.** Neither side budged one _____.
     a. bit   **b.** yard   **c.** mile   **d.** mountain

_____ **6.** His confines, however, are far from _____.
     a. tall   **b.** tiny   **c.** limited   **d.** spacious

_____ **7.** Theories about his death run the _____ from accident to human sacrifice.
     a. opinions   **b.** guesses   **c.** boundary   **d.** range

_____ **8.** Tests found that _____ amounts of blood on his clothing belonged to another person—perhaps his attacker.
     a. tiny   **b.** sticky   **c.** numerous   **d.** decreasing

_____ **9.** No details relevant to Ötzi or his life have been too _____ for curious minds.
     a. limited   **b.** insignificant   **c.** interesting   **d.** large

_____ **10.** Like most human beings, Ötzi likely imagined that his influence on the world would be _____.
     a. significant   **b.** limited   **c.** minute   **d.** eternal

Indicate whether the statements below are TRUE or FALSE according to the passage.

_____ **1.** We can learn about ancient medicine by studying Ötzi's remains.

_____ **2.** Ötzi was mummified in the same style as Egyptian mummies.

_____ **3.** Ötzi is now on display in a museum in Austria.

FINISH THE THOUGHT

Complete each sentence so that it shows the meaning of the italicized word.

1. He was hoping to find at least one *iota* _____

_____

2. A music style that is on the *wane* _____

_____

WRITE THE DERIVATIVE

Complete the sentence by writing the correct form of the word shown in parentheses. You may not need to change the form that is given.

_____ **1.** The U.S. system of checks and balances ensures that the three branches of government have _____ powers. (*finite*)

_____ **2.** We enjoyed the spacious seating in the _____ new airplane. (*commodious*)

_____ 3. Crime scene investigators can get vital information from just a _____ scrap of fabric. *(minuscule)*

_____ 4. Sheila resented what she called her sister's "constant _____ criticisms." *(picayune)*

_____ 5. The _____ of your aims is belied by the questionable methods you use to achieve them. *(lofty)*

_____ 6. The appendix is a _____ organ. *(vestige)*

_____ 7. My grandmother refuses to take any medicines, even when the risks of side effects are _____ small. *(incalculable)*

_____ 8. The forum featured speakers who represented the entire _____ of opinions on the issue. *(gamut)*

_____ 9. His stern expression didn't betray an _____ of sympathy. *(iota)*

_____ 10. The teacher explained the waxing and _____ of the moon. *(wane)*

FIND THE EXAMPLE

Choose the answer that best describes the action or situation.

_____ 1. The *vestiges* of an ancient civilization
   a. dinosaur bones   **b.** history museums   **c.** pottery shards   **d.** grocery stores

_____ 2. A phrase that indicates a *gamut*
   a. for better or worse   **b.** from A to Z   **c.** silver lining   **d.** according to law

_____ 3. A *lofty* thing to do
   a. give to charity   **b.** get a job   **c.** fly in a plane   **d.** climb the stairs

_____ 4. A *minuscule* creature
   a. weasel   **b.** horse   **c.** rat   **d.** mosquito

_____ 5. The person who would most likely need a *commodious* vehicle
   a. a parent of five   **b.** a doctor   **c.** a businesswoman   **d.** an elderly man

_____ 6. Something *incalculable*
   a. distance to moon   **b.** area of Mars   **c.** number of stars   **d.** diameter of Venus

_____ 7. A *picayune* criticism of a used car
   a. gets poor mileage   **b.** has tiny scratch   **c.** has no seat belts   **d.** burns too much oil

_____ 8. The action that would most likely make a band's popularity *wane*
   a. insulting fans   **b.** making a new album   **c.** going on tour   **d.** creating a Web site

_____ 9. An *iota*
   a. stately mansion   **b.** vast desert   **c.** old cheese   **d.** speck of dust

_____ 10. Something that may NOT be *finite*
   a. a ruler's reign   **b.** the universe   **c.** your college years   **d.** the planet Earth

Taking Tests

SAT Critical Reading Tests

The new SAT, first administered in 2005, has a Critical Reading section that presents both short and long reading passages, each of them followed by multiple-choice questions. The strategies below can help you answer such questions successfully.

Strategies

1. *Scan the passage and the test items first.* This will enable you to look for specific information as you read.

2. *Read at an appropriate rate.* Read through the passage once to get the overall idea. Then read it again slowly to make sure you understand it.

3. *Determine the main idea as you read.* The main idea may or may not be directly stated in the passage, but identifying it is critical to understanding what you read.

4. *Identify supporting details.* Details that support main points are often queried in test items.

5. *Be prepared to make inferences and draw conclusions.* These may involve making predictions or generalizations based what you have read, or they may be logical conclusions drawn from the information provided.

6. *Be prepared to make judgments.* Critical reading involves making evaluative judgments about ideas, facts and opinions, or an author's attitude, style, or tone.

7. *Refer to the passage to find information.* You do not need to memorize information from the passage, and may go back to it if necessary.

Practice

Read the following passage. Answer the questions based on what is stated or implied in the passage. For each question, choose the best answer and write the letter of the answer you choose in the space provided.

At one time, the popular adage "The sun never sets on the British Empire" was probably true. For at least two centuries, Britain was the most powerful nation in the world. In the nineteenth century, its possessions included Canada, Australia, parts of Africa, India, colonies in Asia, and numerous islands in the Caribbean, the Atlantic, and the Pacific. Hence, during this period, the sun was always shining on some part of the British Empire somewhere in the world. Over the past century, however, the once-formidable empire has contracted considerably in size and stature.

Officially, what we often refer to as Britain is the United Kingdom of Great Britain and Northern Ireland. The island of Great Britain includes England, Scotland, and Wales; Northern Ireland is the northern region of an island that was once one nation but now encompasses two separate entities (Northern Ireland and Ireland).

Britain has a long and storied past that includes two protracted civil wars (including the War of the Roses, 1455–1485), numerous conflicts with other powers, rebellions among its own colonies (including America), and enormous gains and losses in wealth and properties. The country then known as England emerged as a major naval power in the 1500s during the reign of Queen Elizabeth I. This led to the expansion of trade with Europe and Asia, the exploration of many previously unknown parts of the world, and the establishment of colonies in several places, including North America. The growth of its navy also led to wars with France and Spain, the only other nations that could challenge Britain's supremacy on the seas. By the early 1800s, Britain had lost its American colonies, but industrialization and the expansion of trade with Canada, India, and Asia made Britain—in today's parlance—the world's only superpower.

Two world wars took a major toll on Britain in the twentieth century, and many of its former colonies, such as India, gained independence. Numerous changes also took place within Britain itself. Although it remained a constitutional monarchy, Britain moved more and more toward a socialist government led by the Labour Party, which nationalized several industries and greatly expanded costly social programs to provide health care and social security. Today, Britain is the staunchest ally of the United States and still a strong nation, but the sun actually does set on what is left of the empire—every afternoon, just as it does on every other nation in the modern world.

_____ **1.** Which sentence best states the author's main point in this passage?
    a. For at least two centuries, Britain was the most powerful nation in the world.
    b. Britain once had a worldwide empire, but it has become much smaller and less powerful over the last century.
    c. Today, Britain would be considered the world's only superpower.
    d. Britain's possessions once included Canada, Australia, and India.
    e. Britain has a long, impressive history that includes many wars.

_____ **2.** In the phrase "a long and storied past that includes two *protracted* civil wars," the word *protracted* means
    a. "not justified."
    b. "violent; costly in human losses."
    c. "involving several nations."
    d. "drawn out; lasting a long time."
    e. "successful."

_____ **3.** The overall tone of this passage can best be described as
    a. sarcastic.
    b. tongue-in-cheek.
    c. bitter.
    d. nostalgic.
    e. analytical.

_____ **4.** Which conclusion can be drawn from the information in this passage?
    a. In the 1700s and 1800s, the most powerful nations were those that ruled the seas.
    b. Every European country held overseas possessions and colonies at one time.
    c. Britain lost its North American colonies because it expanded trade with Asia.
    d. Constitutional monarchies have never been as powerful as democratic nations.
    e. Britain should not have allowed America, India, and other colonies to become independent.

_____ **5.** The author mentions that "the sun actually does set on what is left of the empire" to make the point that
    a. the old adage about the setting sun was never true.
    b. Britain remains superior to most nations.
    c. the Labour Party has destroyed Britain's economy.
    d. Britain is no longer one of the world's superpowers.
    e. two world wars nearly destroyed Great Britain.

Reverence and Irreverence

WORD LIST

apathetic	consecrate	credo	heinous	ingrate
piety	sacrilegious	sanctimony	sanctity	timorous

Reverence, a feeling of profound awe, respect, and often love, is experienced by all people from time to time. The words in this lesson refer to various aspects and signs of reverence or the lack of it—irreverence.

1. **apathetic** (ăp´ə-thĕt´ĭk) *adjective* from Greek *a-*, "without" + *pathos*, "feeling"
   Feeling or showing a lack of interest, concern, or emotion; indifferent; unresponsive
   • The **apathetic** student simply shrugged when the guidance counselor asked him about his plans for the future.

   apathy *noun* Public **apathy** toward politics resulted in a low voter turnout and the election of an incumbent with questionable ethics.

apathetic

2. **consecrate** (kŏn´sĭ-krāt´) *verb* from Latin *con-*, "with" + *sacrare*, "to make sacred"
   a. To declare or distinguish as holy; to make sacred for religious use
      • The shaman's blessing **consecrated** the drum that would be used in the healing ceremony.
   b. To make venerable or worthy of reverence; to hallow
      • Many traditions have been **consecrated** by time.
   c. To dedicate solemnly to a service or a goal
      • They **consecrated** their lives to helping the poor.

   consecration *noun* Archaeologists guessed that the stone and clay circle at the center of the ancient ruin had been used for the **consecration** of harvests.

3. **credo** (krē´dō) *noun* from Latin *credere*, "to believe"
   A code, system, or statement of beliefs; a creed
   • The international physicians' **credo** is "First do no harm."

4. **heinous** (hā´nəs) *adjective* from Old French *haine*, "hatred"
   Grossly wicked or evil; abominable
   • The International Criminal Court was established to prosecute leaders accused of **heinous** crimes against humanity.

5. **ingrate** (ĭn´grāt´) *noun* from Latin *in-*, "not" + *gratus*, "pleasing; thankful"
   An ungrateful person
   • Only an **ingrate** would accept an invitation to dinner and then complain about the food.

6. **piety** (pī´ĭ-tē) *noun* from Latin *pius,* "dutiful"
   a. Religious reverence; earnestness in religious matters; devoutness
      • The monk was known throughout the countryside for his **piety.**
   b. Devotion to parents and family
      • Showing her familial **piety,** the woman moved back home to take care of her sick mother.
   c. Possessing a strict sense of morality; high-minded
      • The **pious** woman objected to even the smallest of little white lies.

   pious *adjective* The **pious** man prayed three times a day.

> The word *pious* can also mean "marked by false devoutness; solemnly hypocritical."

7. **sacrilegious** (săk´rə-lĭj´əs) *adjective* from Latin *sacrilegus,* "one who steals sacred things"
   Extremely irreverent or disrespectful toward what is considered sacred
   • The **sacrilegious** youths vandalized the temple.

   sacrilege *noun* In a country as diverse as the United States, what some people consider **sacrilege,** others consider acceptable behavior.

8. **sanctimony** (săngk´tə-mō´nē) *noun* from Latin *sanctus,* "holy; sacred"
   False righteousness; hypocritical devoutness or high-mindedness
   • The cartoon mocked the **sanctimony** of local politicians who had preached "law and order" and then had been caught taking bribes.

   sanctimonious *adjective* The **sanctimonious** preacher encouraged his flock to live simply and within their means, when all the while he was spending church money on fancy cars and vacations.

9. **sanctity** (săngk´tĭ-tē) *noun* from Latin *sanctus,* "holy; sacred"
   Sacredness; holiness of life or disposition
   • The **sanctity** of a promise is something most people agree should not be violated.

10. **timorous** (tĭm´ər-əs) *adjective* from Latin *timere,* "to fear"
    Full of fear or apprehensiveness; timid
    • The **timorous** audience member raised her hand, then withdrew it quickly when the speaker looked her way.

WORD ENRICHMENT

Sanctimonious words

   Sanctimonious is just one of the many words in the English language that refer to putting on a false show of good character. Others include *hypocrisy,* "the practice of professing beliefs, feelings, or virtues that one does not possess"; *pharisaic,* "hypocritically self-righteous and critical"; *tartuffe,* "a hypocrite who feigns religious piety"; and the more colloquial *two-faced,* "hypocritically double-dealing or deceitful."

WRITE THE CORRECT WORD

Write the correct word in the space next to each definition. Use each word only once.

_____ 1. sacredness

_____ 2. religious reverence

_____ 3. apprehensive; fearful

_____ 4. evil; wicked

_____ 5. a code, system, or statement of belief

_____ 6. indifferent

_____ 7. to declare holy

_____ 8. an ungrateful person

_____ 9. false righteousness

_____ 10. extremely disrespectful toward what is sacred

COMPLETE THE SENTENCE

Write the letter for the word that best completes each sentence.

_____ 1. Self-reliance was a major part of philosopher Ralph Waldo Emerson's _____.
    a. credo   **b.** sacrilege   **c.** apathy   **d.** ingrate

_____ 2. The cleric performed a ceremony to _____ the new shrine.
    a. sanctimony   **b.** ingrate   **c.** credo   **d.** consecrate

_____ 3. The judge added ten years to the convict's sentence, saying she had committed "especially _____" crimes.
    a. sanctimonious   **b.** heinous   **c.** timorous   **d.** apathetic

_____ 4. The arrogant man's _____ display of humility was a complete farce.
    a. heinous   **b.** sanctimonious   **c.** apathetic   **d.** consecrated

_____ 5. My least favorite character in the novel was the spoiled _____ who never thanked her parents for anything.
    a. credo   **b.** sanctimony   **c.** ingrate   **d.** apathy

_____ 6. The speaker said, "True _____ is its own reward."
    a. sanctimony   **b.** sacrilege   **c.** apathy   **d.** piety

_____ 7. Hannah was _____ when it came to advancing her career.
    a. apathetic   **b.** sanctified   **c.** sacrilegious   **d.** consecrated

_____ 8. In some religions, it is considered _____ for men and women to sit together during prayer services.
    a. sacrilegious   **b.** sanctimonious   **c.** timorous   **d.** ingrate

_____ 9. The _____ child hid behind the curtains during his parents' party.
    a. apathetic   **b.** pious   **c.** timorous   **d.** sanctimonious

_____ 10. The judge made sure that Alex understood the _____ of the oath he took.
    a. sacrilege   **b.** apathy   **c.** timorousness   **d.** sanctity

Challenge: The minister's lengthy sermon urged congregants to lead a life of _____, but to her disappointment, the congregation remained _____.
_____   **a.** credo...consecrated   **b.** sanctimony...sacrilegious   **c.** piety...apathetic

Joan of Arc

The brief, dramatic life of Joan of Arc (1412–1431) has inspired plays, books, movies, and even television shows. This peasant girl, who long ago led the French to victory against the English, may have perished at an early age, but her story lives on.

(1) Joan was a French farm girl known for her *piety* and kindness. As a child, she witnessed repeated English attacks in the countryside near her village. **(2)** The French ruler, Charles, was weak and *timorous,* and his troops did little to prevent the invaders from devastating his country. In fact, because of the threats to his territory, Charles remained uncrowned.

Joan, however, was determined to save her homeland. Since the age of about twelve, she had been hearing voices that she attributed to saints speaking God's word to her. The voices told her that she should fight the English and liberate her beloved France. **(3)** Her belief that she was divinely inspired to *consecrate* her life to her country gave her great courage. She asked to see Charles, but he refused to meet with her. **(4)** On a second trip, she was granted an audience with Charles and offered to fight for France, but the ruler reacted with *apathy.*

Little by little, though, Joan won acceptance, and Charles finally gave her command of a force of troops. Dressed in men's clothing, she bravely and capably led her soldiers into combat, succeeding in ending the English siege of the city of Orleans. A subsequent string of victories by her troops finally allowed Charles to be crowned king.

Her triumphs were cut short, however, when she was captured by French Burgundians, who sided with the English. Charles, the king who owed his crown to Joan, did not help her. **(5)** Some have judged him to be an *ingrate,* ready to sacrifice the valiant warrior, although the situation may not have been that simple.

Once in the hands of the enemy, however, Joan had no hope of fair treatment. **(6)** The English accused her of *sacrilegious* acts and put her on trial. **(7)** Church officials twisted her piety into *sanctimony,* her bravery into bloodthirsty violence. **(8)** They accused her of violating religious *credos.* In 1431, they burned Joan at the stake. **(9)** This *heinous* act ended her life at the age of only nineteen.

But the reputation of Joan of Arc has lived on long after her death. In 1455 and 1456, the Catholic Church conducted a retrial and declared Joan an innocent martyr of the church. **(10)** In 1920, she was *sanctified* and proclaimed a saint.

Writers have retold Joan's story from many different perspectives. Shakespeare portrayed her as a villainess. Mark Twain and George Bernard Shaw depicted her as a strong woman who was ahead of her time. In France, she is a national hero, and a day in May is celebrated in her honor.

Joan's independence and bravery make her both an example for others and a dramatic inspiration. A recent television show featured a character based on her. She has also been represented in an animated series. There is even a rock group named after her. The poor peasant girl who served her king so valiantly and died so tragically lives on in religion, literature, national pride, and popular culture.

Each sentence below refers to a numbered sentence in the passage. Write the letter of the choice that gives the sentence a meaning that is closest to the original sentence.

_____ **1.** Joan was a French farm girl known for her _____ and kindness.
    a. reverence   **b.** warmth   **c.** creed   **d.** indifference

_____ **2.** The French ruler, Charles, was weak and _____.
    a. timid   **b.** irreverent   **c.** holy   **d.** indifferent

_____ **3.** Joan believed that she was divinely inspired to _____ her life to her country.
    a. timidly bless   **b.** grudgingly give   **c.** wickedly sacrifice   **d.** solemnly dedicate

_____ **4.** She offered to fight for France, but the ruler reacted with _____.
    a. arrogance   **b.** indifference   **c.** holiness   **d.** reverence

_____ **5.** Some have judged him to be a(n) _____, ready to sacrifice the valiant warrior.
    a. holy saint   **b.** reverent person   **c.** ungrateful person   **d.** hypocrite

_____ **6.** The English accused her of _____ acts and put her on trial.
    a. irreverent   **b.** timid   **c.** holy   **d.** hypocritical

_____ **7.** Church officials twisted her piety into _____, her bravery into bloodthirsty violence.
    a. moral fortitude   **b.** indifference   **c.** evil acts   **d.** false righteousness

_____ **8.** They accused her of violating religious _____.
    a. indifference   **b.** crimes   **c.** beliefs   **d.** saints

_____ **9.** This _____ act ended her life at the age of only nineteen.
    a. ungrateful   **b.** abominable   **c.** holy   **d.** justified

_____ **10.** In 1920, she was _____ and proclaimed a saint.
    a. made indifferent   **b.** declared holy   **c.** revered publicly   **d.** portrayed as ungrateful

Indicate whether the statements below are TRUE or FALSE according to the passage.

_____ **1.** Joan of Arc was rescued by French forces and spared from punishment.

_____ **2.** At first, Charles was not interested in Joan's offer to help.

_____ **3.** Joan's exploits helped enthrone Charles.

WRITING EXTENDED RESPONSES

As a young woman of the 1400s, Joan of Arc accomplished great things. In an essay at least three paragraphs long, describe another figure (historical, present-day, or fictional) who made great sacrifices for a cause. Compare and contrast this person to Joan of Arc. Be sure to explain why you think this person is worthy of respect. Use at least three lesson words in your essay and underline them.

WRITE THE DERIVATIVE

Complete the sentence by writing the correct form of the word shown in parentheses. You may not need to change the form that is given.

_____ **1.** We read about the _____ of the oak groves where Druids conducted ceremonies long ago. (*consecrate*)

_____ **2.** Dawn sometimes resents the _____ lectures she gets from her older sister. (*sanctimony*)

_____ **3.** "Renew, reuse, recycle" is the environmental group's _____. (*credo*)

_____ **4.** Mother Teresa was a very _____ person. (*piety*)

_____ **5.** Surprisingly, the news of the policy change was met by public _____ . (*apathetic*)

_____ **6.** During the Middle Ages, anyone suspected of _____ would have most likely been imprisoned. (*sacrilegious*)

_____ **7.** Never known to be _____ , Stephan entered the room with bounding steps and a booming voice. (*timorous*)

_____ **8.** It's ironic that people tend to focus on petty issues when so many _____ things are happening to innocent people around the globe. (*heinous*)

_____ **9.** "That burglar violated the _____ of my home," shouted Jay. (*sanctity*)

_____ **10.** The _____ never even thanked the couple who funded his college education. (*ingrate*)

FIND THE EXAMPLE

Choose the answer that best describes the action or situation.

_____ **1.** A *timorous* creature
    a. mouse   **b.** lion   **c.** horse   **d.** vulture

_____ **2.** How an *apathetic* person would likely react to shocking news
    a. Are you kidding?   **b.** Whatever.   **c.** Oh my!   **d.** How can I help?

_____ **3.** A *heinous* act
    a. tickling   **b.** criticizing   **c.** torturing   **d.** whistling

_____ **4.** How an *ingrate* might respond to receiving a gift certificate
    a. Thank you.   **b.** I like that store.   **c.** How thoughtful!   **d.** I'd rather have cash.

_____ **5.** Usually a sign of *piety*
    a. impulsivity   **b.** wildness   **c.** devotion   **d.** sleepiness

_____ **6.** Something that a *sanctimonious* politician would think about while in a house of worship
    a. the beauty of life   **b.** ethical behavior   **c.** self-improvement   **d.** how it looks to voters

_____ **7.** Something that many people believe has *sanctity*
    a. waste   **b.** life   **c.** sky   **d.** concrete

_____ **8.** Most likely to be part of a soldier's *credo*
    a. Buy low, sell high.   **b.** Early to bed.   **c.** I will be loyal.   **d.** Make that cash.

_____ **9.** A building that would most likely be *consecrated*
    a. temple   **b.** stadium   **c.** restaurant   **d.** warehouse

_____ **10.** An act that some people consider *sacrilegious*
    a. drinking water   **b.** sleeping soundly   **c.** repairing a roof   **d.** destroying a flag

Words from Other Languages

WORD LIST

berserk	jubilee	juggernaut	kowtow	maelstrom
mecca	nabob	saga	shibboleth	trek

As English explorers encountered new languages, they incorporated many foreign words into their own language. For example, the word *cotton* comes from Arabic. Other examples include *boss* (Dutch), *kiosk* (Turkish), and *pajamas* (Hindi). This lesson presents English words that come from other languages.

1. berserk **(bər-sûrk´)** *adjective* from Old Norse *björn,* "bear" + *serkr,* "shirt"
   a. Destructively or frenetically violent
   • When the referee called a foul, the enraged player went **berserk** and was ejected from the game.
   b. Mentally or emotionally upset; deranged
   • Some survivors who had lost many family members in the earthquake went **berserk** with grief.

> Norse warriors, or *berserkers,* wore bear hides and fought like frenzied animals.

2. jubilee **(jōō´bə-lē´)** *noun* from Hebrew *yobel,* "ram's horn"
   a. A specially celebrated anniversary, particularly a fiftieth anniversary
   • The 1887 **jubilee** of Queen Victoria's fifty years on the throne was marked by parades, parties, and even a specially issued coin.
   b. A season or an occasion of joyful celebration
   • The soldier's homecoming was cause for a full-fledged **jubilee,** complete with music, food, and games.

3. juggernaut **(jŭg´ər-nôt´)** *noun* from Hindi *jagannath,* title of Krishna, from Sanskrit jaġannathan, "lord of the world"
   a. An overwhelming, advancing force that crushes or seems to crush everything in its path
   • Successful sports teams are sometimes referred to as **juggernauts.**
   b. Something, such as a belief or institution, that elicits blind and destructive devotion or to which people are ruthlessly sacrificed
   • The Nazi **juggernaut** claimed the lives of many millions of people.

> Both meanings of *juggernaut* come from worshippers who threw themselves under a huge wagon that carried a statue of Krishna in a procession at Puri, India.

4. kowtow **(kou-tou´)** *verb* from Mandarin Chinese *kou,* "to knock" + *tou,* "head"
   a. To kneel, touching the head to the ground in an expression of deep respect, worship, or submission, as formerly done in China
   • Marco Polo **kowtowed** to the powerful emperor.
   b. To show servile submission; to fawn
   • Some bosses expect employees to **kowtow,** but others prefer a more equitable relationship.

kowtowing

5. **maelstrom** (māl´strəm) *noun* from Dutch *malen,* "to grind; to whirl" + *stroom,* "stream"
   a. A violent or turbulent situation
      • The unfortunate family was caught in the **maelstrom** of war.
   b. A whirlpool of extraordinary size or violence
      • The **maelstrom** just below the rapids sucked the canoe down until it lodged beneath a rock at the bottom of the river.

6. **mecca** (mĕk´ə) *noun* from the Saudi Arabian city of *Mecca,* the holiest city of Islam and a destination of pilgrimages
   a. A place that is regarded as the center of an activity or interest
      • Moab, Utah, is a **mecca** for mountain biking.
   b. A place visited by many people
      • New Orleans is a tourist **mecca** for many reasons, including its phenomenal food, music, and nightlife.

7. **nabob** (nā´bŏb´) *noun* from Hindi, derived from Arabic *na'ib,* "deputy"
   A wealthy and prominent person
      • The president held a special lunch for energy industry **nabobs.**

> *Nabob* also means "a governor in India under the Mogul Empire."

8. **saga** (sä´gə) *noun* from Old Norse, "a saying; a narrative"
   a. A prose epic with many episodes, often giving a family history
      • *The Forsyte Saga* tells the story of several generations of that clan.
   b. A long, detailed account
      • The **saga** of their disastrous vacation took an hour to tell.

> *Sagas* were prose narratives written in Iceland between 1120 and 1400. They included histories of Iceland's settlers and legends of their gods and heroes.

9. **shibboleth** (shĭb´ə-lĭth) *noun* from Hebrew *sibbolet,* "torrent of water"
   a. A word or pronunciation that distinguishes people of one group or class from those of another
      • *Y'all* is a **shibboleth** used by U.S. Southerners.
   b. A commonplace saying or idea
      • Is that old **shibboleth** "anyone can become president" really true?

10. **trek** (trĕk) from Afrikaans, "to travel by ox wagon," derived from Dutch *trecken,* "to pull"
   a. *verb* To make a slow, difficult journey; to journey on foot
      • The explorers **trekked** across the continent.
   b. *noun* A journey or leg of a journey, especially if slow and difficult
      • "I'll be happy when this **trek** is over," said the exhausted Boy Scout.

WORD ENRICHMENT

Words from Hebrew

Two of the words in this lesson come from Hebrew. The Bible directed that every fifty years, there would be a year of rest, celebration, and righteousness, called a *jubilee.* The word meant "ram's horn," the instrument to be sounded at the beginning of the *jubilee.*

Shibboleth came from the Hebrew word *sibbolet,* meaning "torrent of water." The ancient Gileadites pronounced this word with an *sh* sound and used it as a password to exclude Ephraimites, because the Ephraimites could not pronounce the *sh* sound. From this meaning, a *shibboleth* has come to mean a word or custom particular to a certain group.

WRITE THE CORRECT WORD

Write the correct word in the space next to each definition. Use each word only once.

_____ **1.** an epic tale

_____ **2.** a prominent person

_____ **3.** wildly violent

_____ **4.** a center of interest

_____ **5.** an unstoppable force

_____ **6.** to kneel before

_____ **7.** a difficult journey

_____ **8.** a special anniversary

_____ **9.** a common saying

_____ **10.** a turbulent situation

COMPLETE THE SENTENCE

Write the letter for the word that best completes each sentence.

_____ **1.** New York City is a _____ of the art world.
  a. mecca   **b.** saga   **c.** jubilee   **d.** maelstrom

_____ **2.** *VIP*, an abbreviation for "very important person," is synonymous with the word
  _____ .
  a. *trek*   **b.** *shibboleth*   **c.** *nabob*   **d.** *jubilee*

_____ **3.** The startled elephant panicked and went _____, charging into the crowd.
  a. saga   **b.** berserk   **c.** kowtow   **d.** mecca

_____ **4.** Do you really think that _____ will make him like or respect you?
  a. trekking   **b.** maelstrom   **c.** juggernaut   **d.** kowtowing

_____ **5.** The interjection *eh* is a _____ used primarily by Canadians.
  a. juggernaut   **b.** kowtow   **c.** shibboleth   **d.** nabob

_____ **6.** The book portrays the _____ of the Cherokees as they were forced off their
  native lands in the late 1830s.
  a. saga   **b.** shibboleth   **c.** mecca   **d.** kowtow

_____ **7.** It was a 500-mile _____ through the jungle to reach the Mayan temple.
  a. trek   **b.** jubilee   **c.** mecca   **d.** maelstrom

_____ **8.** The relentless _____ of the Roman army created a vast empire.
  a. kowtowing   **b.** jubilee   **c.** nabob   **d.** juggernaut

_____ **9.** The _____ that followed the angry speech was like nothing I'd ever seen.
  a. trek   **b.** maelstrom   **c.** nabob   **d.** mecca

_____ **10.** This year, Grant Hospital celebrates its fifty-year _____ .
  a. nabob   **b.** juggernaut   **c.** jubilee   **d.** mecca

Challenge: Accustomed to having people of all walks of life _____ to him, the Hollywood
  _____ almost went berserk when someone told him that he'd have to wait in
  line just like everybody else.
_____   **a.** trek…juggernaut   **b.** kowtow…nabob   **c.** kowtow…maelstrom

Tourists on Top of the World

In 1852, a survey team pointed their instruments toward the horizon and measured the highest point on Earth—at 29,035 feet, Mount Everest was certainly the top of the world.

This king of all mountains towers over the icy Himalayan range, rising more than five miles into the sky like a jagged tooth above Tibet and Nepal. When Everest's height was first measured, the Tibetans (who call the mountain Chomolungma) had long held great respect for it, but no one had ever attempted to climb to the treacherous summit.

(1) Once it was publicized that Everest was the world's tallest peak, it soon became a *mecca* for daring mountaineers. **(2)** In the beginning, their *treks* were rare achievements, at least for those who survived. **(3)** But today, the *juggernaut* of some 27,000 sightseers and climbers per year has brought criticism and left many feeling that Everest is no longer a sacred place. Many people fly in and hike only to the mountain's base. Other rich and inexperienced climbers pay professional guides thousands of dollars to get them to the top. To some people, Everest now seems to be nothing more than a dangerous tourist trap.

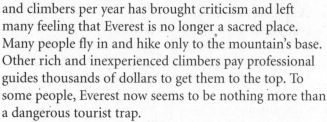

Things were very different as recently as the 1920s. In 1924, two Englishmen, George Leigh Mallory and Andrew Irvine, were the first to attempt to climb Everest. **(4)** When asked why, Mallory answered "because it's there," a phrase that has since become a *shibboleth* for mountaineers and other adventurers.

Driven by stubbornness, ambition, and awe, Mallory and Irvine made their way through shifting fields of ice. They trudged through waist-deep snow and struggled up sheer cliffs toward the dangerous peak. **(5)** But they faced raging winds, subzero temperatures, and low levels of oxygen that can impair judgment and even drive people *berserk*. The combination proved to be too much. **(6)** The pair died on the mountain, unleashing a *maelstrom* of debate as to whether they had made it to the top before they perished.

Not until 1953 did climbers scale the mountain and live to tell about it. For three years, Edmund Hillary of Britain and Tenzing Norgay of Nepal held the honor of being the only humans ever to stand at the highest point on the planet. **(7)** The world *kowtowed* to them, honoring their awesome achievement. Hillary was even knighted for his success by the queen of England.

For more than a quarter-century afterward, only the strongest and most skilled mountaineers followed in Norgay and Hillary's lofty footsteps. Reaching the top was still a glorious feat for each of the twenty-five men who'd done it by 1970. The first woman scaled Everest in 1975. **(8)** But soon, reaching the summit would no longer seem like cause for a *jubilee*.

In 1980, a wealthy, but inexperienced, Texan was guided to the top of the mountain by a skilled mountaineer. **(9)** Soon, more guides were taking inexperienced *nabobs* to the summit, generally charging about $65,000 for the large crew needed to cook, carry equipment, and lead them up.

Meanwhile, a growing number of climbers on the mountain burned refuse for warmth and left heaps of waste and spent oxygen tanks behind. Frozen corpses, too heavy to carry out in that strength-sapping air, lie along the route as grim reminders of those who didn't survive.

For many years, serious climbers warned that something was bound to go wrong, and it did. In 1996, fifteen people from one expedition died on Everest, nine in just one day. Many think the tragedy might have been avoided if there had not been so many inexperienced climbers on the peak.

(10) The *saga* of the nine who died has been described in several books, but some say the lesson of their deaths has not been learned. More and more guides continue to crowd the peak with their clients. But for those who treat the climb as just another expensive adventure, the jury is still out on whether it's the right thing to do.

Each sentence below refers to a numbered sentence in the passage. Write the letter of the choice that gives the sentence a meaning that is closest to the original sentence.

_____ **1.** The mountain became a _____ for daring mountaineers.
    a. tourist trap   **b.** center of interest   **c.** turbulent spot   **d.** buzzword

_____ **2.** Their _____ were rare achievements, at least for those who survived.
    a. difficult journeys   **b.** stirring epics   **c.** common slogans   **d.** personal stories

_____ 3. The _____ of sightseers and climbers has left many feeling that Everest is no longer a sacred place.

a. decline   **b.** unstoppable force   **c.** swirling wave   **d.** celebration

_____ 4. The phrase has since become a _____ for mountaineers and other adventurers.

a. synonym   **b.** motto   **c.** force   **d.** center

_____ 5. Low levels of oxygen can impair judgment and drive people _____.

a. deranged   **b.** arrogant   **c.** submissive   **d.** important

_____ 6. The pair died on the mountain, unleashing a _____ of debate.

a. storm   **b.** submission   **c.** center   **d.** celebration

_____ 7. The world _____ to them, honoring their awesome achievement.

a. sang songs   **b.** paid respect   **c.** gave medals   **d.** was indifferent

_____ 8. But soon, reaching the summit would no longer seem like cause for a _____.

a. blind devotion   **b.** physical hardship   **c.** joyful celebration   **d.** violent situation

_____ 9. Soon, more guides were taking inexperienced _____ to the summit.

a. servile porters   **b.** joyful climbers   **c.** arrogant hikers   **d.** wealthy people

_____ 10. The _____ of the nine who died has been described in several books.

a. painful climb   **b.** epic tale   **c.** solemn occasion   **d.** long journey

Indicate whether the statements below are TRUE or FALSE according to the passage.

_____ 1. In 1852, George Mallory and Andrew Irvine attempted to climb Mount Everest.

_____ 2. Edmund Hillary of Britain and Tenzing Norgay of Nepal were the first to reach the top of Mount Everest in 1953.

_____ 3. Everest has become littered with hikers' refuse.

FINISH THE THOUGHT

Complete each sentence so that it shows the meaning of the italicized word.

1. Our *trek* _____

_____

2. I refuse to *kowtow* _____

_____

WRITE THE DERIVATIVE

Complete the sentence by writing the correct form of the word shown in parentheses. You may not need to change the form that is given.

_____ **1.** I don't understand why some fans go _____ and rampage through a city just because a sports team wins a championship. *(berserk)*

_____ **2.** Many clubs have their own _____. (*shibboleth*)

_____ **3.** The Rices celebrated their fifty-year _____ last week. (*jubilee*)

_____ **4.** Mumbai (formerly Bombay), a huge city in west-central India, is giving Hollywood competition as the world's _____ of moviemaking. (*mecca*)

_____ **5.** The book describes the _____ of Lincoln's long path to the presidency. (*saga*)

_____ **6.** Settlers _____ along behind their wagons as they crossed the plains. (*trek*)

_____ **7.** The 1980 U.S. men's Olympic hockey team miraculously managed to defeat the heavily favored Soviet _____. (*juggernaut*)

_____ **8.** If you _____ to people, they might take advantage of you. (*kowtow*)

_____ **9.** A study of history shows that conquerors must be wary of the potential _____ of unrest that follows successful invasions. (*maelstrom*)

_____ **10.** Economic factors have prompted many carpet industry _____ to settle in the Chattanooga, Tennessee area. (*nabob*)

FIND THE EXAMPLE

Choose the answer that best describes the action or situation.

_____ **1.** Someone LEAST likely to be a *nabob*
  a. movie star   **b.** famous writer   **c.** part-time clerk   **d.** corporate executive

_____ **2.** What one would expect to find at a *mecca*
  a. peace & quiet   **b.** countryside   **c.** lots of people   **d.** lots of stars

_____ **3.** A *shibboleth*
  a. Pass the sock.   **b.** I am Melvin.   **c.** She teaches cats.   **d.** Haste makes waste.

_____ **4.** How one would be most likely to feel just before going *berserk*
  a. extremely angry   **b.** well rested   **c.** cold and indifferent   **d.** very satisfied

_____ **5.** What a person who is *kowtowing* might say
  a. No way.   **b.** Yes, of course, sir.   **c.** I disagree.   **d.** You were rude to her.

_____ **6.** The item most likely to get worn out on a *trek*
  a. hovercraft   **b.** microwave oven   **c.** DVD player   **d.** hiking boots

_____ **7.** Something NOT likely to be found at a *jubilee*
  a. band   **b.** tears   **c.** food   **d.** smiles

_____ **8.** An example of a *maelstrom*
  a. heat wave   **b.** drizzle   **c.** hurricane   **d.** cold snap

_____ **9.** The adjective that best describes a *juggernaut*
  a. overpowering   **b.** gentle   **c.** incompetent   **d.** beneficial

_____ **10.** The most likely title of a *saga*
  a. *Pete the Pebble*   **b.** *Editing for Kids*   **c.** *Manatees*   **d.** *The Wars of Njord*

Movement

WORD LIST

cavort	emanate	meander	retrogress	serpentine
supersede	torpid	transitory	undulate	unremitting

Our world is full of many kinds of movement. The words in this lesson will enhance your ability to describe the motion that is all around us.

1. **cavort** (kə-vôrt´) *verb*
   To leap or dance about in high spirits
   • The young lambs **cavorted** in the pasture, ignoring the collie who was trying to herd them back to the pen.

2. **emanate** (ĕm´ə-nāt´) *verb* from Latin *ex-*, "out of" + *manere* "to flow"
   To send forth; to emit or exude
   • A huge column of smoke **emanated** from the factory.

   emanation *noun* Delicious-smelling **emanations** from the bakery wafted over the neighborhood.

3. **meander** (mē-ăn´dər) *verb* from Greek *maiandros,* after the Maeander River, noted for its winding course
   a. To follow a winding and turning course
      • The river **meandered** through the valley.
   b. To move aimlessly and idly without a fixed direction; to wander
      • It was such a lovely day that we just **meandered** through the park for a few hours.

emanate

> *Meander* and *emanate* can be used in figurative ways. One can *meander* through life, and people can *emanate* emotions.

4. **retrogress** (rĕt´rə-grĕs´, ret´-rə-grĕs´) *verb* from Latin *retro-*, "backward" "backward" + *gradi,* "to go"
   To return to an earlier, inferior, or less complex condition; to go or move backward
   • After taking a bad fall while she was walking, the toddler **retrogressed** to crawling.

   retrogression *noun* "Eliminating government medical assistance programs for the poor would be a tragic **retrogression** in social policy," said the senator.

5. **serpentine** (sûr´pən-tēn´, sûr´pən-tīn´) *adjective* from Latin *serpens,* "serpent"
   Snakelike; resembling a snake in form or movement
   • A **serpentine** path wound its way up the mountainside.

6. **supersede** (soo´pər-sēd´) *verb* from Latin *super-*, "above" + *sedere,* "to sit"
   To replace or supplant; to displace as inferior
   • This new set of operating instructions will **supersede** the old ones.

7. torpid (tôr´pĭd) *adjective* from Latin *torpere*, "to be stiff"
  a. Inactive or apathetic; lethargic; sluggish
    • The heat made us all **torpid**, so little work was done.
  b. Deprived of the power of movement or feeling; numbed
    • The **torpid** patient showed no response when the neurologist poked his feet with sharp sticks.

  torpor *noun* After missing an easy shot, Mark sat on the bench in **torpor**.

Torpid can also mean "dormant; hibernating."

8. transitory (trăn´sĭ-tôr´ē) *adjective* from Latin *transitus*, "passage"
  Existing or lasting only a short while; temporary; short-lived
    • My brother's desire for a cocker spaniel was **transitory**; the next week he wanted a poodle.

9. undulate (ŭn´jə-lāt´) *verb* from Latin *unda*, "wave"
  To move with a smooth, wavelike motion
    • The dancers **undulated** across the stage like gentle waves.

  undulation *noun* The ocean's **undulations** rocked me to sleep, but they made Stuart seasick.

10. unremitting (ŭn´rĭ-mĭt´ĭng) *adjective* from Latin *un-*, "not" + *re-*, "back" + *mittere*, "to send"
  Never letting up or lessening; persistent
    • The **unremitting** rain had a depressing effect.

ANALOGIES

On the answer line, write the letter of the answer that best completes each analogy. Refer to Lessons 19–21 if you need help with any of the lesson words.

_____ **1.** *Saga* is to *story* as _____.
  a. *nabob* is to *laborer*   **c.** *juggernaut* is to *stalemate*
  b. *credo* is to *beliefs*   **d.** *ingrate* is to *thankful*

_____ **2.** *Unremitting* is to *stop* as _____.
  a. *berserk* is to *wildness*   **c.** *torpid* is to *heat*
  b. *heinous* is to *evil*   **d.** *apathetic* is to *act*

_____ **3.** *Piety* is to *sacrilege* as _____.
  a. *torpor* is to *activity*   **c.** *sanctity* is to *holiness*
  b. *shyness* is to *timorousness*   **d.** *jubilee* is to *celebration*

_____ **4.** *Mecca* is to *place* as _____.
  a. *kowtow* is to *rebel*   **c.** *maelstrom* is to *calm*
  b. *transitory* is to *permanent*   **d.** *trek* is to *journey*

WRITE THE CORRECT WORD

Write the correct word in the space next to each definition. Use each word only once.

_____ **1.** not letting up

_____ **2.** to wind or wander

_____ **3.** to supplant

_____ **4.** to go backward

_____ **5.** temporary

_____ **6.** like a snake

_____ **7.** to dance about

_____ **8.** to send forth

_____ **9.** lethargic; sluggish

_____ **10.** to make wavelike motions

COMPLETE THE SENTENCE

Write the letter for the word that best completes each sentence.

_____ **1.** The _____ noise from the car alarm kept us awake for hours.
  a. cavorting   **b.** meandering   **c.** unremitting   **d.** transitory

_____ **2.** Dangerous fumes _____ from the laboratory.
  a. retrogressed   **b.** emanated   **c.** superseded   **d.** cavorted

_____ **3.** People often feel _____ after a big Thanksgiving meal.
  a. serpentine   **b.** superseded   **c.** torpid   **d.** unremitting

_____ **4.** The trail _____ through dunes, meadows, and forests.
  a. meanders   **b.** retrogresses   **c.** cavorts   **d.** supersedes

_____ **5.** The doctors thought they had discovered the cause of the patient's illness, until a(n) _____ in his condition indicated that the treatment wasn't addressing the root of the problem.
  a. emanation   **b.** cavorting   **c.** undulation   **d.** retrogression

_____ **6.** The decisions of the Supreme Court _____ those of lower courts.
  a. cavort   **b.** supersede   **c.** emanate   **d.** retrogress

_____ **7.** Good hula dancers gracefully _____ their bodies.
  a. retrogress   **b.** emanate   **c.** undulate   **d.** meander

_____ **8.** The children _____ on the playground, skipping and running with abandon.
  a. cavorted   **b.** emanated   **c.** retrogressed   **d.** superseded

_____ **9.** The pharmacist assured me that any side effects from the medication would be _____.
  a. serpentine   **b.** undulating   **c.** transitory   **d.** cavorting

_____ **10.** The letter "S" has a(n) _____ shape.
  a. unremitting   **b.** serpentine   **c.** torpid   **d.** transitory

Challenge: The governor's educational policy proved to be only a _____ solution to the _____ problem of chronic budgetary shortfalls.
  a. torpid…emanating   **b.** retrogressive…torpid   **c.** transitory…unremitting

A Climbing Pioneer

The first time Wanda Rutkiewicz went rock climbing, she got impatient. Her friends were using the one safety rope to secure themselves while they scrambled up the wall of rock ahead of her. They were taking too long for Wanda's taste, so she started climbing on her own, balancing on the tiniest of nubs in the surface of the vertical rock face and using her great strength to pull herself upward. Her friends begged her to stop. If she fell without the rope to hold her, she could die. But she didn't stop. She didn't fall. Instead, she smiled all the way to the top.

That was in 1955, in communist Poland, when Wanda was just eighteen. Of that day, she wrote, "I was totally possessed by climbing from that very first moment. The experience was like some inner explosion. I knew it would somehow mark the rest of my life." It did. She became a great and fearless mountain climber.

(1) Wanda grew famous for her *unremitting* efforts to climb the world's most difficult peaks at a time when most mountain expeditions consisted of all-male teams. **(2)** But the fearless woman conquered each mountain alongside the men, *emanating* confidence every step of the way.

Her iron will and daring feats became legendary. With outdated equipment, threadbare climbing clothes, and poorly insulated shoes, she led some of the first all-female expeditions up some of the toughest, coldest, iciest mountain faces on Earth. **(3)** There was no joyful *cavorting*, though, once she reached a summit. In these perilous places, every ounce of energy was needed for the tricky trip down.

(4) At home, Wanda's sense of peace was always *transitory*. Restlessness would drive her back to the mountains, which she said gave her "an exhilarating sense of freedom in the clear, bracing air."

Even after another climber fell onto her, knocking her off a cliff and breaking her leg, she refused to stay home. **(5)** Instead, in a cast and on crutches, she made the grueling ninety-three-mile hike up the *serpentine*

path that leads to the base of the world's most dangerous mountain, K2, in the Himalayas. Once there, she climbed more than 16,000 feet up the mountain before stopping.

In 1978, she became the first Pole to climb the world's tallest mountain, Mount Everest. In 1986, she was the first woman to reach the summit of K2, the world's second tallest mountain, but a climb far more difficult than Everest.

(6) Not wanting to *retrogress* as she aged, she pursued even more ambitious goals. At forty-seven, she announced that she would become the first woman to climb the world's fourteen tallest mountains. All are above 26,000 feet. Only two men had achieved this before. **(7)** With her brown hair *undulating* in the wind, she became a fixture in the forbidding Himalayas.

Sadly, in 1992, Wanda was on her ninth peak when it all came to an end. Just 1,000 feet below the summit of Kanchenjunga, she couldn't go on. Her bad leg slowed her pace. **(8)** The dangerously thin air made her movements *torpid*. Her snowsuit could not ward off the freezing cold once she stopped moving quickly.

(9) Rather than slowly *meander* to her death, she sat down and told her teammates, who were also struggling, to continue on. She said she would rest and go on in the morning, but she was never seen again. Her own words were now proven true: "Living your dreams," she wrote, "instead of just dreaming them, is not without risk."

Wanda Rutkiewicz remains one of the most accomplished female mountaineers in history. **(10)** To this date, no other woman has *superseded* her. She is still the only woman to have climbed eight 26,000-foot mountains. But many who are inspired by her determination continue to climb in her footsteps.

Each sentence below refers to a numbered sentence in the passage. Write the letter of the choice that gives the sentence a meaning that is closest to the original sentence.

_____ **1.** Wanda grew famous for her _____ efforts to climb the world's most difficult peaks.

    a. disturbing   **b.** persistent   **c.** wandering   **d.** temporary

_____ **2.** But the fearless woman conquered each mountain alongside the men, _____ confidence every step of the way.

    a. returning   **b.** shamming   **c.** exuding   **d.** lacking

_____ **3.** There was no joyful _____, though, once she reached a summit.
    a. leaping   **b.** sitting   **c.** dreaming   **d.** wandering

_____ **4.** At home, Wanda's sense of peace was always _____.
    a. lethargic   **b.** strong   **c.** unrelenting   **d.** temporary

_____ **5.** Instead, in a cast and on crutches, she made the grueling ninety-three-mile hike up the _____ path.
    a. frozen   **b.** snaking   **c.** treacherous   **d.** inferior

_____ **6.** Not wanting to _____ as she aged, she pursued even more ambitious goals.
    a. wobble   **b.** slow down   **c.** slip backward   **d.** succeed

_____ **7.** With her brown hair _____ in the wind, she became a fixture in the Himalayas.
    a. waving   **b.** leaping   **c.** covered   **d.** wandering

_____ **8.** The dangerously thin air made her movements _____.
    a. wavelike   **b.** relentless   **c.** regressive   **d.** sluggish

_____ **9.** Rather than slowly _____ her death, she sat down and told her teammates to continue on.
    a. wander to   **b.** fall to   **c.** collapse to   **d.** revert to

_____ **10.** To this date, no other woman has _____ her.
    a. followed   **b.** supplanted   **c.** rivaled   **d.** imagined

Indicate whether the statements below are TRUE or FALSE according to the passage.

_____ **1.** On her first climb, Wanda scaled rocks without a safety rope.

_____ **2.** Mount Everest is considered the most difficult mountain to climb.

_____ **3.** Wanda experienced no accidents during her mountain-climbing career.

WRITING EXTENDED RESPONSES

Mountain climbers like Wanda Rutkiewicz make slow, steady movements as they ascend peaks. Other activities, like dancing, swimming, biking, and various team sports, also require certain precise movements for maximum efficiency. In a descriptive essay of three or more paragraphs, list three activities that depend upon precise movement. Describe the movements that are required for these activities. Use at least three lesson words in your essay and underline them.

WRITE THE DERIVATIVE

Complete the sentence by writing the correct form of the word shown in parentheses. You may not need to change the form that is given.

_____ **1.** The mental _____ in individuals who suffer from Alzheimer's disease is heartbreaking. *(retrogress)*

_____ **2.** "The _____ from the factory are killing us," said the activist at the neighborhood meeting. *(emanate)*

_____ **3.** Earthquakes cause _____ in the land. *(undulate)*

_____ **4.** I blamed my _____ on sleep deprivation. *(torpid)*

_____ **5.** Many people travel to Florida to _____ in warm ocean waters. *(cavort)*

_____ **6.** The slowdown was _____ ; business picked up again after only a few weeks. *(transitory)*

_____ **7.** The _____ stream winds through many towns before it reaches the ocean. *(meander)*

_____ **8.** For some crimes, the authority of the state police _____ that of the local police. *(supersede)*

_____ **9.** The _____ attack of the middleweight boxer brought him the championship belt. *(unremitting)*

_____ **10.** The _____ road looked like a snake on the map. *(serpentine)*

FIND THE EXAMPLE

Choose the answer that best describes the action or situation.

_____ **1.** The thing that is most likely to *undulate*
    a. clouds   **b.** a fast runner   **c.** air   **d.** a sail

_____ **2.** Something that is NOT *transitory*
    a. summer cold   **b.** an eternal flame   **c.** lunch hour   **d.** a snack

_____ **3.** Something LEAST likely to *meander*
    a. interstate highway   **b.** scenic drive   **c.** mountain road   **d.** country road

_____ **4.** A place where it would be very unwise to *cavort*
    a. open field   **b.** the beach   **c.** busy road   **d.** trampoline

_____ **5.** Something that might make you feel *torpid*
    a. police siren   **b.** sudden noise   **c.** tense situation   **d.** heat wave

_____ **6.** Something that would be wise to pursue *unremittingly*
    a. bitter fight   **b.** academic goals   **c.** bad habits   **d.** scared bear

_____ **7.** A *retrogression*
    a. a baby crying   **b.** a cat meowing   **c.** a child adding   **d.** an adult whining

_____ **8.** NOT a *serpentine* object
    a. soccer ball   **b.** metal cable   **c.** winding gorge   **d.** curving road

_____ **9.** The thing that *emanates* the LEAST noise
    a. boom box   **b.** cell phone   **c.** city traffic   **d.** construction paper

_____ **10.** How you would probably feel if someone *superseded* you
    a. gratified   **b.** upset   **c.** indifferent   **d.** lethargic

Prefixes, Roots, and Suffixes

The Word Elements -arch-, -archy, -dem-, -ver-, and -cracy

A number of word elements are relevant to the topics of government and law. A table indicating the meaning and use of four important word elements is given below.

Word Element	Type	Meaning	Word	Word Meaning
arch-	prefix	most important most extreme	archbishop archrival	chief bishop most extreme rival
-archy, -arch	suffix	ruling	monarchy, monarch	government by a monarch a sovereign ruler
-dem-	root	people	democracy	government by the people
-ver-	root	truth	verify	determine the truth of
-cracy	suffix	government; rule	democracy	government by the people

The different meanings of the word element *arch* are related in that the Greek word *arkhein* meant both "to begin" and "to rule." *-Dem-* is based on *demos,* the Greek word for "people." *-Ver-* is from *verus,* the Latin word for truth. Finally, *-cracy* is based upon *kratos,* the Greek word for "strength, power."

You can use your knowledge of word elements to help you understand unknown words, but remember that this process may only give you a hint at the word's meaning. You can combine this meaning with the context of the sentence to formulate a possible definition for the unknown word. Finally, to ensure the accuracy of the definition, check it in the dictionary.

Practice

You can combine the use of context clues with your knowledge of word elements to make intelligent guesses about the meanings of words. Each of the sentences below contains a word formed with the word element *arch-, -archy, -dem-, -ver-,* or *-cracy.* Read the sentences and try to infer what the word in italics means. Then check your definition with the one you find in the dictionary, remembering to choose the definition that best fits in the sentence.

1. In a true *meritocracy,* personal connections and inherited wealth would have little influence on one's success.

   My definition _____

   Dictionary definition _____

2. Many people feel that Shakespeare's Romeo and Juliet are the *archetypal* star-crossed lovers.

My definition _____

Dictionary definition _____

3. The witness *averred* that she had seen the defendant commit the robbery.

My definition _____

Dictionary definition _____

4. The new government was a *diarchy*, in which both the newly elected Prime Minister and the incumbent queen ruled together.

My definition _____

Dictionary definition _____

5. After two years in office, the citizens realized their leader was a *demagogue*, whose impassioned speeches did not translate into wise policies.

My definition _____

Dictionary definition _____

6. Most people agree that a *plutocracy* would be completely unfair to those without significant financial means.

My definition _____

Dictionary definition _____

7. Sherlock Holmes battled with his *archenemy*, Professor Moriarty, near Reichenbach Falls.

My definition _____

Dictionary definition _____

8. Ever *veracious*, the child immediately confessed to accidentally breaking his mother's lamp.

My definition _____

Dictionary definition _____

9. There was great fear that the influenza would spread in *pandemic* proportions.

My definition _____

Dictionary definition _____

10. Though the movie set has *verisimilitude*, you only need to look beyond the room to the cameras, lights, and rigging to remember where you are.

My definition _____

Dictionary definition _____

The Root -ten-

WORD LIST

extenuation	portent	pretentious	retentive	retinue
sustain	sustenance	tenacious	tenement	untenable

The Indo-European root *-ten-* means "to stretch." Several Latin verbs whose roots are used in English words come from the root *-ten-*, including *tendere* (to extend; to stretch), *tenere* (to hold), and *tenuare* (to make thin). Think about how those three verbs are related and about how they relate to the meanings of the lesson words.

1. **extenuation** (ĭk-stĕnʹyōō-āʹshən) *noun* from Latin *ex-*, "out" + *tenuare*, "to make thin"
   A partial excuse or justification
   • The fact that someone else "did it, too" is not an **extenuation** for wrongdoing.

   extenuate *verb* My friend apologized and **extenuated** his bad behavior by explaining that he had just lost his job.

2. **portent** (pôrʹtĕntʹ) *noun* from Latin *pro-*, "before" + *tendere*, "to extend; to stretch"
   An omen; a sign that something important or disastrous is about to occur
   • Authors of mystery novels often include **portents** of crimes.

   portend *verb* Does that vulture circling overhead **portend** trouble?

   portentous *adjective* Ancient people believed that celestial events such as comets and eclipses were **portentous.**

3. **pretentious** (prĭ-tĕnʹshəs) *adjective* from *pre-*, "before" + *tendere*, "to extend; to stretch"
   a. Claiming or demanding a position of distinction or merit, especially when unjustified
   • After writing a letter to the editor that was published in the local paper, the **pretentious** man began referring to himself as a "professional writer."
   b. Showy; marked by extravagant outward display
   • The **pretentious** English professor never used a simple word if she could come up with a longer, more obscure one.

   pretentiousness *noun* After taking a week-long course at Harvard University, Mel's **pretentiousness** was unbearable.

> *Extenuating circumstances* is a common phrase.

> The first syllable of the noun *portent* is stressed; the second syllable of the verb *portend* is stressed.

portents of bad weather

4. **retentive** (rĭ-tĕn´tĭv) *adjective* from Latin *re-*, "back" + *tenere*, "to hold"
Having the ability to keep, maintain, or remember something
• Her mind is so **retentive** that she easily remembers what she reads.

retain *verb* The court set up an affordable plan so that my grandfather could pay the taxes he owed and **retain** his house.

retentiveness *noun* Sponges have great **retentiveness** for liquids.

5. **retinue** (rĕt´n-ōō´) *noun* from Latin *re-*, "back" + *tenere*, "to hold"
The attendants accompanying a high-ranking person; an entourage
• The president is surrounded by a **retinue** of Secret Service agents whenever he leaves the White House.

> *Retinue* is related to *retain*. One definition of *retainer* is "a long-term employee."

6. **sustain** (sə-stān´) *verb* from Latin *sub-*, "up from below" + *tenere*, "to hold"
   a. To support, keep in existence, or supply with necessities; to maintain or provide for
   • We depend on the earth's ability to **sustain** life.
   b. To support from below; to keep from falling or sinking; to prop up
   • A bedrock foundation **sustains** most skyscrapers.
   c. To confirm as correct or valid
   • The court of appeals **sustained** the decision of the lower court.

7. **sustenance** (sŭs´tə-nəns) *noun* from Latin *sub-*, "up from below" + *tenere*, "to hold"
   a. Something, especially food, that supplies life, strength, or health; nutrition
   • Mothers' milk provides **sustenance** to newborn mammals.
   b. Something that provides emotional support or strength
   • The encouragement of parents and teachers provides **sustenance** to children.
   c. The act of sustaining or the condition of being sustained
   • All of us owe our **sustenance** to the sun and to the plants that harness its energy.

> The word *sustenance* and its alternate form *sustenation* are closely related to *sustain*.

8. **tenacious** (tə-nā´shəs) *adjective* from Latin *tenere*, "to hold"
Holding firmly and stubbornly to something
• The three-year-old kept a **tenacious** grip on the toy.

tenacity *noun* The detective's **tenacity** in pursuing the old case finally enabled her to solve the crime.

9. **tenement** (tĕn´ə-mənt) *noun* from Latin *tenere*, "to hold"
A run-down, low-rent apartment building
• Jacob Riis's 1890 book *How the Other Half Lives* acquainted the wealthy with the harsh realities of life in a New York City **tenement.**

10. **untenable** (ŭn-tĕn´ə-bəl) *adjective* from Old English *un-*, "not" + Latin *tenere*, "to hold"
Incapable of being defended, held, or occupied
• "My political enemies have succeeded in putting me in an **untenable** position, so I hereby resign," wrote the mayor.

WRITE THE CORRECT WORD

Write the correct word in the space next to each definition. Use each word only once.

_____ **1.** an omen   _____ **6.** holding stubbornly

_____ **2.** a source of strength   _____ **7.** a partial excuse

_____ **3.** showy   _____ **8.** can't be defended

_____ **4.** a run-down building   _____ **9.** an entourage

_____ **5.** to support   _____ **10.** able to remember

COMPLETE THE SENTENCE

Write the letter for the word that best completes each sentence.

_____ **1.** "That _____ should be condemned by the city," said the engineer.
   a. retinue   **b.** tenement   **c.** portent   **d.** sustenance

_____ **2.** Emotional support can help _____ a person through hard times.
   a. retain   **b.** extenuate   **c.** sustain   **d.** portend

_____ **3.** Celebrities frequently have a(n) _____ of bodyguards to ward off overzealous fans.
   a. sustenance   **b.** portent   **c.** extenuation   **d.** retinue

_____ **4.** In movies, scary music is a(n) _____ that something horrible is about to happen.
   a. portent   **b.** retinue   **c.** tenement   **d.** extenuation

_____ **5.** "In light of the _____ circumstances, I am reducing the defendant's sentence
   to 500 hours of community service," said the judge.
   a. untenable   **b.** pretentious   **c.** portentous   **d.** extenuating

_____ **6.** How does an animal that lives in a desert find _____?
   a. pretentiousness   **b.** sustenance   **c.** retinue   **d.** retention

_____ **7.** The field hockey players smothered their opponents with a _____ defense.
   a. pretentious   **b.** sustaining   **c.** tenacious   **d.** portentous

_____ **8.** The _____ student carried a leather briefcase instead of a book bag like
   everyone else.
   a. pretentious   **b.** portentous   **c.** extenuated   **d.** sustained

_____ **9.** The soldiers knew that their position was _____ when they saw the huge size
   of the advancing enemy army.
   a. retentive   **b.** untenable   **c.** pretentious   **d.** sustained

_____ **10.** Using memory aids such as word association can help people improve their
   _____ abilities.
   a. pretentious   **b.** tenacious   **c.** untenable   **d.** retentive

Challenge: He is so _____ that he pays thousands of dollars each month to sustain a
   _____ of assistants, just so he can appear important.
_____   **a.** pretentious…retinue   **b.** tenacious…sustenance   **c.** retentive…tenement

Hot, Hotter, and Hottest

They look so sweet in their shiny, colorful jackets, but try to eat one and you'll feel like you've been set on fire. The hottest peppers will send you begging for cool relief. Yet these fiery little foods are being used increasingly to help treat illness.

Archeological evidence shows that people have eaten hot peppers since 7,000 B.C. , if not earlier. Both their taste and their medical properties have made them popular around the world.

(1) Hot peppers generally grow best in warm climates, in soil that *retains* moisture. China is currently the largest producer. Thailand and Korea are among the nations that consume the most. **(2)** Once considered a humble food suitable for *tenement* dwellers and homey restaurants, hot peppers have entered the realm of fine dining. Due to their growing popularity, numerous hot sauces now crowd supermarket shelves. They range from mild and tangy to "call-the-fire-department" scorching.

The burning you feel when you eat hot peppers is caused by chemicals called *capsaicinoids,* commonly called *capsaicin.* These chemicals trigger impulses in nerves that normally transmit sensations of pain, heat, and pressure.

So how hot is "hot"? The Scoville scale rates a pepper's hotness based on the amount of capsaicin present. A regular bell, or green, pepper rates a zero. A Jalapeño pepper, common in salsa and Mexican food, can range between 2,500 and 5,000 Scoville units. The hottest peppers can reach a mouth-singeing 350,000 units, and pure capsaicin comes in at 16,000,000! Attempting to eat capsaicin would cause you to choke. In fact, even breathing near the pure substance is dangerous.

(3) Wherever there are hot peppers served, you'll usually find at least one *pretentious* person who claims he can eat even the most fiery ones. **(4)** After putting one in his mouth, he turns bright red, a *portent* of things to come. Suddenly, his eyes are watering and he is gasping for breath. **(5)** He feels as if he needs a *retinue* of helpers standing by with buckets of water. Actually, in part because capsaicin is fat-soluble, milk, sour cream, or bread with butter would be more effective than water, which does little except spread the pain around.

People can develop tolerance to hot peppers. **(6)** Those who are *tenacious* enough to keep eating them despite the initial heat can gradually work their way up the Scoville scale. **(7)** Eating peppers that are too hot, however, will put even the heartiest pepper lover in the *untenable* position of having to ask for help without being able to speak.

Surprisingly, hot peppers do not harm your stomach. **(8)** In fact, they contain many *sustaining* nutrients. They are richer in vitamin C, for example, than citrus fruits are. **(9)** Of course, since we can't eat them in large quantities, they can only be used to complement other forms of *sustenance.*

Long a part of folk remedies, capsaicin is now being examined by the medical profession. **(10)** Scientists have shown that it can *extenuate* chronic pain. It may also fight melanoma, a deadly type of skin cancer. Finally, it can alleviate some heart and stomach problems. These fiery foods may be hot in your mouth, but they are also a hot topic for research.

Each sentence below refers to a numbered sentence in the passage. Write the letter of the choice that gives the sentence a meaning that is closest to the original sentence.

_____ 1. Hot peppers grow best in soil that _____ moisture.
   a. supports and helps   **b.** holds and stores   **c.** needs and lacks   **d.** defends and maintains

_____ 2. They were once considered a humble food suitable for _____ dwellers.
   a. large-house   **b.** small-boat   **c.** rustic-hut   **d.** low-rent apartment

_____ 3. You'll usually find at least one _____ person who claims he can eat even the most fiery ones.
   a. showy   **b.** annoying   **c.** determined   **d.** memorable

_____ **4.** He turns bright red, a(n) _____ of things to come.
   a. eruption   **b.** omen   **c.** support   **d.** excuse

_____ **5.** He feels as if he needs a(n) _____ of helpers standing by with buckets of water.
   a. corporation   **b.** memory   **c.** entourage   **d.** omen

_____ **6.** Those who are _____ enough can work their way up the Scoville scale.
   a. fortunate   **b.** angry   **c.** determined   **d.** inspired

_____ **7.** Eating peppers that are too hot, however, will put even the heartiest pepper lover in the _____ position of having to ask for help without being able to speak.
   a. indefensible   **b.** comfortable   **c.** stubborn   **d.** memorable

_____ **8.** In fact, they contain many _____ nutrients.
   a. excuse-providing   **b.** tongue-burning   **c.** memory-enhancing   **d.** health-supporting

_____ **9.** They can only be used to complement other forms of _____.
   a. amusement   **b.** nutrition   **c.** breathing   **d.** health

_____ **10.** Scientists have shown that it can _____ chronic pain.
   a. maintain   **b.** eliminate   **c.** lessen   **d.** cling to

Indicate whether the statements below are TRUE or FALSE according to the passage.

_____ **1.** Evidence shows that humans have eaten peppers for more than 9,000 years.

_____ **2.** Hot peppers grow best in cold, rocky soil.

_____ **3.** Peppers contain vitamins.

FINISH THE THOUGHT

Complete each sentence so that it shows the meaning of the italicized word.

1. With a *tenacious* grip, _____

_____

2. It is difficult to *sustain* _____

_____

WRITE THE DERIVATIVE

Complete the sentence by writing the correct form of the word shown in parentheses. You may not need to change the form that is given.

_____ **1.** A series of failing grades _____ that he would not graduate. (*portent*)

_____ **2.** Because of _____ circumstances, the principal excused Marc's absence from school. (*extenuation*)

_____ **3.** The judge _____ the prosecutor's objection. *(sustain)*

_____ **4.** The queen entered the reception hall with a _____ of aides and attendants. *(retinue)*

_____ **5.** The old woman showed her _____ by asserting that her bloodline could be traced back to the royal Russian family. *(pretentious)*

_____ **6.** The cornered platoon defended their _____ position down to the last soldier. *(untenable)*

_____ **7.** In the 1800s, many _____ were built in cities where immigrants resided. *(tenement)*

_____ **8.** Trivia experts are known for their _____. *(retentive)*

_____ **9.** The juice from the barrel cactus gave _____ to the lost hiker. *(sustenance)*

_____ **10.** Pit bull terriers have a reputation for _____ and ferociousness. *(tenacious)*

FIND THE EXAMPLE

Choose the answer that best describes the action or situation.

_____ **1.** Something NOT usually thought of as a *portent*
  a. black cat   **b.** gathering clouds   **c.** rock concert   **d.** eerie stillness

_____ **2.** Something you do NOT want to *sustain*
  a. good health   **b.** enjoyable times   **c.** financial success   **d.** severe pain

_____ **3.** An *extenuating* circumstance that might excuse you for causing an automobile accident
  a. speeding   **b.** failed brakes   **c.** talking on cell phone   **d.** daydreaming

_____ **4.** Someone who does NOT usually travel with a *retinue*
  a. U.S. president   **b.** rock star   **c.** salesperson   **d.** governor

_____ **5.** Something that would NOT give physical *sustenance*
  a. loaf of bread   **b.** sheet of paper   **c.** avocado   **d.** chicken soup

_____ **6.** Part of a *tenement*
  a. mansions   **b.** suburban homes   **c.** pricey condominiums   **d.** apartments

_____ **7.** An activity that tests your *retentive* powers
  a. watching TV   **b.** working out   **c.** taking a test   **d.** playing catch

_____ **8.** Something that could make a campsite *untenable*
  a. mosquito swarms   **b.** chipmunks   **c.** nearby waterfall   **d.** pine trees

_____ **9.** An animal that symbolizes *pretentiousness*
  a. beaver   **b.** peacock   **c.** rabbit   **d.** grizzly bear

_____ **10.** How an outlaw would likely feel if pursued by a *tenacious* posse
  a. relieved   **b.** delighted   **c.** lazy   **d.** anxious

The Roots -corp- and -aním-

WORD LIST

animus	corpulent	corpus	corpuscle	equanimity
inanimate	incorporate	incorporeal	magnanimous	pusillanimous

The Latin root *-corp-* means "body," and the Latin root *-anim-* means "mind" or "soul." Many English words come from these roots. This lesson will help you *incorporate* ten of these important words into your vocabulary.

1. **animus** (ăn´ə-məs) *noun* from Latin *anim*, "mind; reason"
   a. A feeling of hatred; enmity; ill will
      • The business rivalry soon developed into personal **animus.**
   b. A disposition; an attitude that informs one's actions
      • Possessing an optimistic **animus,** he invariably embraced new experiences.

   animosity *noun* The **animosity** between the two tribes led to open warfare.

2. **corpulent** (kôr´pyə-lənt) *adjective* from Latin *corp*, "body"
   Excessively fat; obese
   • The actor stuffed his costume with pillows to play Falstaff, Shakespeare's **corpulent** character.

   corpulence *noun* A healthy diet and exercise can help to control a natural tendency toward **corpulence.**

3. **corpus** (kôr´pəs) *noun* from Latin *corp*, "body"
   A large collection of writings of a specific type or on a specific subject
   • A large electronic **corpus** of Irish literature is now available to scholars.

4. **corpuscle** (kôr´pə-səl) *noun* from Latin *corp*, "body"
   An unattached body cell, such as a blood or lymph cell
   • Red **corpuscles** in our blood carry oxygen throughout the body.

   corpuscular *adjective* Our bodies filter waste through **corpuscular** action in our kidneys.

5. **equanimity** (ē´kwə-nĭm´ĭ-tē) *noun* from Latin *equi-*, "equal" + *anim*, "mind"
   The quality of being calm and even-tempered; composure
   • After living through dire poverty and a brutal war, little could disturb my grandfather's **equanimity.**

> In Jungian psychology, the *animus* is the male inner personality present in females. The *anima* is the female inner personality present in males.

> In economics, *corpus* is the capital (wealth) of an estate or trust, or the principal of a bond. The plural of *corpus* is *corpora*.

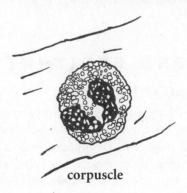

corpuscle

6. **inanimate** (ĭn-ăn´ə-mĭt) *adjective* from Latin *in-*, "not" + *anim*, "mind; soul"
   a. Not alive; not having the qualities associated with life
      • A table is an **inanimate** object.
   b. Dull; not energetic
      • The director tried to enliven the actor's **inanimate** performance.

   animated *adjective* His face and voice were **animated** as he described his adventures to his friends.

   > In grammar, *inanimate* refers to nouns that stand for nonliving things. Examples include *car* and *room*.

7. **incorporate** (ĭn-kôr´pə-rāt´) *verb* from *in-*, "to cause" + *corp*, "body"
   a. To include something as part of a larger whole
      • Please **incorporate** specific examples into your essay.
   b. To embody; to give material or physical form to
      • Wilma Rudolph **incorporates** the ideal of a great runner.
   c. To form into a legal corporation
      • My mother's firm **incorporated** in 1980.

8. **incorporeal** (ĭn´kôr-pôr´ē-əl) *adjective* from Latin *in-*, "not" + *corp*, "body"
   Lacking physical form and substance; immaterial
   • Great thoughts are **incorporeal,** yet they shape the physical world.

9. **magnanimous** (măg-năn´ə-məs) *adjective* from Latin *magnus*, "great" + *anim*, "soul; mind"
   a. Courageously noble in mind and heart
      • According to legend, the **magnanimous** hero rescued many children.
   b. Generous in forgiving; not seeking revenge
      • The **magnanimous** man publicly forgave the eyewitness who had falsely identified him as the suspect.

   magnanimity *noun* Nelson Mandela showed **magnanimity** by working with his former persecutors.

10. **pusillanimous** (pyōō´sə-lăn´ə-məs) *adjective* from Latin *pusillus*, "weak" + *anim*, "mind; soul"
    Cowardly; lacking courage
    • At the first critical comment, the **pusillanimous** man claimed that his assistant had written the controversial report.

    pusillanimity *noun* In an act of pure **pusillanimity,** the general abandoned the town he had been ordered to defend.

WORD ENRICHMENT

Cowardly words

Many words besides *pusillanimous* refer to a lack of courage. *Dastardly* connotes a malicious cowardice. *Craven* means "characterized by abject fear; cowardly." *Timorous* refers to a timid type of fear. *Petrified*, used metaphorically, means "paralyzed with terror."

Animals and colors can also connote cowardice. Since the 1400s, *chicken* has been used to describe someone lacking in courage. Since the 1800s, the color yellow—as in *yellow-bellied*—has also been used as a synonym for *cowardly*.

WRITE THE CORRECT WORD

Write the correct word in the space next to each definition. Use each word only once.

_____ **1.** lacking physical form

_____ **2.** generous in forgiving

_____ **3.** very fat

_____ **4.** a disposition

_____ **5.** a collection of writings on a specific topic

_____ **6.** cowardly

_____ **7.** unattached body cell

_____ **8.** not alive

_____ **9.** calmness; composure

_____ **10.** to include as part of a whole

COMPLETE THE SENTENCE

Write the letter for the word that best completes each sentence.

_____ **1.** The odes of John Keats are part of the _____ of English poetry.
    a. animus   **b.** corpulence   **c.** corpus   **d.** equanimity

_____ **2.** Rocks, books, and bicycles are all _____ objects.
    a. corpulent   **b.** incorporeal   **c.** pusillanimous   **d.** inanimate

_____ **3.** The _____ of many different ethnic traditions has enriched U.S. culture.
    a. equanimity   **b.** incorporation   **c.** corpuscle   **d.** corpulence

_____ **4.** Jun always seems calm and faces his problems with _____.
    a. animus   **b.** incorporation   **c.** equanimity   **d.** pusillanimity

_____ **5.** Being _____ can lead to health problems such as heart disease and diabetes.
    a. corpulent   **b.** pusillanimous   **c.** magnanimous   **d.** inanimate

_____ **6.** In a(n) _____ gesture, the winner of the election praised her opponent.
    a. pusillanimous   **b.** magnanimous   **c.** inanimate   **d.** incorporeal

_____ **7.** White _____ defend the body against infection.
    a. magnanimities   **b.** incorporations   **c.** corpora   **d.** corpuscles

_____ **8.** A(n) _____ wrestler will win few matches.
    a. incorporeal   **b.** animated   **c.** incorporated   **d.** pusillanimous

_____ **9.** In folklore, ghosts are almost always _____ beings.
    a. magnanimous   **b.** corpulent   **c.** incorporeal   **d.** pusillanimous

_____ **10.** A(n) _____ developed between fans of the opposing teams.
    a. animus   **b.** equanimity   **c.** corpus   **d.** corpulence

Challenge: Our host's _____ was shattered when he was confronted with the evidence that a(n) _____ guest had knocked over a priceless vase and then fled.

_____   **a.** magnanimity…inanimate   **b.** animus…corpuscular   **c.** equanimity…pusillanimous

Bodyspeak

Most of us think that we communicate with words. **(1)** But human beings are not *incorporeal.* **(2)** While our words are traveling between us, our bodies do not remain *inanimate;* we smile, cross our arms, and blush. Our postures and movements send powerful signals. In his book *Silent Messages*, psychologist Albert Mehrabian estimates that a mere 7 percent of our total message is delivered by words, while over 50 percent is communicated by our gestures (the rest comes through in our tone of voice). **(3)** Our "body language" *incorporates* much of what we are feeling at any given moment.

(4) Young or old, tall or short, lean or *corpulent,* everyone communicates through body language. **(5)** The large *corpus* of research articles on this subject gives insight into the meanings of our nonverbal communication. Although this field is still evolving, some preliminary conclusions can be drawn.

(6) For example, blushing, which occurs when blood vessels carrying red *corpuscles* to our faces dilate, is a many-layered response. Blushing involves imagining others' perceptions of us. It says, silently, that we know that others are aware that we have done something shameful or embarrassing. **(7)** A loss of *equanimity* often results. Interestingly, we usually don't blush in private because no one is around to "catch" our actions. And babies don't blush because they have not yet internalized social norms.

A more pleasant example of common body language is the smile. All primates smile. Unlike humans, however, animals do not infer a feeling of happiness from this gesture. Among apes, a "fear grin" often signals submission to a more powerful animal. **(8)** In other words, a facial expression that indicates happiness in humans actually shows a degree of *pusillanimity* in apes.

Smiling is thought to be universal among humans. The behavior appears in babies when they are just a few weeks old. **(9)** It is also observed in blind children who have never seen a smile, according to the *magnanimous* people who teach them. Still, cultures differ in the meanings they attach to the gesture. According to Professor Anna Wierzbicka, people in Poland value the smile of true happiness, but talk disapprovingly about the "false smile." In contrast, people from the United States cultivate quick smiles that often indicate mere politeness.

(10) Finally, crossing one's arms is often interpreted as a sign of defensiveness or even *animus.* One theory is that the gesture originated in motions meant to protect against a physical attack. Interestingly, a report summarizing the behavior of North American college students found that women use a crossed-arm posture with men they do not like and an open-arms posture with men they do like. In contrast, men did not vary their behavior toward women in this way.

Much research on body language remains to be done. In many ways, even the simple smile remains a mystery. Whatever the ultimate interpretations, though, people already agree on the power of the body to convey information. So the next time you shrug or cross your arms, think of the message you are communicating silently, but eloquently.

Each sentence below refers to a numbered sentence in the passage. Write the letter of the choice that gives the sentence a meaning that is closest to the original sentence.

_____ **1.** Human beings are not _____ .
    a. immaterial   **b.** important   **c.** calm   **d.** cowardly

_____ **2.** Our bodies do not remain _____ ; we smile, cross our arms, and blush.
    a. hateful   **b.** calm   **c.** disembodied   **d.** lifeless

_____ **3.** Our "body language" _____ much of what we are feeling at any given moment.
    a. camouflages   **b.** includes   **c.** exaggerates   **d.** removes

_____ **4.** Young or old, tall or short, lean or _____ , everyone communicates through body language.
    a. thin   **b.** detached   **c.** overweight   **d.** composed

_____ **5.** The large _____ of research articles on this subject gives insight into the meanings of our nonverbal communication.
   a. business   **b.** bulky body   **c.** collection   **d.** inclusion

_____ **6.** Blushing occurs when blood vessels carrying red _____ to our faces dilate.
   a. anger   **b.** fats   **c.** clots   **d.** cells

_____ **7.** A loss of _____ often results.
   a. composure   **b.** generosity   **c.** energy   **d.** life

_____ **8.** The facial expression actually shows a degree of _____ in apes.
   a. cowardice   **b.** victory   **c.** calmness   **d.** generosity

_____ **9.** It is also observed in the _____ people who teach them.
   a. embarrassed   **b.** jubilant   **c.** noble   **d.** overweight

_____ **10.** Crossing one's arms is often interpreted as a sign of defensiveness or even _____.
   a. liveliness   **b.** hatred   **c.** composure   **d.** fright

Indicate whether the statements below are TRUE or FALSE according to the passage.

_____ **1.** Most communication among people is done with words.

_____ **2.** Blushing has to do with blood flow to the face.

_____ **3.** Men and women use body language the same way.

WRITING EXTENDED RESPONSES

The passage you have just read describes the meanings commonly ascribed to different body postures and movements. These behaviors correspond to certain emotions. In an essay of at least three paragraphs, describe body language you have observed in others. You may describe body language associated with anger, surprise, happiness, fear, or embarrassment. Use at least three lesson words in your essay and underline them.

WRITE THE DERIVATIVE

Complete the sentence by writing the correct form of the word shown in parentheses. You may not need to change the form that is given.

_____ **1.** The _____ of the composer's work spans many styles and many years. *(corpus)*

_____ **2.** The _____ jazz performance quickly brought the cheering audience to its feet. *(inanimate)*

_____ **3.** The public values _____ in victorious athletes. *(magnanimous)*

_____ **4.** Because of his _____, King George IV had to be lowered onto his horse by a mechanical device. *(corpulent)*

_____ **5.** Last year, the school play _____ the work of many students. *(incorporate)*

_____ **6.** Outwardly undisturbed by the defeat, the general retained the appearance of _____ . *(equanimity)*

_____ **7.** Your excuse better not involve any scary, _____ beings, Nick. *(incorporeal)*

_____ **8.** Calmly and without _____, Martin explained the seriousness of the errors. *(animus)*

_____ **9.** In *The Wizard of Oz*, the lion hopes to replace his _____ with courage. *(pusillanimous)*

_____ **10.** The blood test revealed that the patient did not have enough white _____ to fight the infection. *(corpuscle)*

FIND THE EXAMPLE

Choose the answer that best describes the action or situation.

_____ **1.** An example of a *corpuscle*
    a. lofty theory   **b.** red blood cell   **c.** sensory organ   **d.** military unit

_____ **2.** Something that might *incorporate*
    a. individual   **b.** bones   **c.** foes   **d.** business

_____ **3.** The usual object of *animus*
    a. loved one   **b.** friend   **c.** enemy   **d.** president

_____ **4.** An example of a *corpus*
    a. song   **b.** anthology   **c.** military unit   **d.** business

_____ **5.** Something a *magnanimous* gesture does NOT represent
    a. generosity   **b.** sensitivity   **c.** vengeance   **d.** care

_____ **6.** The person most likely to be *corpulent*
    a. sumo wrestler   **b.** marathon runner   **c.** downhill skier   **d.** lifeguard

_____ **7.** Something that is *inanimate*
    a. fishing rod   **b.** flying dove   **c.** growing grass   **d.** blossoming tree

_____ **8.** Something that a person known for *equanimity* rarely loses
    a. rival   **b.** tenderness   **c.** contest   **d.** temper

_____ **9.** Something that is *incorporeal*
    a. a bird   **b.** a rock   **c.** a theory   **d.** a snowflake

_____ **10.** A *pusillanimous* act
    a. sacrificing   **b.** hiding   **c.** rescuing   **d.** parachuting

The Roots -onym- and -nomín-

WORD LIST

anonymous	cognomen	denomination	ignominious	misnomer
moniker	nomenclature	nominal	patronymic	renown

The ancient Greek root *-onym-* and the subsequent Latin version *-nomin-* (also spelled *nomen*) both mean "name." Each root stems from the Indo-European root *nomen*. As you will see in this lesson and elsewhere, many English words include these roots that mean "name."

anonymous

1. **anonymous** (ə-nŏn´ə-məs) *adjective* from Greek *a-*, "without" + *onym*, "name"
   a. Having an unknown or unacknowledged name or authorship
      • The stirring contents of the **anonymous** note made her wish she knew who had written it.
   b. Having no distinctive or recognizable character
      • At the huge rally, I was just an **anonymous** speck in the crowd.

   anonymity *noun* The reporter promised to protect her source's **anonymity**.

2. **cognomen** (kŏg-nō´mən) *noun* from Latin *com-*, "together" (influenced by *cognoscere*, "to know") + *nomen*, "name"
   a. A surname; a family name
      • My mom's **cognomen,** "Jensen," comes from her Swedish ancestors.
   b. A descriptive nickname
      • Yuri was always darting around, so his parents gave him the **cognomen** "Speedy."

3. **denomination** (dĭ-nŏm´ə-nā´shən) *noun* from Latin *de-*, "from" + *nomin*, "name"
   a. A united group of religious organizations
      • Methodists represent one of many Christian **denominations.**
   b. One of a series of kinds, values, or sizes
      • Though a relatively rare **denomination,** two-dollar bills are still in circulation.

4. **ignominious** (ĭg´nə-mĭn´ē-əs) *adjective* from Latin *in-*, "not" + *nomin*, "name"
   Shameful; disgraceful; degrading
      • The conviction brought his career to an **ignominious** end.

   ignominy (ĭg´ nə mĭn´-ē) *noun* The cadet suffered the **ignominy** of a **dishonorable** discharge.

5. misnomer (mĭs-nō′mər) *noun* from Latin *mis-*, "wrong"
+ *nomen*, "name"
An unsuitable name; a name wrongly applied
• In my opinion, "Cutie Pie" is a **misnomer** for a pit bull.

6. moniker (mŏn′ĭ-kər) *noun* from Old Irish *ainm*, "name"
A distinctive name or nickname
• Bands that became popular in the 1960s had strange but catchy
monikers like "Three Dog Night" and "The Grateful Dead."

7. nomenclature (nō′mən-klā′chər) *noun* from Latin *nomen*, "name"
+ *calare*, "to call"
A system of names used in a science or an art
• Much of the **nomenclature** used in biology comes from Latin.

8. nominal (nŏm′ə-nəl) *adjective* from Latin *nomin*, "name"
  a. Existing in name only
   • Although the monarch is the **nominal** ruler, the prime minister
     and Parliament actually govern the country.
  b. Insignificantly small; trifling
   • He paid his parents the **nominal** rent of twenty dollars a month.

nominally *adverb* Though he was on the football team, James was
only **nominally** interested in the sport.

9. patronymic (păt′rə-nĭm′ĭk) *adjective* from Greek *pater*, "father"
+ *onym*, "name
Of or relating to the name of one's father
• "Hansen" is a **patronymic** name meaning "son of Hans."

10. renown (rĭ-noun′) *noun* from Latin *re-*, "again" + *nomen*, "name"
Fame; widespread honor and acclaim
• Albert Einstein was a physicist of great **renown**.

renowned *adjective* Jamaica is **renowned** for its beautiful beaches.

> *Patronymic* is also a noun
> that refers to any name taken
> from one's father. Note that
> *patronymic* is spelled the
> same way whether it is an
> adjective or a noun.

ANALOGIES

On the answer line, write the letter of the answer that best completes
each analogy. Refer to lessons 22–24 if you need help with any of the
lesson words.

_____ **1.** *Tenement* is to *building* as _____ .
   a. *retinue* is to *solitude*   **c.** *patronymic* is to *name*
   b. *corpulence* is to *food*   **d.** *renown* is to *infamy*

_____ **2.** *Portent* is to *omen* as _____ .
   a. *moniker* is to *anonymity*   **c.** *animus* is to *love*
   b. *equanimity* is to *hysteria*   **d.** *corpus* is to *collection*

_____ **3.** *Incorporeal* is to *material* as _____ .
   a. *pretentious* is to *humble*   **c.** *untenable* is to *indefensible*
   b. *tenacious* is to *stubborn*   **d.** *ignominious* is to *shameful*

_____ **4.** *Pusillanimous* is to *brave* as _____ .
   a. *sustain* is to *neglect*   **c.** *magnanimous* is to *forgiving*
   b. *inanimate* is to *lifeless*   **d.** *extenuating* is to *moderating*

WRITE THE CORRECT WORD

Write the correct word in the space next to each definition. Use each word only once.

_____ **1.** a surname

_____ **2.** a distinctive name

_____ **3.** disgraceful

_____ **4.** relating to the name of one's father

_____ **5.** a religious group

_____ **6.** fame; acclaim

_____ **7.** insignificantly small

_____ **8.** an unsuitable name

_____ **9.** the names used in a science or an art

_____ **10.** having an unknown name

COMPLETE THE SENTENCE

Write the letter for the word that best completes each sentence.

_____ **1.** Lisa Summers-Smith has a hyphenated _____.
   a. misnomer   **b.** nomenclature   **c.** renown   **d.** cognomen

_____ **2.** The actor earned _____ for his wonderful portrayals of Ibsen's characters.
   a. ignominy   **b.** renown   **c.** anonymity   **d.** nomenclature

_____ **3.** She humbly insisted that her donations remain _____.
   a. anonymous   **b.** patronymic   **c.** ignominious   **d.** renowned

_____ **4.** It would be a _____ to call former champion Tiger Woods an "underdog" in the golf tournament.
   a. nomenclature   **b.** misnomer   **c.** patronymic   **d.** denomination

_____ **5.** We belong to the same religious _____ but attend different churches.
   a. moniker   **b.** ignominy   **c.** misnomer   **d.** denomination

_____ **6.** In a(n) _____ act, the soldier sold military secrets to the enemy.
   a. renowned   **b.** patronymic   **c.** ignominious   **d.** nominal

_____ **7.** The truck driver used the _____ "Motor Mouth" when talking on his CB radio.
   a. ignominy   **b.** renown   **c.** moniker   **d.** patronymic

_____ **8.** John F. Kennedy, Jr.'s, name was a(n) _____ reference to his father, John F. Kennedy.
   a. nominal   **b.** anonymous   **c.** ignominious   **d.** patronymic

_____ **9.** In order to be a biologist, you must master scientific _____.
   a. nomenclature   **b.** cognomen   **c.** ignominy   **d.** denomination

_____ **10.** Our family lawyer charged a(n) _____ fee of $10 to handle my minor legal problem.
   a. patronymic   **b.** ignominious   **c.** anonymous   **d.** nominal

Challenge: Although the baseball player was _____ for his all-around play, he made only a _____ contribution in the World Series games.
_____
   a. ignominious…renowned   **b.** renowned…nominal   **c.** anonymous…nominal

What's in a Surname?

We are listed by them, we answer to them, and we use them in our official signatures. **(1)** Where would we be without our *cognomens*? Yet despite their importance today, last names were once quite uncommon. In the small communities of the early Middle Ages, no one needed two names, for there was likely only one John or one Mary in the neighborhood.

By the 1200s, as urban populations grew, it became necessary to further distinguish people, so last names became more common. Not surprisingly, people's surnames often described the places where they lived. **(2)** George Washington and Abraham Lincoln, the U.S. presidents who grace bills of one- and five-dollar *denominations,* respectively, have surnames rooted in locations. *Washington* is the surname of two parishes in England. Lincoln means "from the lake colony." **(3)** The surname *Churchill* is one of considerable *renown* in English history. The name originally referred to someone living by a church on a hill.

Other people took names from their occupations. The most common surname in the United States, *Smith,* used to refer to blacksmiths. Another, *Cooper,* referred to one who made wooden barrels and tubs. **(4)** Today, the bearers of such names might as well be *anonymous.*

Few *Smiths* and *Coopers* deal in their family's original professions. **(5)** Similarly, it is doubtful that many modern *Millers* have even a *nominal* interest in grinding wheat into flour. **(6)** Although these common last names are now *misnomers,* they continue to be passed down through generations.

(7) Surnames have also been taken from *monikers.* *Short* and *Brown* are thought to have come from physical traits or even the color of clan garments. *Fox, Moody,* and *Rich* came from people's characters and reputations. **(8)** Despite what the adjective now means, the surname *Stout* once referred to a rather noisy, *ignominious* character.

Many common last names originated with a father's name. *Jones* meant "son of John," as did *Johnson.* The Scottish prefix *Mc* or *Mac* also meant "son of." The Spanish surname *Ramirez* meant "son of Ramon."

(9) It is not clear who devised the traditional geneological *nomenclature* used in the United States, whereby a father's last name is passed down through the generations. Today, though, it is increasingly common for people to have surnames that combine the last names of both parents.

Naming customs vary across countries and cultures. In many Spanish-speaking countries, it is customary to give a child two surnames. The first one comes from the father, and the second from the mother. So Eugenio Cortez Portillo has a father named *Cortez* and a mother named *Portillo.* **(10)** In Russia, *patronymics* are used as middle names. If Alexander Tupikov has a son, Gennady, his name is Gennady *Alexandrovich* Tupikov; a daughter, Sophia, would be called Sophia *Alexandrovna* Tupikov.

So, now that you've read a little about the subject, what's in *your* surname?

Each sentence below refers to a numbered sentence in the passage. Write the letter of the choice that gives the sentence a meaning that is closest to the original sentence.

_____ **1.** Where would we be without our _____?
a. church groups   **b.** personalities   **c.** last names   **d.** hopes and dreams

_____ **2.** George Washington and Abraham Lincoln, the U.S. presidents who grace bills of one- and five-dollar _____, have surnames rooted in locations.
a. high debts   **b.** first names   **c.** rent payments   **d.** money units

_____ **3.** The surname *Churchill* is one of considerable _____ in English history.
a. fame   **b.** controversy   **c.** unsuitability   **d.** shame

_____ **4.** The bearers of such names might as well be _____.
      a. unsubstantial   **b.** unnamed   **c.** indistinct   **d.** insignificant

_____ **5.** Similarly, it is doubtful that many modern *Millers* have even a _____ interest in grinding wheat into flour.
      a. nameless   **b.** legal   **c.** small   **d.** shameful

_____ **6.** These common last names are now _____.
      a. endangered   **b.** misleading   **c.** famous   **d.** unusual

_____ **7.** Surnames have also been taken from _____.
      a. nicknames   **b.** countries   **c.** father's names   **d.** scientific names

_____ **8.** The surname *Stout* once referred to a rather noisy, _____ character.
      a. acclaimed   **b.** philosophical   **c.** disgraceful   **d.** famous

_____ **9.** It is not clear who devised the traditional geneological _____ used in the United States.
      a. values   **b.** naming system   **c.** nicknames   **d.** inheritance rules

_____ **10.** In Russia, _____ are used as middle names.
      a. last names   **b.** nicknames   **c.** mothers' names   **d.** fathers' names

Indicate whether the statements below are TRUE or FALSE according to the passage.

_____ **1.** Some surnames originally described the places where people lived.

_____ **2.** The use of last names in early medieval England was very common.

_____ **3.** *Lincoln* is mentioned in the passage as the most common American surname.

FINISH THE THOUGHT

Complete each sentence so that it shows the meaning of the italicized word.

1. His *ignominious* deed _____

_____

2. Her *renowned* ancestor _____

_____

WRITE THE DERIVATIVE

Complete the sentence by writing the correct form of the word shown in parentheses. You may not need to change the form that is given.

_____ **1.** There were at least a dozen people in my high school with the _____ Smith. (*cognomen*)

_____ **2.** The senator worked hard to counteract the _____ that plagued her after she was alleged to have been involved in a scandal. (*ignominious*)

_____ **3.** One of the _____ given to the St. Louis Rams football team was "The Greatest Show on Turf." *(moniker)*

_____ **4.** I'm guessing that your surname *Robinson* is _____, but do you know if it means "son of Rob" or "son of Robin"? *(patronymic)*

_____ **5.** Even before winning the Nobel Peace Prize, the group Doctors Without Borders was _____ throughout the world. *(renown)*

_____ **6.** The NATO official agreed to the secret interview on the condition that she would retain her _____. *(anonymous)*

_____ **7.** The bank teller gave me money in ten- and twenty-dollar _____. *(denomination)*

_____ **8.** The _____ we use to identify living things has developed over centuries of learning and discovery. *(nomenclature)*

_____ **9.** Although _____ based in Britain, the company actually operates out of Malaysia. *(nominal)*

_____ **10.** It is a _____ to describe the actor as a "newcomer" to Broadway because he has been playing minor roles for years. *(misnomer)*

FIND THE EXAMPLE

Choose the answer that best describes the action or situation.

_____ **1.** An example of a U.S. *denomination*
   a. ten pesos   **b.** twenty-pound note   **c.** five yen   **d.** ten-dollar bill

_____ **2.** A likely *moniker* for a champion weightlifter
   a. Ox   **b.** Feather   **c.** Joseph   **d.** Jelly

_____ **3.** Activity LEAST likely to involve using *nomenclature*
   a. biology   **b.** walking   **c.** journalism   **d.** chemistry

_____ **4.** Something that might bring an actor widespread *renown*
   a. filming a scene   **b.** memorizing lines   **c.** ability to cry   **d.** winning an Oscar

_____ **5.** The *cognomen* of the first president of the United States
   a. Washington   **b.** George   **c.** general   **d.** place

_____ **6.** An example of an *ignominious* act
   a. winning a prize   **b.** eating a salad   **c.** stealing from friends   **d.** keeping watch

_____ **7.** The relative a *patronymic* name is taken from
   a. uncle   **b.** father   **c.** cousin   **d.** mother

_____ **8.** A situation in which one is supposed to be *anonymous*
   a. at a masquerade   **b.** on a date   **c.** talking to a friend   **d.** at a birthday party

_____ **9.** A *misnomer* for an elephant
   a. Big Boy   **b.** Tantor   **c.** Tiny   **d.** Bubba

_____ **10.** An example of an activity that requires *nominal* effort
   a. hiking up hills   **b.** doing sit-ups   **c.** lifting furniture   **d.** brushing hair

Prefixes, Roots, and Suffixes

The Prefixes *bene-, eu-,* and *mal-*

The prefixes in this lesson deal with concepts of good and bad. The prefix *bene-* means "well" in Latin and is now used to describe something good. Similarly, *eu-* means "good; well; true" in Greek. In contrast to these two prefixes, *mal-* means "bad" or "abnormal" and comes from the Latin *malus*. The chart below gives the meanings of these prefixes and how they are used.

Prefix	Meaning	Word	Word Meaning
bene-	good, well	beneficial	producing a favorable result
eu-	good, well	eulogy	speech or expression praising someone
mal-	bad, abnormal	maladjusted	poorly adjusted

Practice

You can combine the use of context clues with your knowledge of prefixes to make intelligent guesses about the meanings of words. Each of the sentences below contains a word formed with the prefix *bene-, eu-,* or *mal-*. Read the sentences and try to infer what the word in italics means. Then check your definition with the one you find in the dictionary, remembering to choose the definition that best fits in the sentence.

1. I am such a *maladroit* dancer that I am always bumping into people or stepping on their toes.

   My definition_____

   Dictionary definition_____

2. The news that she had won a million-dollar lottery filled her with *euphoria*.

   My definition_____

   Dictionary definition_____

3. At the graduation ceremony, the speaker offered the *benediction* "May your lives be peaceful and happy."

   My definition_____

   Dictionary definition_____

4. Angered that she had not been invited to the wedding, the mythological goddess hissed the *malediction* "May the earth dry up and wither!"

   My definition_____

   Dictionary definition_____

5. Many car dealers use the *euphemism* "previously owned vehicle" in place of the phrase "used car."

My definition _____

Dictionary definition _____

6. The *benevolent* man donated both his time and his money to the children's hospital.

My definition _____

Dictionary definition _____

7. The beautiful sounds made by the choir provided a *euphonious* experience for listeners.

My definition _____

Dictionary definition _____

8. The *benefactor* donated enough money to build a new library for the college.

My definition _____

Dictionary definition _____

9. Often, just before I come down with the flu or a cold, I have a vague feeling of *malaise*.

My definition _____

Dictionary definition _____

10. It is difficult to believe that someone could commit such a *malevolent* act.

My definition _____

Dictionary definition _____

Review Word Elements

Reviewing word elements helps you to remember them and use them in your reading. Below, write the meaning of the word elements you have studied.

Word	Word Element	Type of Element	Meaning of Word Element
anarchy	*-archy*	suffix	_____
extenuation	*-ten-*	root	_____
demographic	*-dem-*	root	_____
corpus	*-corp-*	root	_____
anonymous	*-onym-*	root	_____
veracity	*-ver-*	root	_____
meritocracy	*-cracy*	suffix	_____
inanimate	*-anim-*	root	_____

The Root -pend-

WORD LIST

append	dispense	expendable	impend	penchant
pending	preponderance	propensity	recompense	suspension

The root -pend- comes from the Latin verb *pendere*, meaning "to hang," "to weigh," or "to pay." The root is used in many common English words. A *pendant* "hangs" from a necklace. To *ponder* something is to "weigh" it in one's mind. An *expense* is something that is "paid."

1. **append** (ə-pěnd´) *verb* from Latin *ad-*, "upon" + *pend*, "hang"
   a. To add something to the end of a document
   • The researcher **appended** a series of charts and tables to the report.
   b. To attach to
   • The teacher **appended** name tags to the kindergarteners' shirts.

   appendix *noun* The **appendix** of the article presented the author's research data.

2. **dispense** (dĭ-spěns´) *verb* from Latin *dis-*, "free from" + *pend*, "weigh"
   a. To distribute in parts and portions
   • The relief agency **dispensed** some of the food to each family.
   b. To exempt from a duty or obligation
   • Because time was short, we **dispensed** with the reading of the minutes.

dispense

> The common phrase *to dispense with* means "to get rid of" or "to manage without."

3. **expendable** (ĭk-spěn´də-bəl) *adjective* from Latin *ex-*, "out" + *pend*, "pay; weigh"
   a. Not strictly necessary
   • The manager decided that the high-salaried, temperamental player was **expendable,** so he traded him to another team.
   b. Not worth keeping or reusing
   • These flimsy paper plates are **expendable.**

   expend *verb* To spend or use up
   • The calories you **expend** while exercising will help you lose weight.

4. **impend** (ĭm-pěnd´) *verb* from Latin *im-*, "over" + *pend*, "hang"
   a. To be about to happen
   • The dark sky and still air indicates that a storm is **impending.**
   b. To threaten to happen
   • As war **impended,** people fled the area.

5. **penchant** (pěn´chənt) *noun* from Latin *pend*, "hang"
   A strong liking; an inclination to be good at something
   • He turned his **penchant** for tinkering with engines into a career as an auto mechanic.

6. pending (pĕn′dĭng) from Latin *pend*, "hang"
   a. *adjective* Awaiting conclusion; not yet decided or settled
      • I'm hoping to attend Wilson College, but my application is
        still **pending.**
   b. *preposition* During; while awaiting
      • **Pending** the arrival of my passport, I cannot leave the country.

7. preponderance (prĭ-pŏn′dər-əns) *noun* from Latin *pre-*, "before"
   + *pend*, "weigh"
   Superiority in number, weight, influence, or importance
   • A **preponderance** of evidence supports the existence of global
     warming.

   preponderant *adjective* Music plays a **preponderant** role in the
   arts curriculum.

8. propensity (prə-pĕn′sĭ-tē) *noun* from Latin *pro-*, "forward"
   + *pend*, "hang"
   An inborn tendency or inclination
   • New studies show that some people are born with a **propensity** to be
     restless and may have problems sitting or standing still.

9. recompense (rĕk′əm-pĕns′) from Latin *re-*, "back" + *com-*,
   "together" + *pend*, "weigh"
   a. *verb* To pay or award compensation to
      • The judge ordered the car dealer to **recompense** his customer for
        selling her a defective vehicle.
   b. *noun* A payment in return for something
      • The **recompense** from the insurance company covered repair costs
        after the fire damaged the house.

10. suspension (sə-spĕn′shən) *noun* from Latin *sub-*, "under"
   + *pend*, "hang"
   a. A temporary stopping of a law or a rule
      • There is a **suspension** of parking fees on Sunday.
   b. A temporary loss of a privilege or right to do something, such as
       attend work or school
      • The officers are on **suspension** while awaiting a decision about
        possible wrongdoing.

   suspend *verb* Train service was **suspended** while workers repaired
   the tracks.

WORD ENRICHMENT

Hanging around

   Suspension has different meanings in various fields of knowledge.
In music, it refers to a tone of a chord that is held into the following chord
to create temporary dissonance. In engineering, it refers to a type of device
from which a mechanical part is hung. And in chemistry, *suspension* refers
existence of undissolved particles in a solution.

WRITE THE CORRECT WORD

Write the correct word in the space next to each definition. Use each word only once.

_____ **1.** to threaten to happen

_____ **2.** an inborn tendency

_____ **3.** to attach to

_____ **4.** to compensate

_____ **5.** superiority in number or influence

_____ **6.** to distribute in parts

_____ **7.** a strong liking

_____ **8.** not yet decided

_____ **9.** not totally necessary

_____ **10.** a temporary stopping of a law

COMPLETE THE SENTENCE

Write the letter for the word that best completes each sentence.

_____ **1.** My mischievous little sister has shown a great _____ for getting into trouble.
   a. suspension   **b.** recompense   **c.** propensity   **d.** preponderance

_____ **2.** I have an updated version of this map, so the old one you're holding is _____.
   a. preponderant   **b.** expendable   **c.** pending   **d.** penchant

_____ **3.** Would you please _____ your resumé to this job application?
   a. impend   **b.** expend   **c.** append   **d.** suspend

_____ **4.** The starting center was given a five-game _____ for fighting.
   a. penchant   **b.** propensity   **c.** recompense   **d.** suspension

_____ **5.** Ever since he was a boy, the chef had a(n) _____ for cooking.
   a. penchant   **b.** appendix   **c.** pending   **d.** recompense

_____ **6.** A jury ruled that the _____ of the evidence supported the defendant's alibi.
   a. append   **b.** suspension   **c.** recompense   **d.** preponderance

_____ **7.** When the sky turned pea-green, we knew that the tornado was _____.
   a. dispensing   **b.** impending   **c.** suspended   **d.** expending

_____ **8.** I took my prescription to the drugstore, and the pharmacist _____ the medicine.
   a. recompensed   **b.** impended   **c.** appended   **d.** dispensed

_____ **9.** The U.S. Congress is currently debating the bill, but its passage is still _____.
   a. preponderant   **b.** expendable   **c.** pending   **d.** propensity

_____ **10.** Each week, my elderly grandmother _____ a young woman for shopping for her groceries, mowing her lawn, and doing small household repairs.
   a. appends   **b.** recompenses   **c.** suspends   **d.** impends

Challenge: My English teacher has a _____ for writing personal notes of encouragement to his students and then _____ them to our essays.
_____   **a.** penchant…appending   **b.** suspension…impending   **c.** propensity…expending

Denise Taylor: Reporter

"Reporting is a thrill for curious people, because each week you learn something new," offers Denise Taylor. Taylor is a reporter for the *Boston Globe*, specializing in food and the arts. In addition to a weekly column, she writes frequent restaurant reviews for the paper.

(1) As a child, Taylor showed a *penchant* for writing, winning awards as early as the second grade. But reporting was not her first career. Because she is interested in the environment and youth issues, Taylor spent ten years working for nonprofit organizations. Still, the writing bug remained, so she came up with a unique idea for a food story, pitched it to the *Boston Globe*, and has been a journalist ever since.

Taylor covers arts topics that range from hip-hop dance to sculpture shows. **(2)** Her pieces must be concise but thorough, as journalists don't have the luxury of *appending* explanatory notes. **(3)** And there are always deadlines *pending*. Once, Taylor researched, wrote, and submitted an entire story—all in one day.

Despite daunting deadlines, Taylor searches for the human story behind the facts. **(4)** A reporter's *propensity* to chat may prompt celebrities to divulge unusual information. Taylor once told Tony Butala, lead singer of The Lettermen, about a youngster who had so little confidence that he would only sing behind closed doors. Butala then revealed that, as a child, he had the same problem.

(5) Sometimes what appears to be an *expendable* question guides Taylor to a great insight. Once, she made a polite inquiry about a popular singer's family. The performer went on to discuss her uncle, who had been a vaudeville star, and her father, who had owned a famous nightclub. The singer then revealed that watching their performances had inspired her own career.

(6) When Taylor writes restaurant reviews, she doesn't simply conform to the *preponderance* of public opinion. Instead, she makes certain to exercise and express her own independent judgment. **(7)** But her role is also more than just giving a rating and *dispensing* criticism. Taylor believes that her restaurant reviews should tell a story. "It's important to remember that 'story' is part of the phrase 'news story.' Often, the people who run restaurants are just as interesting as the food," she says.

As a reviewer, Taylor feels lucky that she gets to try foods ranging from Lebanese pastries to Tibetan soups. But sampling untried restaurants has its drawbacks, too. "I've eaten far more than my share of really bad food," she says.

Professional reporters like Taylor must carefully follow a professional code of ethics. **(8)** A reporter who breaks any part of this code can be *suspended* or fired. **(9)** Because Taylor serves as a critic, restaurants may not *recompense* her in any way. After all, it would be unethical for a journalist to accept free food from a restaurant or tickets to a performance that she is reviewing.

(10) Taylor often finds herself racing to meet one *impending* deadline after another. But the chance to share rich experiences with her readers more than makes up for the stress. As for aspiring writers, Taylor believes anyone with the desire can become a writer. "As long as you have something to say and the will to learn how to say it well, the world of writing can be yours," she advises.

Each sentence below refers to a numbered sentence in the passage. Write the letter of the choice that gives the sentence a meaning that is closest to the original sentence.

_____ **1.** As a child, Taylor showed a _____ for writing.
   a. distaste   **b.** strong liking   **c.** superior influence   **d.** frustration

_____ **2.** Journalists don't have the luxury of _____ explanatory notes.
   a. attaching   **b.** translating   **c.** distributing   **d.** giving out

_____ **3.** And there are always deadlines _____ .
   a. awaiting completion   **b.** being extended   **c.** being unreasonable   **d.** that are unnecessary

_____ **4.** A reporter's _____ to chat may prompt celebrities to divulge unusual information.
   a. compensation   **b.** threat   **c.** refusal   **d.** tendency

_____ **5.** Sometimes what appears to be an _____ question guides Taylor to a great insight.
　a. unanswerable　　**b.** insulting　　**c.** unnecessary　　**d.** exemplary

_____ **6.** When Taylor writes restaurant reviews, she doesn't simply conform to the _____ of public opinion.
　a. pointlessness　　**b.** temporary ceasing　　**c.** variations　　**d.** weight

_____ **7.** But her role is also more than just giving a rating and _____ criticism.
　a. threatening　　**b.** distributing　　**c.** ignoring　　**d.** adding to

_____ **8.** A reporter who breaks any part of this code can be _____ or fired.
　a. demoted　　**b.** paid off　　**c.** prosecuted　　**d.** stopped from working

_____ **9.** Because Taylor serves as a critic, restaurants may not _____ her in any way.
　a. compensate　　**b.** applaud　　**c.** photograph　　**d.** attach themselves to

_____ **10.** Taylor often finds herself racing to meet one _____ deadline after another.
　a. unnecessary　　**b.** impossible　　**c.** approaching　　**d.** ridiculous

Indicate whether the statements below are TRUE or FALSE according to the passage.

_____ **1.** Taylor often regrets her career choices.

_____ **2.** Taylor enjoys reporting the human element in her stories.

_____ **3.** Two of the perks of Taylor's job are free concert tickets and discounted restaurant meals.

WRITING EXTENDED RESPONSES

As you have just read, Denise Taylor works under tight deadlines. Would you enjoy a job with this much pressure? In a persuasive essay, try to either convince an employer that you would be good at a high-pressure job, or explain why you do not want to take such a job. Your piece should be at least three paragraphs in length and include a minimum of two well-supported points. Use at least three lesson words in your essay and underline them.

WRITE THE DERIVATIVE

Complete the sentence by writing the correct form of the word shown in parentheses. You may not need to change the form that is given.

_____ **1.** My physician has a _____ to be conservative about recommending surgery to his patients. (*propensity*)

_____ **2.** Construction crews will _____ work on the new bridge until they determine why one of the cables snapped. (*suspension*)

_____ **3.** I knew my sister had a _____ for great literature when she began reading Jane Austen in the fourth grade. (*penchant*)

4. After working all day, we were too exhausted to _____ the energy to move the sofa. (*expendable*)

5. The pump would not _____ the liquid soap properly. (*dispense*)

6. In the _____ of her book on overpopulation, there's a chart showing which nations have experienced the greatest growth over the past decade. (*append*)

7. We know we will travel to Canada this summer, but the date of our trip is still _____. (*pending*)

8. With their wedding _____, the couple wrote special vows to say during the ceremony. (*impend*)

9. In the folktale, the lost prince tried to _____ the kind stranger for giving him food and lodging, but the stranger refused the money. (*recompense*)

10. The _____ opinion of the state legislators was that the bill they passed constituted a necessary step in protecting consumers from identity theft. (*preponderance*)

FIND THE EXAMPLE

Choose the answer that best describes the action or situation.

_____ 1. The item most likely to be *expendable*
a. used plastic wrap   b. new DVD player   c. water glass   d. rare baseball card

_____ 2. What you would most likely do to *dispense* with an old computer
a. refurbish it   b. donate it to charity   c. take it apart   d. install games on it

_____ 3. The person most likely to be *suspended*
a. a model employee   b. a sick coworker   c. a violent student   d. a strict principal

_____ 4. What someone with a *propensity* to experience stress would most likely do
a. sleep peacefully   b. bite finger nails   c. concentrate well   d. work calmly

_____ 5. A suitable job for someone with a *penchant* for traveling
a. librarian   b. custodian   c. architect   d. airline pilot

_____ 6. Something you would most likely *append* to a research report
a. an introduction   b. a doctor's note   c. a list of sources   d. a humorous story

_____ 7. The person likely to have the *preponderant* opinion in a company
a. CEO   b. accountant   c. Director of Sales   d. intern

_____ 8. How a surfer feels when a perfect wave is *impending*
a. disappointed   b. excited   c. bored   d. exhausted

_____ 9. The reason why an employee would expect *recompense* from a company
a. taking sick days   b. organizing a team   c. writing a report   d. getting injured at work

_____ 10. A question whose answer is still *pending*
a. How do birds fly?   b. Is Earth flat?   c. Can fish read?   d. How many stars exist?

The Roots -dic- and -loq-

WORD LIST

benediction	colloquium	dictum	edict	elocution
grandiloquence	indict	interlocutor	loquacious	soliloquy

The root *-dic-* (or *-dict-*) comes from the Latin verb *dicere,* meaning "to say." The root *-loq-* (or *-locu-*) derives from the Latin *loqui,* which means "to speak." Many common English words contain these roots. To *predict* something is to state or tell about it in advance. To *contradict* is to express the opposite of what someone has said. An *eloquent* person speaks persuasively and fluently. In this lesson, you will learn more words containing these roots.

1. **benediction** (běn´ĭ-dĭk´shən) *noun* from Latin *bene-,* "well" + *dict,* "say"
   A blessing or expression of good wishes
   • At the graduation ceremony, the headmistress gave a **benediction** wishing health and peace to students and their families.

2. **colloquium** (kə-lō´kwē-əm) *noun* from Latin *col-,* "together" + *loq,* "speak"
   a. An informal meeting held in order to exchange views
   • Medical-school deans participated in a **colloquium** on new trends in nursing education.
   b. An academic seminar on a broad field of study, typically with several different lecturers
   • The Modern Language Association **colloquium** included presentations on language learning, historical studies, and comparative linguistics.

> The plural of *colloquium* is *colloquiums* or *colloquia.*

3. **dictum** (dĭk´təm) *noun* from Latin *dict,* "say"
   A noteworthy statement; an authoritative, often formal, pronouncement
   • One of Hippocrates's most famous **dictums** is "All excess is hostile to nature."

4. **edict** (ē´dĭkt´) *noun* from *e-,* "out" + *dict,* "say"
   A formal command; a decree or proclamation issued by an authority and having the force of law
   • The head of the new government issued an **edict** forbidding opposition groups to meet.

5. **elocution** (ĕl´ə-kyōō´shən) *noun* from *ex-,* "out" + *locu,* "speak"
   The art or manner of public speaking that emphasizes gesture, vocal projection, and delivery
   • Without electric sound systems, public speaking in the 1800s often relied on dramatic **elocution.**

edict

6. **grandiloquence** (grăn-dĭl´ə-kwəns) *noun* from Latin *grandis*, "great" + *loqu*, "speak"
A pompous, self-important manner in speech or expression
• The **grandiloquence** and formality of the play's dialogue makes the characters seem unnatural.

grandiloquent *adjective* We rolled our eyes at the **grandiloquent** speech the administrator had prepared for what was supposed to be a simple ceremony.

7. **indict** (ĭn-dīt´) *verb* from Latin *in-*, "in" + *dict*, "say"
   a. To charge with or accuse of wrongdoing
      • The nutrition advocates **indicted** the advertising agency for trying to tempt children to eat junk food.
   b. To make a formal, legal charge against
      • The defendant was **indicted** for grand larceny.

indictment *noun* At the trial, the court officer read the **indictment** for obstruction of justice.

indictable *adjective* At times, there is a thin line between aggressive business practices and **indictable** crimes.

> Often, *indictments* result from a grand-jury investigation, a process to determine whether someone should be prosecuted.

8. **interlocutor** (ĭn-tər-lŏk´yə-tər) *noun* from Latin *inter-*, "between" + *locu*, "speak"
A participant in a dialogue or conversation, often in a formal setting
• During the international conference, the U.S. president gained the respect of his **interlocutors** from Japan and China.

interlocution *noun* The **interlocution** between the two heads of state helped them develop an understanding that would ultimately lead to a peace agreement.

9. **loquacious** (lō-kwā´shəs) *adjective* from *loq*, "speak"
Extremely talkative
• The talk-show host finally silenced the **loquacious** guest by calling for a commercial break.

loquaciousness *noun* Because she had friends all across the country, her **loquaciousness** resulted in large phone bills.

10. **soliloquy** (sə-lĭl´ə-kwē) *noun* from Latin *solis*, "alone" + *loq*, "speak"
A dramatic speech in which one talks to oneself, revealing one's thoughts; the act of speaking to oneself; a monologue
• A famous **soliloquy** about the nature of existence from Shakespeare's play *Hamlet* begins, "To be or not to be; that is the question."

soliloquize *verb* It is inappropriate to **soliloquize** when you are supposed to be discussing something at a meeting.

WORD ENRICHMENT

Lots of talk!

Loquacious, an adjective used to describe those who talk a lot, has some synonyms. *Garrulous*, a somewhat more negative word, is reserved for those who talk annoyingly or pointlessly. The word can also be used to refer to a speech. A *garrulous* speech is excessively long and rambling. In contrast, *voluble* has no negative connotations, but characterizes fluent speech.

WRITE THE CORRECT WORD

Write the correct word in the space next to each definition. Use each word only once.

_____ **1.** a formal decree

_____ **2.** very talkative

_____ **3.** an academic seminar

_____ **4.** to charge with a crime

_____ **5.** the art of public speaking

_____ **6.** pompous speech

_____ **7.** a blessing

_____ **8.** a noteworthy statement

_____ **9.** a speech to oneself

_____ **10.** a participant in a dialogue

COMPLETE THE SENTENCE

Write the letter for the word that best completes each sentence.

_____ **1.** A(n) _____ that news reporters should heed is "Always strive to be objective."
  a. dictum   **b.** benediction   **c.** soliloquy   **d.** indictment

_____ **2.** In Olalla's _____, the audience learned her character's true motives.
  a. benediction   **b.** colloquium   **c.** edict   **d.** soliloquy

_____ **3.** After the meeting of the food aid volunteers, the organizer offered a(n) _____, wishing them safety and success in their endeavor.
  a. benediction   **b.** dictum   **c.** soliloquy   **d.** edict

_____ **4.** _____ by nature, Phillip found the perfect job as a radio host.
  a. Elocution   **b.** Indictable   **c.** Loquacious   **d.** Grandiloquent

_____ **5.** In televised debates, _____ ask questions of presidential candidates.
  a. colloquia   **b.** interlocutors   **c.** indicters   **d.** benedictions

_____ **6.** The _____ of Rafael's everyday speech made people think he was a snob.
  a. grandiloquence   **b.** colloquium   **c.** soliloquy   **d.** benediction

_____ **7.** Ana thinks that lessons in _____ might improve her chances for a successful political career.
  a. loquacious   **b.** benediction   **c.** grandiloquent   **d.** elocution

_____ **8.** Tempers flared during the faculty _____ on cost-cutting measures in the school district.
  a. elocution   **b.** soliloquy   **c.** benediction   **d.** colloquium

_____ **9.** After the grand jury made its decision, the authorities issued a(n) _____ of the suspect.
  a. soliloquy   **b.** elocution   **c.** indictment   **d.** colloquium

_____ **10.** The dictator's _____ made it illegal to be on the streets after 9:00 P.M.
  a. benediction   **b.** edict   **c.** elocution   **d.** interlocutor

Challenge: Seemingly living by the _____ "no pain, no gain," the sergeant issued a(n) _____ that all new recruits were to do five-hundred pushups before breakfast.
_____   **a.** colloquium…indictment   **b.** dictum…edict   **c.** elocution…interlocutors

The Gettysburg Addresses

In 1863, the small town of Gettysburg, Pennsylvania, was the site of the U.S. Civil War's most brutal battle. An estimated 7,000 lives were lost, and another 44,000 soldiers were wounded. **(1)** When it came time to memorialize the dead, two important men were asked to give speeches and *benedictions* to pay tribute to the fallen soldiers. The solemn words these men spoke would mark a turning point in the art of public speaking.

The two Gettysburg addresses clearly show the contrast between the new and the old styles of public presentation of the time. **(2)** One speech recalled the *grandiloquent* style of ancient Greek rhetoric. **(3)** The other evoked the short, intimate deliveries one might now find in academic *colloquia* or on radio and television news shows.

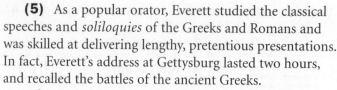

(4) Edward Everett, the principal speaker at the ceremony, was an expert in the classic *elocution* of his day. At that time—with no radio, television, or movies—the public address, or oratory, was a popular form of entertainment. Speakers delivered long, dramatic speeches, complete with sweeping, theatrical gestures. Unequipped with amplifiers, they spoke in booming voices loud enough to be heard by large crowds. Such showy presentations made orators like Everett celebrities. Their addresses were published, quoted, and accompanied by "behind the scenes" glimpses of the great men, much like articles in the popular magazines of today.

(5) As a popular orator, Everett studied the classical speeches and *soliloquies* of the Greeks and Romans and was skilled at delivering lengthy, pretentious presentations. In fact, Everett's address at Gettysburg lasted two hours, and recalled the battles of the ancient Greeks.

After Everett's presentation, the second speaker, Abraham Lincoln, took the podium. **(6)** Though not *loquacious* by nature, Lincoln had built a legal and political career using his ability to tell stories, and he knew how to hold an audience. **(7)** Lincoln lived in the days before professional writers crafted presidential speeches and held practice sessions with *interlocutors* who analyzed every word. So, the president simply composed his own 270-word, two-minute address. **(8)** In that brief speech, Lincoln charged the nation with an *edict* not to let the fallen soldiers' deaths be "in vain," but rather to ensure that there be a "new birth of freedom." In other words, Lincoln strove to rally the nation's spirit behind the war to end slavery. **(9)** In doing so, he was recalling his own *dictum:* "Force is all-conquering, but its victories are short lived."

When Lincoln sat down, he wasn't certain his words had been well received. In fact, he remarked to a friend that his speech was "a flat failure." **(10)** Indeed, various newspapers *indicted* it as "silly remarks" and a "dishwatery utterance." Others, however, admired Lincoln's concise style. The next day, Everett sent a letter to Lincoln, saying, "I should be glad, if I could flatter myself, that I came as near to the central idea of the occasion, in two hours, as you did in two minutes."

Today, Lincoln's Gettysburg Address is one of the bestknown examples of American oratory. In its conciseness and simplicity, it foreshadowed the more succinct public speaking of today.

Each sentence below refers to a numbered sentence in the passage. Write the letter of the choice that gives the sentence a meaning that is closest to the original sentence.

_____ **1.** Two men were asked to give speeches and_____ to pay tribute to the fallen soldiers.

    a. reparations   **b.** goodbyes   **c.** blessings   **d.** greetings

_____ **2.** One speech recalled the_____ style of ancient Greek rhetoric.

    a. spontaneous   **b.** pompous   **c.** concise   **d.** analytical

_____ **3.** The other evoked the deliveries one might now find in academic_____ .

    a. ceremonies   **b.** informal meetings   **c.** anthologies   **d.** retrospectives

_____ **4.** Edward Everett was an expert in the classic _____ of his day.
   a. arguments   **b.** music   **c.** literature   **d.** speaking style

_____ **5.** As a popular orator, Everett studied the classical speeches and _____ of the Greeks and Romans.
   a. personal views   **b.** formal commands   **c.** descriptions   **d.** words to oneself

_____ **6.** Though not _____ by nature, Lincoln had built a legal and political career using his ability to tell stories, and he knew how to hold an audience.
   a. confident   **b.** soft-spoken   **c.** talkative   **d.** pompous

_____ **7.** Lincoln lived in the days before professional writers crafted presidential speeches and held practice sessions with _____ who analyzed every word.
   a. coconspirators   **b.** speech teachers   **c.** dialogue participants   **d.** adversaries

_____ **8.** Lincoln charged the nation with a _____ not to let the soldiers' deaths be "in vain."
   a. statement   **b.** request   **c.** command   **d.** plea

_____ **9.** He was recalling his own _____: "Force is all-conquering, but its victories are short lived."
   a. pronouncement   **b.** argument   **c.** definition   **d.** explanation

_____ **10.** Various newspapers _____ his speech as "silly remarks."
   a. praised   **b.** summarized   **c.** condemned   **d.** reported

Indicate whether the statements below are TRUE or FALSE according to the passage.

_____ **1.** To improve their skills, orators like Edward Everett studied addresses delivered centuries earlier by speakers in other cultures.

_____ **2.** In his speech, Lincoln invoked the grandeur of Greece and Rome.

_____ **3.** Lincoln's Gettysburg Address was popular with everyone who reported on it.

FINISH THE THOUGHT

Complete each sentence so that it shows the meaning of the italicized word.

1. We reacted to her *grandiloquence* by _____

_____

2. My *loquacious* friend _____

_____

WRITE THE DERIVATIVE

Complete the sentence by writing the correct form of the word shown in parentheses. You may not need to change the form that is given.

_____ **1.** "I think, therefore I am" is René Descartes' famous _____. *(dictum)*

_____ **2.** The three _____ met in a closed session. *(interlocutor)*

_____ 3. Alejandro's boss issues ――― just as a czar or dictator would. *(edict)*

_____ 4. The ――― of the people seated behind us ruined our enjoyment of the movie. *(loquacious)*

_____ 5. The newspaper editorial was an ――― of rising insurance rates. *(indict)*

_____ 6. Following the ―――, the bride and groom slowly made their way up the aisle. *(benediction)*

_____ 7. Explaining his evil intentions to the audience, the play's villain ――― at the side of the stage. *(soliloquy)*

_____ 8. After the banquet, the ambassador spoke ――― about the traditions of his country. *(grandiloquence)*

_____ 9. The chair of the arts department scheduled a series of ――― on the history and influence of African-American music. *(colloquium)*

_____ 10. The comedian studied ――― to improve his timing and voice control. *(elocution)*

FIND THE EXAMPLE

Choose the answer that best describes the action or situation.

_____ 1. Someone LEAST likely to be *loquacious*
    a. comedian   **b.** talk-show host   **c.** politician   **d.** mime

_____ 2. Of the following, the one that is a *dictum*
    a. Waste not, want not   **c.** Fourscore and twenty years ago
    b. What are your thoughts?   **d.** The true meaning of happiness

_____ 3. The person most likely to deliver a *soliloquy*
    a. reporter   **b.** actor   **c.** essayist   **d.** illustrator

_____ 4. Something that frequently includes a *benediction*
    a. sports event   **b.** jury trial   **c.** formal ceremony   **d.** family barbecue

_____ 5. A likely adjective describing someone whose language is *grandiloquent*
    a. humble   **b.** intelligent   **c.** stuck-up   **d.** persuasive

_____ 6. The person most likely to issue an *edict*
    a. salesperson   **b.** grocer   **c.** emperor   **d.** entertainer

_____ 7. Someone most concerned with *elocution*
    a. computer expert   **b.** debater   **c.** painter   **d.** grand juror

_____ 8. What one does in a *colloquium*
    a. exchange views   **b.** talk alone   **c.** accuse of wrongdoing   **d.** issue orders

_____ 9. An event that features *interlocutors*
    a. Italian opera   **b.** dance recital   **c.** theater review   **d.** panel discussion

_____ 10. How you would probably feel if you were *indicted*
    a. humble   **b.** grateful   **c.** helpful   **d.** afraid

The Root -cap-

WORD LIST

cadet	caper	capital	capitalism	capitulate
caprice	chieftain	mischievous	per capita	recapitulate

The root *-cap-* means "head." This root is taken from the Latin word for *head,* which is *caput.* Such words as *chapter* (the "head" of a piece of writing) and *chef* (the "head" of a kitchen) come from *-cap-.* This root should not be confused with a separate *-cap-* root that comes from the Latin word *capere,* "to take or seize," and forms such words as *captivate* and *capture.* Try to determine how the words in this lesson relate to the root *-cap-* that means "head."

"AT EASE, cadets!"

cadets

1. cadet (kə-dĕt´) *noun* from Latin *cap,* "head"
A student at a military school who is training to be an officer
- The **cadet** was proud to be enrolled in the U.S. Military Academy at West Point.

> A *cadet* can also mean "a younger son or brother."

2. caper (kā´pər) from Latin *caper,* "goat," derived from *cap,* "head"
a. *noun* A daring adventure or prank
- The boys thought it was just an innocent **caper** to dress the statue in ladies' clothes, but the town officials were not amused.
b. *verb* To leap about; frolic
- It made us smile to see the playful otters **capering** in the water.

3. capital (kăp´ĭ-tl) from Latin *cap,* "head"
a. *noun* The official location of a government; a center of a specific activity or industry
- The city of Springfield is the **capital** of the state of Illinois.
b. *noun* Wealth in the form of money or property
- Juan saved for years in order to build up enough **capital** to start his own business.
c. *adjective* First and foremost
- This decision is of **capital** importance.

> The word *capitol* refers to the building in which a legislature meets.

4. capitalism (kăp´ĭ-tl-ĭz´əm) *noun* from Latin *cap,* "head"
An economic system based on private ownership of resources and industry
- Economic conditions promoted by **capitalism** often result in lower prices for consumers.

capitalistic or **capitalist** *adjective* China is currently moving from a state-run economy to a more **capitalistic** system.

> *Capitalist* can also be used as a noun.

5. capitulate (kə-pĭch´ə-lāt´) *verb* from Latin *cap,* "head"
To surrender under specified conditions; to yield or give up
- My mother finally **capitulated** and let us get a dog.

capitulation *noun* The army's **capitulation** ended many years of fighting.

6. **caprice** (kə-prēs´) *noun* from Latin *cap*, "head"
A sudden, unpredictable action or change of mind; a whim; an inclination to change one's mind
• In an act of **caprice**, the president suddenly fired his top advisor.

capricious *adjective* Three-year-olds have **capricious** tastes in food.

7. **chieftain** (chēf´tən) *noun* from Latin *cap*, "head"
The leader of a group, especially a clan or tribe
• The **chieftain** called a meeting of the council of elders.

8. **mischievous** (mĭs´chə-vəs) *adjective* from Middle English *mis-*, "badly" + *chever*, "to come to a head," from Latin *cap*, "head"
Playful in a naughty or troublesome way
• The **mischievous** boy hid his brother's homework.

mischief *noun* I knew our cat was up to its usual **mischief** when I heard a loud crash in the next room.

> Note the pronunciation of *mischievous*, a word that is often mispronounced.

9. **per capita** (pər kăp´ĭ-tə) *adverb* and *adjective* from Latin *per*, "according to" + *cap*, "head"
For each individual; per person
• The small country of Luxembourg has the highest **per capita** income of any nation.

10. **recapitulate** (rē-kə-pĭch´ə-lāt´) *verb* from Latin *re-*, "back" + *cap*, "head"
To repeat in shortened form; to summarize
• The president **recapitulated** the highlights of his State of the Union address at a press conference.

recapitulation *noun* The conclusion at the end of a textbook chapter often provides a **recapitulation** of the main points.

ANALOGIES

On the answer line, write the letter of the answer that best completes each analogy. Refer to lessons 25–27 if you need help with any of the lesson words.

_____ **1.** *Dispense* is to *collect* as _____.
   a. *edict* is to *order*
   b. *penchant* is to *liking*
   c. *appendix* is to *addition*
   d. *capital* is to *debt*

_____ **2.** *Indict* is to *defendant* as _____.
   a. *chieftain* is to *follower*
   b. *suspend* is to *rule*
   c. *cadet* is to *officer*
   d. *grandiloquence* is to *inarticulateness*

_____ **3.** *Caprice* is to *whim* as _____.
   a. *soliloquy* is to *dialogue*
   b. *propensity* is to *skill*
   c. *capitulation* is to *combative*
   d. *colloquium* is to *conference*

_____ **4.** *Loquacious* is to *quiet* as _____.
   a. *pending* is to *unsettled*
   b. *caper* is to *prank*
   c. *expendable* is to *necessary*
   d. *mischievous* is to *playful*

WRITE THE CORRECT WORD

Write the correct word in the space next to each definition. Use each word only once.

_____ **1.** tribal leader

_____ **2.** to summarize

_____ **3.** to surrender

_____ **4.** an adventure

_____ **5.** a government's central location

_____ **6.** playfully naughty

_____ **7.** an officer-in-training

_____ **8.** per person

_____ **9.** whim

_____ **10.** economy based on private ownership

COMPLETE THE SENTENCE

Write the letter for the word that best completes each sentence.

_____ **1.** In an act of _____, my neighbor filled his front yard with pink flamingos.
    a. capitulation   **b.** cadet   **c.** capitalism   **d.** caprice

_____ **2.** My parents don't possess enough _____ to retire from their jobs yet.
    a. capital   **b.** capitulation   **c.** mischief   **d.** recapitulation

_____ **3.** People living in New Hampshire pay some of the lowest taxes, _____, in the United States.
    a. mischievous   **b.** capitalistic   **c.** per capita   **d.** capital

_____ **4.** The small brochure in the glove compartment _____ the main safety features listed in the car's instruction manual.
    a. recapitulates   **b.** capers   **c.** capitulates   **d.** caprices

_____ **5.** My cousin knew I was responsible for the trick because of my _____ smile.
    a. capitalistic   **b.** mischievous   **c.** capricious   **d.** per capita

_____ **6.** In the movie, the gang of thieves pulled off a clever _____.
    a. caprice   **b.** chieftain   **c.** caper   **d.** capitulation

_____ **7.** These Air Force _____ are currently taking classes on military history.
    a. caprices   **b.** recapitulations   **c.** capitals   **d.** cadets

_____ **8.** Despite the fact that she doesn't agree with him, the vice president is expected to _____ to the president's wishes.
    a. capitulate   **b.** caper   **c.** caprice   **d.** recapitulate

_____ **9.** Most people agree that the cold war between the Soviet Union and the United States was a battle between communism and _____.
    a. mischief   **b.** capitalism   **c.** cadets   **d.** caprice

_____ **10.** On our tour of the Amazon, we were greeted by a village _____.
    a. caper   **b.** capitulation   **c.** capital   **d.** chieftain

Challenge: Although the _____ prank was, in actuality, a harmless _____, the lieutenant insisted that the troops be reprimanded.
_____   **a.** per capita…caprice   **b.** capital…cadet   **c.** mischievous…caper

Sequoya: Cherokee Leader

The great Cherokee Sequoya invented a writing system that brought literacy, books, and newspapers to his people. **(1)** Sequoya was the son of a Cherokee mother, who came from a distinguished line of *chieftains,* and a British trader. Born in 1776, Sequoya lived in the southeastern states of Tennessee and Georgia, where the Cherokee tribe occupied considerable land.

It is thought that Sequoya suffered from a physical disability, for his name means "pig's foot," in Cherokee. However, if he did, the disability didn't stop him from becoming an accomplished farmer, blacksmith, and silversmith. **(2)** He was also a soldier who fought alongside U.S. government troops and *cadets.* As he watched the men write letters home and read military orders, he became fascinated with their "talking leaves" of paper.

Sequoya began to feel that literacy was essential to power. **(3)** Literacy is an important basis of *capitalism.* **(4)** Complex financial transactions cannot be left to the *caprices* of verbal agreements and memory. **(5)** In the modern world, for example, nations with high literacy rates have higher *per capita* incomes than those with low rates. Literacy is also a cornerstone of politics, for treaties and contracts are much more enforceable when they are recorded in writing.

Sequoya was determined to create a writing system for the Cherokee people. To his immense credit, he did in a few years what most civilizations only accomplish over the course of multiple generations. Analyzing the speech of his native tongue, he was able to devise a "syllabary" of eighty-six characters that represented the entire Cherokee language.

At first, fellow Cherokees treated Sequoya's breakthrough with suspicion. **(6)** According to one story, Sequoya's own wife thought he was involved in a useless, time-wasting *caper.* **(7)** She was alleged to have committed the *mischievous* act of setting fire to his workshop.

Sequoya gave public demonstrations to convince his people of the value of writing. He taught his syllabary to his daughter Ayoka. During a demonstration, Sequoya would ask someone a question when Ayoka was outside and could not hear. **(8)** Sequoya would then write down a *recapitulation* of the answer. Ayoka would come back inside and read out loud what he had written. To the amazement of all, it was the answer the person had given. Within a year, his alphabet gained acceptance, and thousands of Cherokees were reading and writing. **(9)** In 1824, the Cherokee National Council met at their *capital* of New Echota. They honored Sequoya with a silver medal.

Unfortunately, Sequoya's triumph was followed by tragedy for his people. **(10)** The U.S. government forced the Cherokees to *capitulate* their lands. The tribe had to relocate west of the Mississippi River. Many were part of the brutal march called the "Trail of Tears."

Throughout this difficult time, Sequoya's writing system allowed Cherokees in different states to communicate. In commemoration of Sequoya's legacy, the giant trees in Sequoia National Park in California bear his name.

Each sentence below refers to a numbered sentence in the passage. Write the letter of the choice that gives the sentence a meaning that is closest to the original sentence.

_____ **1.** Sequoya was the son of a British trader and a Cherokee mother, who came from a distinguished line of _____.
     a. leaders   **b.** samurai   **c.** gentlemen   **d.** officers

_____ **2.** He was also a soldier who fought alongside U.S. government troops and _____.
     a. adventures   **b.** musicians   **c.** politicians   **d.** officers-in-training

_____ **3.** It is an important basis of _____.
     a. surrender   **b.** military strategy   **c.** camouflage   **d.** an economic system

_____ **4.** Complex financial transactions cannot be left to the _____ of verbal
agreements and memory.
    a. leadership   **b.** naughtiness   **c.** whims   **d.** systems

_____ **5.** Nations with high literacy rates have higher _____ incomes than those with
low rates.
    a. taxable   **b.** per person   **c.** unpredictable   **d.** economic

_____ **6.** According to one story, Sequoya's own wife thought he was involved in a useless,
time-wasting _____ .
    a. prank   **b.** act of mercy   **c.** change of mind   **d.** summary

_____ **7.** She was alleged to have committed the _____ act of setting fire to his workshop.
    a. strange   **b.** naughty   **c.** daring   **d.** mysterious

_____ **8.** Sequoya would then write down a(n) _____ of the answer.
    a. summary   **b.** translation   **c.** approximation   **d.** change

_____ **9.** In 1824, the Cherokee National Council met at their _____ of New Echota.
    a. secret place   **b.** arena   **c.** country   **d.** government
headquarters

_____ **10.** The U.S. government forced the Cherokees to _____ their lands.
    a. improve   **b.** frolic on   **c.** surrender   **d.** change

Indicate whether the statements below are TRUE or FALSE according to the passage.

_____ **1.** Sequoya interacted with people of European descent.

_____ **2.** Sequoya's writing system was greeted with immediate public acceptance.

_____ **3.** Sequoya's triumph with language helped ensure that the Cherokees would be
allowed to keep their land.

WRITING EXTENDED RESPONSES

**The passage you have just read describes some differences between
Native Americans and settlers of European descent. In an essay of at
least three paragraphs, compare and contrast two different countries or
societies, showing ways in which they are alike and different (including
their economic situations). Your essay should include at least two well-
supported points. Use three or more lesson words in your piece and
underline them.**

WRITE THE DERIVATIVE

**Complete the sentence by writing the correct form of the word shown in
parentheses. You may not need to change the form that is given.**

_____ **1.** Jumping high into the air, the frogs _____ across the lily pads that spanned the
pond. *(caper)*

_____ **2.** When our basketball coach replaced our starters with bench players in the fourth
quarter, we knew that our team was _____ . *(capitulate)*

_____ **3.** One of the classes the _____ take is the Law of Armed Conflict. *(cadet)*

_____ **4.** Spray painting the stop sign wasn't mere _____, but an act of vandalism. *(mischievous)*

_____ **5.** The _____ boy told his parents he wanted a fire truck, then immediately changed his mind and asked for a video game. *(caprice)*

_____ **6.** Some people refer to Austin, Texas, as the "Live Music _____ of the World." *(capital)*

_____ **7.** The driving instructor offered her student a _____ of traffic rules before they began driving around the neighborhood. *(recapitulate)*

_____ **8.** The tribal _____ spoke out today against the Mining Act, which he felt would lead to massive destruction of animal habitats. *(chieftain)*

_____ **9.** Author Ayn Rand wrote novels showing the benefits of a _____ society. *(capitalism)*

_____ **10.** This county spends the lowest amount of money on education, _____, in the entire state. *(per capita)*

FIND THE EXAMPLE

Choose the answer that best describes the action or situation.

_____ **1.** Something a *chieftain* would be most likely to do
   a. play pranks   **b.** obey orders   **c.** call a meeting   **d.** weave some cloth

_____ **2.** A day when people are most likely to commit acts of *mischief*
   a. April Fool's   **b.** Thanksgiving   **c.** Memorial Day   **d.** Valentine's Day

_____ **3.** When a speaker might *recapitulate* the main points of his or her speech
   a. at the beginning   **b.** in the middle   **c.** toward the end   **d.** before the speech begins

_____ **4.** Something that a person would be least likely to make a *capricious* decision about
   a. what to wear   **b.** where to eat   **c.** what film to see   **d.** whom to marry

_____ **5.** A movement we make when we *caper*
   a. crawl   **b.** walk   **c.** leap   **d.** hobble

_____ **6.** A word describing something of *capital* importance
   a. little   **b.** significant   **c.** average   **d.** some

_____ **7.** A reason that you might *capitulate* to another
   a. you are proud   **b.** you are winning   **c.** you are stubborn   **d.** you are losing

_____ **8.** What a *cadet* is learning to do
   a. lead   **b.** stroll   **c.** sing   **d.** play

_____ **9.** An idea central to a *capitalistic* society
   a. no prisons   **b.** silly pranks   **c.** free trade   **d.** universal health care

_____ **10.** Information needed to determine a state's *per capita* income
   a. number of TV stars   **b.** number of households   **c.** number of people   **d.** number of millionaires

Prefixes, Roots, and Suffixes

The Word Elements *ante-* and *-ann-*

The prefixes in this skill feature both deal with time. *Ante-* means "prior to; before" as well as "in front of." The prefix is derived from the word *ante,* meaning "before" in Latin. The Latin root *-ann-,* or *-enn-,* meaning "year," comes from *annus,* which means "year."

Element	Type	Meaning	Word	Word Meaning
ante-	prefix	before; in front of	antedate	to precede
ann, enn	root	year	annual	happening each year

Practice

You can combine the use of context clues with your knowledge of these word elements to make intelligent guesses about word meanings. Each of the sentences below contains a word formed with the word element *ante-* or *ann (enn).* Read the sentences and try to infer what the word in italics means. Then check your definition with the one you find in the dictionary, remembering to choose the definition that best fits in the sentence.

1. We waited in the *anteroom* until we were escorted to the meeting room.

My definition _____

Dictionary definition _____

2. The *biennial* meeting was held in 2002, 2004, and 2006.

My definition _____

Dictionary definition _____

3. The bodybuilder admired her own *anterior* shoulder muscles.

My definition _____

Dictionary definition _____

4. The American Revolutionary War *anteceded* the U.S. Civil War.

My definition _____

Dictionary definition _____

5. The number of people who live to their *centennial* birthday is rapidly rising.

My definition _____

Dictionary definition _____

6. The common abbreviation A.M. stands for *antemeridian*.

My definition _____

Dictionary definition _____

7. Pollution has been a *perennial* problem in many cities.

My definition _____

Dictionary definition _____

8. He invested in an *annuity* and now receives payments for life.

My definition _____

Dictionary definition _____

Review Word Elements

Reviewing word elements helps you to remember them while you read.
Below, write the meaning of the word elements you have studied.

Word	Word Element	Type of Element	Meaning of Word Element
maladjusted	*mal-*	prefix	_____
democracy	*-dem-*	root	_____
monarch	*-arch*	suffix	_____
verify	*-ver-*	root	_____
euphemism	*eu-*	prefix	_____
autocracy	*-cracy*	suffix	_____
tenacious	*-ten-*	root	_____
colloquium	*-loq-*	root	_____
capitulate	*-cap-*	root	_____
impend	*-pend-*	root	_____
benediction	*bene-*	prefix	_____
magnanimous	*-anim-*	root	_____
dictum	*-dict-*	root	_____
incorporeal	*-corp-*	root	_____
misnomer	*-nom-*	root	_____
patronymic	*-onym-*	root	_____

Words and Phrases from French

WORD LIST

coup d'état	dilettante	élan	entrée	esprit de corps
laissez faire	nouveau riche	potpourri	savoir-faire	tête-à-tête

English has borrowed many words from the French language, including numerous terms dealing with *cuisine*—a French word that means "cook." If you have ever asked for an *hors d'oeuvre* before dinner, looked at a *menu*, eaten an *éclair* or a *soufflé*, or *sautéed* vegetables, then you have used words with French origins.

1. coup d'état (ko͞o´ dā-tä´) *noun* from French *coup*, "blow; stroke" + *de-*, "of" + *état*, "state"
A sudden overthrow of an existing government, usually by a small group
• In a surprising **coup d'état**, the rebel forces overtook the capital.

> The plural of *coup d'état* can be *coups d'état* or *coup d'états*.

2. dilettante (dĭl´ĭ-tänt´) from Old French *delitier*, "to please; to charm"
a. *noun* A dabbler in an art or a field of knowledge
• Pat is a **dilettante**, not an authority, when it comes to music.
b. *noun* A lover of the fine arts; a connoisseur
• A devoted **dilettante**, Jacques knew every art dealer in New York.
c. *adjective* Superficial; amateurish
• The critic referred to the author's first novel as a **dilettante** attempt.

3. élan (ā-län´) *noun* from Old French *eslan*, "rush"
a. Distinctive style or flair
• Tossing one end of the glorious silk scarf over her shoulder, Bridget made her exit with **élan.**
b. Enthusiastic vigor and liveliness
• The child's **élan** as he played the piano impressed the audience at the recital.

4. entrée (ŏn´trā) *noun* from French *entrer*, "to enter"
a. The power, permission, or liberty to enter; admittance
• **Entrée** to the golf course is limited to members of the club.
b. The main dish of a meal
• After eating several appetizers, we were too full to enjoy the **entrée**.

entrée

> On very formal occasions, an *entrée* can be the dish served directly before the main course or between two main courses.

5. esprit de corps (ĕ-sprē´ də kôr´) *noun* from French *esprit*, "spirit" + *de-*, "of" + *corps*, "group; body"
A common spirit of comradeship, enthusiasm, and devotion to a cause among group members
• Athletes demonstrate **esprit de corps** when they sacrifice making individual points so that the team can perform more effectively.

6. **laissez faire** (lĕs´ā fâr´, lā´zā fâr´) *noun* from French *laisser*, "to let; to allow" + *faire*, "to do"
   a. An economic doctrine that opposes governmental regulation of or interference in commerce beyond the minimum necessary
   • Principles of **laissez faire** were popularized by the physiocrats of eighteenth-century France, who sought to free trade and agriculture from governmental controls.
   b. Noninterference in the affairs of others
   • Dad had a **laissez faire** attitude about our curfews, letting us set our own.

7. **nouveau riche** (nōō´vō rēsh´) *noun* from French, *nouveau*, "new" + *riche*, "rich"
   One who has recently become rich, especially one who vulgarly displays wealth
   • Henry James's novels are filled with the disdain that European aristocrats felt for the American **nouveaux riches** in the late 1800s.

> The plural of *nouveau riche* is *nouveaux riches.* The expression is generally a negative, pejorative one.

8. **potpourri** (pō´pŏŏ-rē´) *noun* from French *pot*, "pot" + *pourrir*, "to rot"
   a. A combination of assorted and oddly matched things
   • Dana cooked a stew from a **potpourri** of leftover vegetables.
   b. A miscellaneous anthology or collection
   • The book was a **potpourri** of poetry, essays, and short stories.
   c. A mixture of dried flower petals and spices used to scent the air
   • The scent of the **potpourri** perfumed the bedroom.

9. **savoir-faire** (săv´wär-fâr´) *noun* from French *savoir*, "to know how" + *faire*, "to do"
   The ability to say or do the right or graceful thing
   • With her usual **savoir-faire**, Andrea avoided an awkward moment by subtly changing the direction of the conversation.

10. **tête-à-tête** (tĕt´ə-tĕt´) from French *tête*, "head" + *à*, "to" + *tête*, "head"
    a. *noun* A private conversation between two persons
    • During our **tête-à-tête**, Ellen confidentially told me of her plans to look for another job.
    b. *adjective* or *adverb* Without the intrusion of a third person; in intimate privacy
    • Michael offered to watch the younger children so that his parents could have dinner **tête-à-tête**.

WORD ENRICHMENT

Nouveau and nouvelle

The word *nouveau* means "new, different, and fashionable." Another spelling of the word is *nouvelle,* as in *nouvelle cuisine,* a contemporary school of French cooking that emphasizes healthy eating. *Art nouveau* is a decorative style of the early twentieth century that was noted for flowing, curved lines. *Nouvelle vague*—"new wave" in English—refers to a French cinematic movement of the 1960s that featured symbolism and alienation. *New wave* also refers to a kind of rock music popularized in the United States in the early 1980s.

WRITE THE CORRECT WORD

Write the correct word in the space next to each definition. Use each word only once.

_____ **1.** style; flair

_____ **2.** a mixed assortment

_____ **3.** noninterference

_____ **4.** a main dish

_____ **5.** newly wealthy

_____ **6.** private conversation

_____ **7.** social grace

_____ **8.** dabbler in the arts

_____ **9.** political overthrow

_____ **10.** comradeship

COMPLETE THE SENTENCE

Write the letter for the word that best completes each sentence.

_____ **1.** Rose had the _____ and poise to enter the palace with perfect confidence.
    a. entrée   **b.** coup d'état   **c.** élan   **d.** nouveau riche

_____ **2.** The _____ went to exhibits only if they were near his house.
    a. laissez faire   **b.** dilettante   **c.** potpourri   **d.** esprit de corps

_____ **3.** The reporter was excited when the star asked for a _____ meeting.
    a. tête-à-tête   **b.** coup d'état   **c.** nouveau riche   **d.** savoir-faire

_____ **4.** Etiquette books can help improve your _____ by giving you a good overview of appropriate behavior for all social occasions.
    a. laissez faire   **b.** coup d'état   **c.** esprit de corps   **d.** savoir-faire

_____ **5.** Our boss treated us in a(n) _____ way, trusting us to manage our own projects.
    a. potpourri   **b.** dilettante   **c.** laissez faire   **d.** nouveau riche

_____ **6.** The band's latest CD is a(n) _____ of old hits and new songs.
    a. potpourri   **b.** entrée   **c.** élan   **d.** coup d'état

_____ **7.** Spending money lavishly on showy clothes, cars, and homes can mark a person as one of the _____.
    a. tête-à-tête   **b.** nouveau riche   **c.** savoir-faire   **d.** esprit de corps

_____ **8.** I couldn't decide whether to order lobster or chicken for my _____.
    a. coup d'état   **b.** dilettante   **c.** élan   **d.** entrée

_____ **9.** Successful combat units often develop a strong _____.
    a. tête-à-tête   **b.** esprit de corps   **c.** nouveau riche   **d.** élan

_____ **10.** The dictator was toppled by his generals in a stunning _____.
    a. savoir-faire   **b.** dilettante   **c.** coup d'état   **d.** laissez faire

Challenge: It takes practice, a natural _____, and a thorough knowledge of etiquette to develop the poise and _____ that is essential to feel comfortable at elegant functions.
_____   **a.** tête-à-tête…entrée   **b.** dilettante…potpourri   **c.** élan … savoir-faire

Searching for the Real Molly

Many books and films recount the life of Molly Brown, the *Titanic's* most famous survivor. But most of these tales distort the truth. **(1)** The legend of "The Unsinkable Molly Brown" is a *potpourri* of exaggerations, untruths, and fantasy—starting with her name. It was Margaret, not Molly.

Recently, author Kristen Iversen decided to research why history got this story wrong. She found that the myth was started by two writers. After the *Titanic* sank in icy waters in 1912, Margaret Brown became a hero. She helped keep up the spirits of the shivering people in her lifeboat, enabling them to row to a rescue ship. **(2)** Once safe, she built needed *esprit de corps* among the survivors.

While most of the passengers who escaped the sinking ship never thought to help the less wealthy survivors, Mrs. Brown worked tirelessly to aid them. She organized efforts to make sure everyone was provided with warm clothes and food. Aware that many immigrants on the *Titanic* lost their life savings when the ship went down, she collected donations for them from wealthy passengers.

Because Mrs. Brown became famous for these simple acts of kindness, Gene Fowler and Caroline Bancroft decided to write about her, but their entertaining tales held little truth.

According to Fowler and Bancroft, Molly Brown was born poor and raised only by her father. **(3)** As a child, she skipped school, ran wild, and created all kinds of mischief with *élan*. She married a rich man for his wealth, and hid all his money in the stove, then accidentally burned it all up. **(4)** Once her husband regained his wealth, she struggled to gain *entrée* to high society. But high-class ladies wanted nothing to do with the impolite and uneducated Molly Brown.

(5) So she went to Europe, where she became a *dilettante* of the arts. For amusement, the European royalty befriended the silly American. **(6)** It was not until after her ordeal on the *Titanic* that she was able to gain admittance to high society in America, a feat nearly as impressive as a *coup d'état* for a person of her low breeding. In short, Fowler and Bancroft made Molly look like a loveable but shallow fool. Nothing could be further from the truth.

In reality, Margaret grew up in a strict household, with both parents, and attended school every day. She married for love, not for riches, and never burned money up in a stove. **(7)** Her husband did strike gold, becoming fabulously wealthy, but Mrs. Brown never behaved like a *nouveau riche*. She was not desperate to be adored by the rich.

In fact, she befriended people of all backgrounds and incomes, from her maids to princesses. **(8)** In top social circles, everyone longed for a *tête-à-tête* with the respected Mrs. Brown. **(9)** Eventually, she did go overseas, where she dazzled Europe's upper class with her *savoir-faire* and her ability to speak five languages.

So why did Fowler, Bancroft, and later writers get it wrong? Iversen argues that they were more interested in a good rags-to-riches story than the truth. **(10)** Margaret Brown's family took a *laissez faire* approach to the made-up tales. Hoping to avoid more publicity, they never bothered to correct the facts.

Iversen also believes that the public was not ready for her real story. In a time of rigid class distinctions, here was a woman who befriended rich and poor alike. Mrs. Brown also fought for workers' and women's rights, which were unpopular among the elite of the day. Had the true story of Margaret Brown's charitable acts been publicized, more than a few feathers would have been ruffled.

Each sentence below refers to a numbered sentence in the passage. Write the letter of the choice that gives the sentence a meaning that is closest to the original sentence.

_____ **1.** The legend of "The Unsinkable Molly Brown" is a(n) _____ of exaggerations, untruths, and fantasy.

    a. tale   **b.** doctrine   **c.** assortment   **d.** narration

_____ **2.** Once safe, she built needed _____ among the survivors.

    a. confidence   **b.** interactions   **c.** style   **d.** team spirit

_____ **3.** As a child, she skipped school, ran wild, and created all kinds of mischief with _____ .

    a. style and flair   **b.** enthusiasm   **c.** wealth   **d.** bad luck

_____ **4.** Once her husband regained his wealth, she struggled to gain _____ high society.
    a. admittance to   **b.** trust from   **c.** comradeship with   **d.** recognition by

_____ **5.** So she went to Europe, where she became a(n) _____ the arts.
    a. donor for   **b.** force for   **c.** appreciator of   **d.** savior of

_____ **6.** She was able to gain admittance to high society in America, a feat nearly as impressive as a(n) _____.
    a. intimate conversation   **b.** bribe   **c.** invitation   **d.** sudden overthrow

_____ **7.** Mrs. Brown never behaved like a(n) _____ person.
    a. important   **b.** newly wealthy   **c.** amateurish   **d.** self-absorbed

_____ **8.** In top social circles, everyone longed for a _____ with the respected Mrs. Brown.
    a. stroll   **b.** dinner   **c.** fashion show   **d.** personal meeting

_____ **9.** Eventually, she did go overseas, where she dazzled Europe's upper class with her _____.
    a. dancing   **b.** social graces   **c.** main courses   **d.** smile

_____ **10.** Margaret Brown's family took a(n) _____ approach to the made-up tales.
    a. hands-off   **b.** defensive   **c.** unusual   **d.** irritated

Indicate whether the statements below are TRUE or FALSE according to the passage.

_____ **1.** Kristen Iversen recently published a book that tells the true story of Margaret Brown.

_____ **2.** Fowler and Bancroft created the legend of Molly Brown to embarrass the Brown family.

_____ **3.** The real Margaret Brown was a sophisticated socialite who was well received in many circles.

FINISH THE THOUGHT

Complete each sentence so that it shows the meaning of the italicized word.

1. She showed her *élan* when _____

_____

2. Because the government believed in a *laissez faire* policy, _____

_____

WRITE THE DERIVATIVE

Complete the sentence by writing the correct form of the word shown in parentheses. You may not need to change the form that is given.

_____ **1.** To demand recognition of their grievances, the students carried out a temporary _____ by staging a sit-in in the college president's office. (*coup d'état*)

_____ 2. John's _____ performance revealed that he had a lot of work ahead if he hoped to earn a seat in the orchestra. (*dilettante*)

_____ 3. The appetizers were tasty, but I couldn't wait to try the beef Wellington, which was one of the restaurant's best _____. (*entrée*)

_____ 4. The rooms in many bed-and-breakfast inns feature sweet-smelling _____. (*potpourri*)

_____ 5. Effective public speakers have a certain _____ that makes them a pleasure to listen to. (*élan*)

_____ 6. The two leaders solved many of their differences during their _____. (*tête-à-tête*)

_____ 7. Thanks to their diplomatic training, the Boltons had the _____ required to host a member of the royal family. (*savoir-faire*)

_____ 8. Talent, good coaching, and _____ are attributes of most championship teams. (*esprit de corps*)

_____ 9. Despite growing unrest, the government pursued a _____ attitude toward the injustices. (*laissez faire*)

_____ 10. It is often thought that "old money" disdains the _____. (*nouveau riche*)

FIND THE EXAMPLE

Choose the answer that best describes the action or situation.

_____ 1. An event that would most likely require a high degree of *savoir-faire*
   a. lunch with friends   **b.** staff meeting   **c.** family reunion   **d.** White House reception

_____ 2. Someone LEAST likely to grant you a *tête-à-tête*
   a. parent   **b.** physician   **c.** pop star   **d.** sibling

_____ 3. A group least likely to develop *esprit de corps*
   a. soldiers   **b.** commuters   **c.** rowing team   **d.** bird watchers

_____ 4. A meal that contains a *potpourri* of ingredients
   a. seafood stew   **b.** steak and potatoes   **c.** roasted turkey   **d.** hot dogs and beans

_____ 5. The person most likely to be considered a *nouveau riche*
   a. laborer   **b.** pauper   **c.** lottery winner   **d.** wealthy heir

_____ 6. Something required for legal *entrée* to a foreign country
   a. warm personality   **b.** passport   **c.** map   **d.** fresh ingredients

_____ 7. Someone most likely to be described as a *dilettante*
   a. leading expert   **b.** virtuoso   **c.** amateur actor   **d.** master chef

_____ 8. A situation it might be best to treat with a *laissez faire* attitude
   a. two friends arguing   **b.** an important test   **c.** an interview   **d.** a new job

_____ 9. How a dictator would likely feel if citizens staged a successful *coup d'état*
   a. entertained   **b.** threatened   **c.** enriched   **d.** content

_____ 10. A job that would be the LEAST likely to require *élan*
   a. maitre d'   **b.** fashion model   **c.** baggage handler   **d.** actor

Words About Art

WORD LIST

| abstract | avant-garde | eclectic | expressionism | grotesque |
| hackneyed | perspective | representational | surrealistic | verisimilitude |

The words in this lesson relate to the visual arts and are used to describe styles, techniques, or time periods when a particular style of art was in fashion. As you read through the definitions and sample sentences, notice that some words can also apply to situations outside of the art world.

1. **abstract** (ăb-străkt´, ăb´-străkt) from Latin *ab-*, "away from" + *trahere*, "to draw"
   a. *adjective* Made with designs or shapes that do not realistically represent people or things
   • The artist dripped paint on canvases to make her **abstract** pieces.
   b. *adjective* Not applied or practical; theoretical
   • Peace seems easy to achieve when it is an **abstract** idea, but it can be hard to achieve in reality.
   c. *noun* (ăb´-străkt) A statement or summary of the important points of a text
   • Please submit an **abstract** of your paper for the journal.

   abstraction *noun* Until you put your theory into practice, it is nothing but an **abstraction.**

abstract

Notice that the adjective form of *abstract* has two acceptable pronunciations, but the noun form has only one.

2. **avant-garde** (ä´vänt-gärd´) from Old French *avant*, "before" + *garder*, "to guard"
   a. *noun* A group active in the invention of new techniques in a given field, especially the arts
   • Painter Pablo Picasso, member of the **avant-garde**, was a founder of the artistic movement called *cubism*.
   b. *adjective* Relating to an innovative group, especially one in the arts
   • Actors in the **avant-garde** play spoke in nonsensical languages.

3. **eclectic** (ĭ-klĕk´tĭk) *adjective* from Greek *eklektikos*, "selective"
   Employing elements from a variety of sources, systems, or styles
   • The art museum's **eclectic** collection included Greek statues, Renaissance oil paintings, and modern video presentations.

4. **expressionism** (ĭk-sprĕsh´ə-nĭz´ĕm) *noun* from Latin *ex-*, "out of" + *premere*, "to press"
   An early twentieth-century art movement that emphasized the artist's personal, subjective expression of inner experiences
   • Paintings done in the style of **expressionism** often have subjects with exaggerated and distorted appearances.

   expressionist *noun* The **expressionist** portrayed his own feelings of helplessness by painting people who were falling in space.

   expressionistic or **expressionist** *adjective* The **expressionistic** painting conveyed anger through bold red streaks across the canvas.

The adjective *expressionist* is generally used to refer to a painter or work, especially one that was part of the original art movement, whereas *expressionistic* refers to the style of an individual artist or work.

5. **grotesque** (grō-těsk´) *adjective* from Italian *grotta*, "grotto; cave"
Outlandish or bizarre; distorted or monstrous
   • The paintings of Hieronymus Bosch, a fifteenth-century Flemish artist, show **grotesque** creatures floating in visually disturbing spaces.

   grotesqueness *noun* The small child was shocked by the **grotesqueness** of her reflection in the fun-house mirror.

Grotesque is also a noun that refers to a style of art that depicts fanciful combinations of natural forms and monstrous figures.

6. **hackneyed** (hăk´nēd) *adjective*
Overfamiliar through overuse; trite
   • The artistic style was imitated so often that it became **hackneyed.**

7. **perspective** (pər-spĕk´tĭv) *noun* from Latin *per-*, "thoroughly" + *specere*, "to look; to see"
   a. A particular view or outlook, either physical or mental
      • Lee could not understand his father's **perspective** on the need for an early curfew.
   b. The technique of representing three dimensions on a two-dimensional surface
      • The student practiced **perspective** by sketching a road that narrowed and finally disappeared at the horizon.

8. **representational** (rĕp´rĭ-zĕn-tā´shə-nəl) *adjective* from Latin *re-*, "again; anew" + *praesentare* "to present"
Relating to realistic depiction in the visual arts
   • Portraits are almost always examples of **representational** art.

Abstract and representational could be considered opposites.

9. **surrealistic** (sə-rē´ə-lĭs´tĭk) *adjective* from French *sur-*, "beyond," + *réalité*, "reality"
   a. Referring to a twentieth-century artistic movement that produced fantastic imagery and odd combinations of subject matter
      • Salvador Dali's **surrealistic** work *The Persistence of Memory* (1931) depicts several melting clocks.
   b. Having an oddly dreamlike or unreal quality
      • I keep having the same **surrealistic** dream in which my teacher grows wings and flies out the classroom window.

   surrealist *noun* Many **surrealists** sought to portray spontaneity uninhibited by reason.

   surrealism *noun* Some say that **surrealism** was sparked by Sigmund Freud's explorations of the human subconscious.

Surreal, a word derived from the word surrealism, means the same thing as the lesson word surrealistic.

10. **verisimilitude** (věr´ə-sĭ-mĭl´ĭ-tōōd´) *noun* from Latin *verus*, "true" + *similis*, "similar"
The quality of appearing to be true or real
   • Especially when compared with abstract art, a photograph has a high degree of **verisimilitude.**

WORD ENRICHMENT

Horses and hackneyed

Hackney once referred to a part of London where special horses that pulled taxis were raised. These horses soon "wore out," hence the current meaning of *hackneyed*.

WRITE THE CORRECT WORD

Write the correct word in the space next to each definition. Use each word only once.

_____ **1.** bizarre or distorted   _____ **6.** trite; overused

_____ **2.** oddly dreamlike   _____ **7.** a particular outlook

_____ **3.** realness of appearance   _____ **8.** using a variety of elements

_____ **4.** realistically depicted   _____ **9.** theoretical

_____ **5.** art style emphasizing inner   _____ **10.** innovative group, especially
          experiences   in the arts

COMPLETE THE SENTENCE

Write the letter for the word that best completes each sentence.

_____ **1.** My _____ music collection includes hip-hop, blues, reggae, and jazz.
    a. abstract   **b.** surrealistic   **c.** representational   **d.** eclectic

_____ **2.** This photographer seems to be able to see things from the _____ of a child.
    a. avant-garde   **b.** perspective   **c.** expressionism   **d.** abstraction

_____ **3.** The _____ bronze statue depicted a human figure with snakes for arms.
    a. grotesque   **b.** representational   **c.** hackneyed   **d.** eclectic

_____ **4.** The _____ fashion designer's dresses were beautiful and interesting—but the
    critics thought that they were too futuristic for the public to accept.
    a. eclectic   **b.** grotesque   **c.** avant-garde   **d.** hackneyed

_____ **5.** I drew a _____ sketch of ocean waves that turned into tongues.
    a. surrealistic   **b.** representational   **c.** hackneyed   **d.** perspective

_____ **6.** The Brazilian artist is famous for her _____ paintings, which consist of solid
    blocks of green and yellow that fill the entire canvas.
    a. hackneyed   **b.** surrealistic   **c.** grotesque   **d.** abstract

_____ **7.** The writer used slang in his dialogue to give the street scene _____.
    a. surrealism   **b.** abstraction   **c.** verisimilitude   **d.** expressionism

_____ **8.** The coach tried to cheer us up after our seventh straight loss, but his words
    sounded _____ and meaningless.
    a. eclectic   **b.** hackneyed   **c.** representational   **d.** avant-garde

_____ **9.** This _____ landscape painting captures the true appearance of Machu Picchu.
    a. representational   **b.** abstract   **c.** avant-garde   **d.** surrealistic

_____ **10.** The class we took on visual _____ gave us windows into the minds of many great
    artists.
    a. verisimilitude   **b.** perspective   **c.** eclecticism   **d.** grotesqueness

Challenge: We were hoping that the new museum's exhibits would offer a fresh _____,
    but most of the featured artwork was derivative and _____.
_____   **a.** abstraction…eclectic   **b.** perspective…hackneyed   **c.** verisimilitude…surrealistic

A Champion of Surrealism

(1) When it first appeared on the art scene, *surrealistic* art shocked the public. With dreamlike and often disturbing images, this unrestrained art form was a hard sell. **(2)** But from one young gallery owner's *perspective*, the surrealists were the great minds of their time.

So at the age of twenty-five, Julien Levy opened a gallery in New York City, dedicated to cutting-edge art. **(3)** It was 1931, a time when people were accustomed to viewing *representational* art such as landscapes and portraits. Levy also sold photography, which was not yet accepted as an art form. Many thought the gallery would fail.

But Levy proved to be a visionary. He mounted New York City's first exhibition of surrealistic art, including Salvador Dali's now-famous dripping clocks. **(4)** Like other surrealistic works, Dali's paintings did not even attempt *verisimilitude*. **(5)** Levy was also the first to show work by master painters Max Ernst, René Magritte, and Frida Kahlo, whose strange and bold works were anything but *hackneyed*. With each show, this innovative style of art became more popular. **(6)** In fact, largely because of Levy, the *avant-garde* art scene began to shift from Paris to New York.

As artists flocked to New York City, Levy's gallery became the place to be. Levy himself became close friends with many artists and even collaborated with a few on film and photography projects. His parties drew the rich, the famous, and the talented. As artist Dorothea Tanning once put it, Levy's gallery "was truly making art history."

(7) Levy's tastes were *eclectic*, as were his gallery shows. Besides masterful paintings and photographs, he displayed painted trash cans and lampshades. He even exhibited cartoons: He was one of the first to show Walt Disney's animation in a gallery.

Experimental art films also debuted at Levy's gallery parties. Film-great Luis Buñuel screened his *Un Chien Andalou* at Levy's. **(8)** The film promptly horrified New York City's polite society with its *grotesque* images, including the famous scene of a woman's eye being sliced with a razor.

As influential people attended Levy's parties, they began to see the value of the work he showed. This helped lay the groundwork for the first American modern-art movement. By the mid-1940s, a daring young artist named Jackson Pollock began splattering paint onto canvases. Another renegade, Arshile Gorky, filled his paintings with curvy, almost balloonlike shapes. **(9)** Other artists, too, began to create highly emotional, *abstract* images.

(10) This was the start of abstract *expressionism*, the movement that made New York City the center of the art world. This new group of artists was greatly inspired by the surrealists. In turn, the expressionists also went on to influence new generations of creative talent. Levy closed his gallery in 1948, but his vision continues to affect the art world even today.

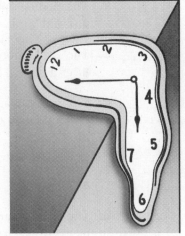

Each sentence below refers to a numbered sentence in the passage. Write the letter of the choice that gives the sentence a meaning that is closest to the original sentence.

_____ **1.** When it first appeared on the art scene, _____ art shocked the public.
    a. overfamiliar   **b.** impractical   **c.** oddly dreamlike   **d.** realistic

_____ **2.** But from one young gallery owner's _____, the surrealists were the great minds of their time.
    a. ambition   **b.** outlook   **c.** creativity   **d.** emotion

_____ **3.** People were accustomed to viewing _____ art.
    a. traditional   **b.** expensive   **c.** distorted   **d.** realistic

_____ **4.** Dali's paintings did not even attempt _____.
    a. emotional force   **b.** mental outlook   **c.** a point of view   **d.** real appearance

_____ **5.** Levy showed work by master painters Max Ernst, René Magritte, and Frida
Kahlo, whose strange and bold works were anything but _____.
a. diverse   b. repugnant   c. bizarre   d. trite

_____ **6.** The _____ art scene began to shift from Paris to New York.
a. cutting-edge   b. bizarre   c. realistic   d. varied

_____ **7.** Levy's tastes were _____, as were his gallery shows.
a. varied   b. overfamiliar   c. earnest   d. realistic

_____ **8.** The film promptly horrified New York's polite society with its _____ images.
a. true-to-life   b. bizarre   c. innovative   d. unoriginal

_____ **9.** Other artists, too, began to create highly emotional, _____ images.
a. amateurish   b. realistic   c. overused   d. unrealistic

_____ **10.** This was the start of abstract _____, the movement that made New York City
the center of the art world.
a. innovation   b. realism   c. subjectivism   d. view

Indicate whether the statements below are TRUE or FALSE according to the passage.

_____ **1.** Surrealistic art was an instant success with the public.

_____ **2.** Levy's inventory in his new gallery was limited to paintings, for he believed that
canvas was the only true medium for art.

_____ **3.** Abstract expressionism came after surrealism.

WRITING EXTENDED RESPONSES

Most of us have specific likes and dislikes when it comes to the visual
arts. In an essay, describe the kind of art that you like. You may include
styles, subjects, specific paintings, or even the kinds of colors you enjoy
the most. Your essay should be three or more paragraphs in length. Use at
least three lesson words in your essay and underline them.

WRITE THE DERIVATIVE

Complete the sentence by writing the correct form of the word shown in
parentheses. You may not need to change the form that is given.

_____ **1.** By featuring Cajun, Caribbean, and Mexican cuisine, our restaurant earned a
reputation for _____ food. *(eclectic)*

_____ **2.** I want to get my mother a birthday card that expresses my love, but most of the
messages in the cards at the store seem _____. *(hackneyed)*

_____ **3.** Stop talking in _____; use concrete examples! *(abstract)*

_____ 4. Reading this book on suffrage gave me a fresh _____ on how hard women struggled to win the right to vote. *(perspective)*

_____ 5. _____ had its heyday back in the 1930s, but the art movement continues to interest people today. *(surrealistic)*

_____ 6. Last night, we saw an _____ opera that included humanoid robots with video screens mounted in their midsections. *(avant-garde)*

_____ 7. His monster costume was so _____ effective that his little sister gasped in fear when he came downstairs. *(grotesque)*

_____ 8. Norman Rockwell is one of my favorite creators of _____ paintings. *(representational)*

_____ 9. The video game, with its realistic landscapes and detailed characters, was a model of _____. *(verisimilitude)*

_____ 10. In 2004, thieves brazenly pulled Edvard Munch's famous _____ painting, *The Scream,* off the wall of an Oslo museum. *(expressionism)*

FIND THE EXAMPLE

Choose the answer that best describes the action or situation.

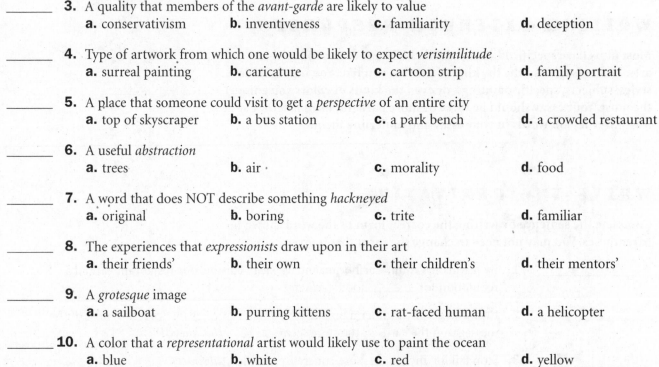

_____ 1. Most likely subject of *surrealistic* painting
   a. levitating piano   **b.** bowl of fruit   **c.** soaring hawk   **d.** Greek battle scene

_____ 2. By definition, an *eclectic* creation
   a. photograph   **b.** portrait   **c.** collage   **d.** song

_____ 3. A quality that members of the *avant-garde* are likely to value
   a. conservativism   **b.** inventiveness   **c.** familiarity   **d.** deception

_____ 4. Type of artwork from which one would be likely to expect *verisimilitude*
   a. surreal painting   **b.** caricature   **c.** cartoon strip   **d.** family portrait

_____ 5. A place that someone could visit to get a *perspective* of an entire city
   a. top of skyscraper   **b.** a bus station   **c.** a park bench   **d.** a crowded restaurant

_____ 6. A useful *abstraction*
   a. trees   **b.** air   **c.** morality   **d.** food

_____ 7. A word that does NOT describe something *hackneyed*
   a. original   **b.** boring   **c.** trite   **d.** familiar

_____ 8. The experiences that *expressionists* draw upon in their art
   a. their friends'   **b.** their own   **c.** their children's   **d.** their mentors'

_____ 9. A *grotesque* image
   a. a sailboat   **b.** purring kittens   **c.** rat-faced human   **d.** a helicopter

_____ 10. A color that a *representational* artist would likely use to paint the ocean
   a. blue   **b.** white   **c.** red   **d.** yellow

Agreeable and Disagreeable

WORD LIST

convivial	ebullience	felicitous	irascible	placid
querulous	sardonic	surly	truculent	unctuous

Smiling, laughing, joking—all these are agreeable activities. Arguing and feeling irritable are disagreeable. The words in this lesson will help you describe agreeable and disagreeable activities, events, people, and places.

1. **convivial** (kən-vĭv´ē-əl) *adjective* from Latin *con-*, "together" + *vivere*, "to live"
   a. Fond of feasting, drinking, and good company; sociable
   • Our **convivial** friend never refused an invitation to a party.
   b. Merry; festive
   • The **convivial** atmosphere at the reunion reminded us of what good times we had in high school.

   conviviality *noun* The lively atmosphere of the outdoor café encouraged **conviviality**.

> The Latin word *convivium* means "banquet."

2. **ebullience** (ĭ-bŏŏl´yəns) *noun* from Latin *ex-*, "up; out" + *bullire*, "to bubble"
   Zestful enthusiasm; exuberance
   • My uncle's natural **ebullience** always raised our spirits.

   ebullient *adjective* We could hear **ebullient** voices as we approached the party, and we couldn't wait to get there.

convivial

3. **felicitous** (fĭ-lĭs´ĭ-təs) *adjective* from Latin *felix-*, "fortunate"
   a. Well chosen, well suited; apt
   • Judging by appearance alone, Danny didn't seem like a **felicitous** choice to play Romeo, but he was wonderful in the part.
   b. Marked by happiness or good fortune
   • Josephine's safe return home from overseas duty was a **felicitous** event celebrated by family and friends.

   felicity *noun* A wedding is an occasion of great **felicity**.

4. **irascible** (ĭ-răs´ə-bəl) *adjective* from Latin *irasci*, "to be angry"
   Prone to outbursts of temper; easily angered
   • "Get that dog off my property," yelled our **irascible** neighbor.

   irascibility *noun* The ornery supervisor was known for his foul temperament and his **irascibility**.

5. **placid** (plăs´ĭd) *adjective* from Latin *placere*, "to please"
   a. Undisturbed by commotion or disorder; calm; not easily upset
   • Immediately after the storm, the lake was **placid** again.
   b. Satisfied; complacent
   • My little brother was a **placid** baby who rarely cried.

> The noun forms of *placid* are *placidity* and *placidness*.

6. querulous (kwĕr´ə-ləs) *adjective* from Latin *queri*, "to complain"
Tending to complain; irritable; expressing a complaint
- I was tired of the customer's **querulous** remarks about the merchandise.

7. sardonic (sär-dŏn´ĭk) *adjective* from Greek *sardonios*, "of scornful laughter"
Scornfully or cynically mocking
- When Mrs. Gilford appeared at the dinner table in her bathrobe and curlers, her husband greeted her with the **sardonic** remark, "My dear, there's no need to dress elegantly on my account."

8. surly (sûr´lē) *adjective* from Middle English *sirly*, "masterful; lordly"
Sullenly ill humored; gruff
- Gerald's **surly** behavior prevented him from being promoted.

surliness *noun* We tried to humor him out of his disagreeable **surliness**.

> *Surly* can also refer to threatening weather.

9. truculent (trŭk´yə-lənt) *adjective* from Latin *trux-*, "fierce"
Disposed to fight; expressing bitter opposition; scathing
- My mother says that my sister's **truculent** behavior is only a phase, but I'm not sure how many more arguments I can stand.

truculence *noun* The leader's **truculence** created a tense, warlike atmosphere with neighboring countries.

10. unctuous (ŭngk´chōō-əs) *adjective* from Latin *unctum*, "ointment"
a. Characterized by affected, exaggerated, or insincere earnestness
- Dickens's character Uriah Heep is noted for his **unctuous** insistence that he is a humble person.
b. Having the quality or characteristics of oil or ointment; slippery
- The **unctuous** frog slipped from my hands.

> To form nouns from the words *querulous* and *unctuous*, simply add the suffix *-ness*.

ANALOGIES

On the answer line, write the letter of the answer that best completes each analogy. Refer to lessons 28–30 if you need help with any of the lesson words.

_____ **1.** *Grotesque is to beautiful as* _____.
    a. *placid is to calm*   **c.** *ebullient is to somber*
    b. *querulous is to complaining*   **d.** *unctuous is to insincere*

_____ **2.** *Verisimilitude is to abstraction as* _____.
    a. *nouveau riche is to wealth*   **c.** *truculence is to anger*
    b. *eclectic is to homogeneous*   **d.** *élan is to style*

_____ **3.** *Savoir-faire is to manners as* _____.
    a. *abstraction is to concrete*   **c.** *entrée is to dessert*
    b. *esprit de corps is to morale*   **d.** *potpourri is to sameness*

_____ **4.** *Truculent is to fight as* _____.
    a. *felicitous is to sorrow*   **c.** *irascible is to complain*
    b. *sardonic is to complimentary*   **d.** *hackneyed is to fresh*

WRITE THE CORRECT WORD

Write the correct word in the space next to each definition. Use each word only once.

_____ **1.** easily angered

_____ **2.** scornfully mocking

_____ **3.** calm; complacent

_____ **4.** anxious to fight

_____ **5.** well suited; apt

_____ **6.** ill humored

_____ **7.** insincere earnestness

_____ **8.** sociable; festive

_____ **9.** irritable; complaining

_____ **10.** exuberance

COMPLETE THE SENTENCE

Write the letter for the word that best completes each sentence.

_____ **1.** "Enjoy life!" might be the motto of a(n) _____ person.
   a. truculent   **b.** convivial   **c.** unctuous   **d.** surly

_____ **2.** My sister-in-law is a(n) _____ person whom I try to avoid whenever she is in
   a bad mood.
   a. irascible   **b.** placid   **c.** felicitous   **d.** ebullient

_____ **3.** My boss had such a _____ disposition that almost every conversation became
   an argument.
   a. truculent   **b.** placid   **c.** convivial   **d.** unctuous

_____ **4.** The best man gave a toast, wishing the newlyweds a(n) _____ life together.
   a. surly   **b.** irascible   **c.** unctuous   **d.** felicitous

_____ **5.** Knowing that I was a novice, the riding teacher gave me the most _____ horse.
   a. truculent   **b.** irascible   **c.** placid   **d.** querulous

_____ **6.** The _____ union leader was in no mood for minor concessions from
   management.
   a. placid   **b.** surly   **c.** convivial   **d.** felicitous

_____ **7.** Most tragic melodramas feature a(n) _____ villain who is a smooth-talking hypocrite.
   a. placid   **b.** ebullient   **c.** unctuous   **d.** convivial

_____ **8.** "Why do we have to do that?" asked Lily in her _____ way.
   a. querulous   **b.** placid   **c.** convivial   **d.** felicitous

_____ **9.** The critic for the *Examiner* was quite _____ in his review, referring to the play
   as a "paragon of mediocrity."
   a. placid   **b.** ebullient   **c.** convivial   **d.** sardonic

_____ **10.** The teacher greeted the kindergarteners with _____ on their first day of school.
   a. irascibility   **b.** ebullience   **c.** surliness   **d.** truculence

Challenge: The Navy captain gave this advice to his sailors before they headed into town:
   "Enjoy the _____ atmosphere, but be careful not to be drawn into arguments
   with any _____ individuals."
_____   **a.** convivial…irascible   **b.** querulous…convivial   **c.** irascible…ebullient

What Makes Us Happy?

Scientists study everything from cures for disease to the size of the universe. One rarely discussed field of science, however, is happiness research. Some lucky scientists get to spend their time figuring out who feels that life is good and why.

(1) The mere mention of this field can bring on *sardonic* responses from those who think the subject is not worthy of being called scientific. But happiness research is well respected and provides much needed information. One use for this research is in the workplace.

(2) To prevent employees from becoming *querulous,* and thus more likely to quit, business managers rely on studies that show what people like and dislike about their jobs. Not all the answers that researchers gather are obvious ones.

For example, people might think that a larger salary makes for a bigger smile. Generally, this is true. **(3)** But researchers found that most workers are even more *ebullient* when they receive a promotion. As it turns out, money alone does not buy happiness. An employee's rank in an organization sometimes matters even more than his or her salary.

Happiness studies can also help shape government policy. For instance, some popular but unhealthy products, such as tobacco, are often taxed highly, both to raise funds and to discourage people from buying them. **(4)** Analyzing thirty years of happiness data in the United States and Canada, economists found surprising results that indicate such taxation often elicits a *felicitous* reaction from those affected by it.

(5) Rather than making people *irascible,* these taxes had the overall effect of making many happier.

The higher prices helped some smokers to kick their bad habit, which made them feel better about themselves, and therefore happier. And many who did not quit smoking felt hopeful that the taxes would help them quit later. So they, too, felt happier.

Other results simply provide insight into where we live. In Australia, surveys of 20,000 people found that those living in the country were happier than those living in the city. **(6)** This may come as no surprise to anyone who has encountered the *surly* behavior of some city dwellers.

But knowing the reasons behind these differences can help people improve their lives. **(7)** Surprisingly, country dwellers did not cite clean air, *placid* lakes, or any aspect of nature as the source of their contentment. **(8)** Instead, among other factors, rural residents reported that their neighbors were more *convivial,* and that the friendships they formed made them more content.

(9) In contrast, city living was shown to cause stress, and therefore unhappiness, perhaps due to the more frequent confrontations with *truculent* strangers. A decreased sense of safety was also cited. This indicates that increasing safety measures and opportunities to meet neighbors might increase urbanites' happiness.

Rankings of happiness levels in different countries are also enlightening. Based on studies from 1990 to 2000, the five happiest nations are Denmark, Malta, Switzerland, Iceland, and Ireland. The United States fell somewhere in the middle of the ninety-nation list.

(10) This, however, is no reason for the residents of the cheeriest countries to *unctuously* send their condolences to the rest of us. Other studies indicate that, within countries, happiness varies widely for many reasons. Happy and unhappy people can be found everywhere.

Each sentence below refers to a numbered sentence in the passage. Write the letter of the choice that gives the sentence a meaning that is closest to the original sentence.

_____ **1.** Just the mention of this field can bring on _____ responses from those who think the subject is not scientific.
    a. unexpected   **b.** angry   **c.** pleasant   **d.** mocking

_____ **2.** To prevent employees from becoming _____, business managers rely on studies showing what people like and dislike about their jobs.
    a. curious   **b.** irritable   **c.** enthusiastic   **d.** peaceful

_____ **3.** But most workers are even more _____ when they receive a promotion.
    a. exuberant   **b.** irritable   **c.** suspicious   **d.** friendly

_____ **4.** Economists have found striking results that indicate such taxation often elicits a(n) _____ reaction from those affected by it.
    a. unjust   **b.** cynical   **c.** happy   **d.** slippery

_____ **5.** Rather than making people _____, these taxes had the overall effect of making them happier.
    a. more friendly   **b.** more suspicious   **c.** easily angered   **d.** more unhealthy

_____ **6.** This may come as no surprise to those who have encountered the _____ behavior of some city dwellers.
    a. gruff   **b.** friendly   **c.** calm   **d.** unpredictable

_____ **7.** Surprisingly, country dwellers did not cite clean air, _____ lakes, or any aspect of nature as the source of their contentment.
    a. choppy   **b.** windswept   **c.** calm   **d.** festive

_____ **8.** Rural residents reported that their neighbors were more _____.
    a. irritated   **b.** enthusiastic   **c.** sociable   **d.** argumentative

_____ **9.** City living was shown to cause stress, perhaps due to the more frequent confrontations with _____ strangers.
    a. combative   **b.** friendly   **c.** welcoming   **d.** cynical

_____ **10.** This is no reason for the residents of the cheeriest countries to _____ send their condolences to the rest of us.
    a. scornfully   **b.** insincerely   **c.** complacently   **d.** nastily

Indicate whether the statements below are TRUE or FALSE according to the passage.

_____ **1.** Happiness research is well respected and can provide valuable information.

_____ **2.** Most workers would prefer a raise rather than a promotion.

_____ **3.** The study showed that the tediousness of country life created less happiness than a fast-paced urban life.

FINISH THE THOUGHT

Complete each sentence so that it shows the meaning of the italicized word.

1. At the *convivial* gathering _____

_____

2. His *sardonic* comment was _____

_____

WRITE THE DERIVATIVE

Complete the sentence by writing the correct form of the word shown in parentheses. You may not need to change the form that is given.

_____ **1.** The _____ of the plumber's manner intimidated me. *(surly)*

_____ **2.** The writhing fish's _____ made it difficult to hold. *(unctuous)*

_____ 3. The _____ of the early morning was interrupted by sanitation workers emptying trash cans in the alley. (*placid*)

_____ 4. Comedians are known for their _____ insights on modern life. (*sardonic*)

_____ 5. Maria's _____ demeanor was infectious. (*ebullience*)

_____ 6. Displaying _____ in a debate is considered poor form. (*truculent*)

_____ 7. The Smith's _____ made them excellent neighbors. (*convivial*)

_____ 8. The birth of their first child was a moment of great _____. (*felicitous*)

_____ 9. Many great actors have earned Oscars portraying disagreeable characters known for their foul temperaments and _____. (*irascible*)

_____ 10. Sometimes a _____ demeanor is a sign of deep unhappiness. (*querulous*)

FIND THE EXAMPLE

Choose the answer that best describes the action or situation.

_____ 1. How you would likely feel if someone described you in a *sardonic* manner
  a. hurt and angry   **b.** gratified   **c.** enriched   **d.** happy and calm

_____ 2. How you would probably feel if you encountered some *surly* strangers
  a. calm   **b.** joyful   **c.** anxious   **d.** sociable

_____ 3. The person with whom you would be most likely to have a *felicitous* encounter
  a. a tax collector   **b.** an archrival   **c.** a rude neighbor   **d.** a long-lost friend

_____ 4. A gathering most likely to have a *convivial* atmosphere
  a. family reunion   **b.** math class   **c.** business meeting   **d.** political debate

_____ 5. An occasion for *ebullience*
  a. making toast   **b.** winning an award   **c.** swimming laps   **d.** running laps

_____ 6. The character in a detective show most likely to display *unctuous* behavior
  a. elderly woman   **b.** detective   **c.** swindler   **d.** store clerk

_____ 7. The person likely to spend the most time in a *placid* environment
  a. mother of toddlers   **b.** soccer coach   **c.** racecar driver   **d.** librarian

_____ 8. What a *truculent* person is most likely to say
  a. No, I won't go!   **b.** Thank you.   **c.** May I help you?   **d.** You did a great job.

_____ 9. A job where *irascible* behavior might be considered an asset
  a. therapist   **b.** drill sergeant   **c.** sales clerk   **d.** diplomat

_____ 10. Section of a store where you would most likely find *querulous* people
  a. housewares   **b.** produce section   **c.** automotive   **d.** returns department

Prefixes, Roots, and Suffixes

The Word Elements *hyper-, hypo-,* and *-dyn-*

The three word elements in this feature refer to some aspect of power or force. *Hyper-,* from the Greek *huper,* means "over; above; beyond; excessive." *Hypo-* means "below; beneath; or less than normal," and comes from the Greek *hupo.* The root *dyn* means "power" and comes from the Greek *dunamis.*

Element	Type	Meaning	Word	Word Meaning
hyper-	prefix	over; excessive	hyperactive	having excessive activity
hypo-	prefix	below; less than normal	hypoallergenic	having decreased tendency to provoke allergies
-dyn-	root	powerful	dynamic	forceful, vigorous

Practice

You can combine the use of context clues with your knowledge of these word elements to make intelligent guesses about word meanings. Each of the sentences below contains a word formed with the word element *hyper-, hypo-,* or *dyn.* Read the sentences and try to infer what the word in italics means. Then check your definition with the one you find in the dictionary, remembering to choose the definition that best fits in the sentence.

1. The medicine was delivered through an injection by *hypodermic* needle.

   My definition _____

   Dictionary definition _____

2. Some people are *hypersensitive* to social pressures during their early teenage years.

   My definition _____

   Dictionary definition _____

3. That *dynamo* of a CEO turned a losing venture into a profitable business.

   My definition _____

   Dictionary definition _____

4. You don't have to resort to *hyperbole* like "I am dead on my feet" to describe how you feel.

   My definition _____

   Dictionary definition _____

5. The man who was rescued from the blizzard was suffering from *hypothermia.*

   My definition _____

   Dictionary definition _____

6. He was so nervous that he began twitching and *hyperventilating*.

My definition _____

Dictionary definition _____

7. Engineers often use *dynamometers*.

My definition _____

Dictionary definition _____

8. Our dog was suffering from *hypoxia* after being stuck in the small box all night.

My definition _____

Dictionary definition _____

Review Word Elements

Reviewing word elements helps you to remember them and use them in your reading. Below, write the meaning of the word elements you have studied.

Word	Word Element	Type of Element	Meaning of Word Element
benefactor	*bene-*	prefix	_____
epidemic	*-dem-*	root	_____
soliloquy	*-loq-*	root	_____
veritable	*-ver-*	root	_____
nominal	*-nom-*	root	_____
eulogy	*eu-*	prefix	_____
incorporate	*-corp-*	root	_____
untenable	*-ten-*	root	_____
capital	*-cap-*	root	_____
suspension	*-pend-*	root	_____
annuity	*-ann-*	root	_____
equanimity	*-anim-*	root	_____
edict	*-dict-*	root	_____
anteroom	*ante-*	prefix	_____
anonymous	*-onym-*	root	_____
archenemy	*arch-*	prefix	_____
malaise	*mal-*	prefix	_____
democracy	*-cracy*	suffix	_____

LESSON 1	LESSON 1	LESSON 1	LESSON 1	LESSON 1
cognate	inflection	orthography	paradigm	philology
phonology	rejoinder	rhetoric	succinct	syntax
belie	clandestine	disingenuous	dissemble	forthright
nefarious	perfidious	probity	scrupulous	spurious
concomitant	eon	extant	hiatus	inure
irrevocable	millennium	perpetuity	pristine	transience

LESSON 1 cognate
LESSON 1 inflection
LESSON 1 orthography
LESSON 1 paradigm
LESSON 1 philology

LESSON 1 phonology
LESSON 1 rejoinder
LESSON 1 rhetoric
LESSON 1 succinct
LESSON 1 syntax

LESSON 2 belie
LESSON 2 clandestine
LESSON 2 disingenuous
LESSON 2 dissemble
LESSON 2 forthright

LESSON 2 nefarious
LESSON 2 perfidious
LESSON 2 probity
LESSON 2 scrupulous
LESSON 2 spurious

LESSON 3 concomitant
LESSON 3 eon
LESSON 3 extant
LESSON 3 hiatus
LESSON 3 inure

LESSON 3 irrevocable
LESSON 3 millennium
LESSON 3 perpetuity
LESSON 3 pristine
LESSON 3 transience

cognate (kŏg´nāt´) *n.* A word related to another word in a different language © Great Source	inflection (ĭn-flĕk´shən) *n.* A change in the form of a word © Great Source	orthography (ôr-thŏg´rə-fē) *n.* The study of a language's writing or spelling system © Great Source	paradigm (păr´ə-dīm´) *n.* A model for a way of viewing things © Great Source	philology (fĭ-lŏl´ə-jē) *n.* Study of the history of language © Great Source
phonology (fə-nŏl´ə-jē) *n.* The sound system of a language © Great Source	rejoinder (rĭ-join´dər) *n.* An answer to a reply; witty response © Great Source	rhetoric (rĕt´ər-ĭk) *n.* The study of using language effectively © Great Source	succinct (sək-sĭngkt´) *adj.* Clear and precise; using few words © Great Source	syntax (sĭn´tăks´) *n.* How words are arranged © Great Source
belie (bĭ-lī´) *v.* To misrepresent © Great Source	clandestine (klăn-dĕs´tĭn) *adj.* Done in secret © Great Source	disingenuous (dĭs´ĭn-jĕn´yōō-əs) *adj.* Not telling the whole truth © Great Source	dissemble (dĭ-sĕm´bəl) *v.* To hide one's feelings or motives behind a false appearance © Great Source	forthright (fôrth´rīt´) *adj.* Direct, honest © Great Source
nefarious (nə-fâr´ē-əs) *adj.* Infamous © Great Source	perfidious (pər-fĭd´ē-əs) *adj.* Treacherous © Great Source	probity (prō´bĭ-tē) *n.* Total integrity; uprightness © Great Source	scrupulous (skrōō´pyə-ləs) *adj.* Conscientious and exact © Great Source	spurious (spyōōr´ē-əs) *adj.* Fake; not authentic © Great Source
concomitant (kən-kŏm´ĭ-tənt) *adj.* Occurring simultaneously © Great Source	eon (ē´ŏn´) *n.* Longest division of geologic time © Great Source	extant (ĕk´stənt) *adj.* Still in existence © Great Source	hiatus (hī-ā´təs) *n.* Gap in space, time, or continuity © Great Source	inure (ĭn-yŏŏr´) *v.* Accustom to hardship © Great Source
irrevocable (ĭ-rĕv´ə-kə-bəl) *adj.* Irreversible © Great Source	millennium (mə-lĕn´ē-əm) *n.* One thousand years © Great Source	perpetuity (pûr´pĭ-tōō´ĭ-tē) *n.* An eternity © Great Source	pristine (prĭs´tēn´) *adj.* Unspoiled © Great Source	transience (trăn´zē-əns) *n.* Brief existence © Great Source

LESSON 4 buffoon	LESSON 4 farce	LESSON 4 irony
LESSON 4 levity	LESSON 4 parody	LESSON 4 raillery
LESSON 5 adumbrate	LESSON 5 arcane	LESSON 5 covert
LESSON 5 impenetrable	LESSON 5 impervious	LESSON 5 limpid
LESSON 6 adjunct	LESSON 6 amalgamate	LESSON 6 compatriot
LESSON 6 diffuse	LESSON 6 diverge	LESSON 6 parity

LESSON 4 jocular	LESSON 4 lampoon	
LESSON 4 regale	LESSON 4 satirical	
LESSON 5 educe	LESSON 5 fathom	
LESSON 5 manifest	LESSON 5 nebulous	
LESSON 6 conclave	LESSON 6 contiguous	
LESSON 6 synergy	LESSON 6 transcend	

buffoon (bə-fōōn´) *n.* A clown or jester	**farce** (färs) *n.* An exaggerated comic play	**irony** (ī´rə-nē) *n.* Deliberate use of words to convey the opposite of their literal meaning	**jocular** (jŏk´yə-lər) *adj.* Characterized by a joking manner	**lampoon** (lăm-pōōn´) *n.* A written piece that pokes fun or ridicules
© Great Source	© Great Source	© Great Source	© Great Source	© Great Source
levity (lĕv´ĭ-tē) *n.* A light and humorous manner	**parody** (păr´ə-dē) *n.* A comic imitation that exaggerates	**raillery** (rā´lə-rē) *n.* Good-natured teasing	**regale** (rĭ-gāl´) *v.* To entertain	**satirical** (sə-tĭr´ĭ-kəl) *adj.* Humorously critical; using sarcasm
© Great Source	© Great Source	© Great Source	© Great Source	© Great Source
adumbrate (ăd´əm-brāt´) *v.* To describe vaguely	**arcane** (är-kān´) *adj.* Mysterious	**covert** (kō´vərt) *adj.* Hidden or concealed	**educe** (ĭ-dōōs´) *v.* To draw out	**fathom** (făth´əm) *v.* To comprehend
© Great Source	© Great Source	© Great Source	© Great Source	© Great Source
impenetrable (ĭm-pĕn´ĭ-trə-bəl) *adj.* Impossible to break through	**impervious** (ĭm-pûr´vē-əs) *adj.* Incapable of being affected	**limpid** (lĭm´pĭd) *adj.* Calm and serene	**manifest** (măn´ə-fĕst´) *v.* To show or demonstrate plainly; to reveal	**nebulous** (nĕb´yə-ləs) *adj.* Cloudy; hazy
© Great Source	© Great Source	© Great Source	© Great Source	© Great Source
adjunct (ăj´ŭngkt´) *n.* Attached in a subordinate position	**amalgamate** (ə-măl´gə-māt´) *v.* To unite	**compatriot** (kəm-pā´trē-ət) *n.* A colleague	**conclave** (kŏn´klāv´) *n.* A secret meeting	**contiguous** (kən-tĭg´yōō-əs) *adj.* Adjacent
© Great Source	© Great Source	© Great Source	© Great Source	© Great Source
diffuse (dĭ-fyōōs´) *adj.* Widely spread or scattered	**diverge** (dĭ-vûrj´) *v.* To branch out	**parity** (păr´ĭ-tē) *n.* Equality	**synergy** (sĭn´ər-jē) *n.* The interaction of merged forces resulting in greater effect	**transcend** (trăn-sĕnd´) *v.* To surpass
© Great Source	© Great Source	© Great Source	© Great Source	© Great Source

LESSON 7	axiomatic
LESSON 7	definitive
LESSON 7	dialectic
LESSON 7	empirical
LESSON 7	presuppose
LESSON 7	rationalize
LESSON 7	rebuttal
LESSON 7	repudiate
LESSON 7	tenuous
LESSON 7	verifiable
LESSON 8	bedlam
LESSON 8	bowdlerize
LESSON 8	chauvinism
LESSON 8	draconian
LESSON 8	martinet
LESSON 8	maudlin
LESSON 8	mesmerize
LESSON 8	silhouette
LESSON 8	stentorian
LESSON 8	titanic
LESSON 9	exalt
LESSON 9	exhort
LESSON 9	garrulous
LESSON 9	gist
LESSON 9	histrionic
LESSON 9	laconic
LESSON 9	peremptory
LESSON 9	polemic
LESSON 9	vivacious
LESSON 9	vociferous

axiomatic
(ăk´sē-ə-măt´ĭk) *adj.*
Self-evident

definitive
(dĭ-fĭn´ĭ-tĭv) *adj.*
Authoritative and complete

dialectic
(dī´ə-lĕk´tĭk) *n.*
The exchange of opposing logical arguments

empirical
(ĕm-pîr´ĭ-kəl) *adj.*
Relying on observation

presuppose
(prē´sə-pōz´) *v.*
To assume beforehand

rationalize
(răsh´ə-nə-līz´) *v.*
To explain away with self-satisfying but incorrect reasons

rebuttal
(rĭ-bŭt´l) *n.*
Disproving an argument

repudiate
(rĭ-pyōō´dē-āt´) *v.*
To reject the validity of

tenuous
(tĕn´yōō-əs) *adj.*
Flimsy

verifiable
(vĕr´ə-fī´ə-bəl) *adj.*
Provable

bedlam
(bĕd´ləm) *n.*
Noisy confusion

bowdlerize
(bōd´lə-rīz´) *v.*
To abridge and simplify a work

chauvinism
(shō´və-nĭz´əm) *n.*
A prejudiced belief in the superiority of one's group

draconian
(drā-kō´nē-ən) *adj.*
Very severe

martinet
(mär´tn-ĕt´) *n.*
A rigid disciplinarian

maudlin
(môd´lĭn) *adj.*
Overly sentimental

mesmerize
(mĕz´mə-rīz´) *v.*
To enthrall

silhouette
(sĭl´ōō-ĕt´) *n.*
An outline against a dark background

stentorian
(stĕn-tôr´ē-ən) *adj.*
Extremely loud

titanic
(tī-tăn´ĭk) *adj.*
Enormous

exalt
(ĭg-zôlt´) *v.*
To glorify or praise

exhort
(ĭg-zôrt´) *v.*
To appeal strongly

garrulous
(găr´ə-ləs) *adj.*
Wordy and rambling

gist
(jĭst) *n.*
The essence; the central idea

histrionic
(hĭs´trē-ŏn´ĭk) *adj.*
Excessively dramatic

laconic
(lə-kŏn´ĭk) *adj.*
Terse

peremptory
(pə-rĕmp´tə-rē) *adj.*
Not allowing refusal

polemic
(pə-lĕm´ĭk) *n.*
A controversial argument

vivacious
(vĭ-vā´shəs) *adj.*
Lively

vociferous
(vō-sĭf´ər-əs) *adj.*
Offensively loud or forceful

LESSON 10	LESSON 10	LESSON 10	LESSON 10	LESSON 10
atrophy	debilitate	livid	moribund	noxious
LESSON 10	**LESSON 10**	**LESSON 10**	**LESSON 10**	**LESSON 10**
pestilence	prostrate	salubrious	scourge	unscathed
LESSON 11	**LESSON 11**	**LESSON 11**	**LESSON 11**	**LESSON 11**
audacious	contumacy	dour	éclat	indefatigable
LESSON 11	**LESSON 11**	**LESSON 11**	**LESSON 11**	**LESSON 11**
irresolute	obdurate	obsequious	pertinacity	stoic
LESSON 12	**LESSON 12**	**LESSON 12**	**LESSON 12**	**LESSON 12**
austere	avarice	florid	insatiable	inundate
LESSON 12	**LESSON 12**	**LESSON 12**	**LESSON 12**	**LESSON 12**
myriad	parsimony	prodigal	replete	voluminous

atrophy
(ăt´rə-fē) v.
To wither away

© Great Source

debilitate
(dĭ-bĭl´ĭ-tāt´) v.
To sap the energy of

© Great Source

livid
(lĭv´ĭd) adj.
Black-and-blue

© Great Source

moribund
(môr´ə-bŭnd´) adj.
About to die

© Great Source

noxious
(nŏk´shəs) adj.
Poisonous

© Great Source

---

pestilence
(pĕs´ta-ləns) n.
A usually fatal
epidemic disease

© Great Source

prostrate
(prŏs´trāt´) v.
To reduce to
extreme weakness

© Great Source

salubrious
(sə-loo´brē-əs) adj.
Favorable to
good health

© Great Source

scourge
(skûrj) n.
A cause of great
devastation

© Great Source

unscathed
(ŭn-skāthd´) adj.
Completely uninjured

© Great Source

---

audacious
(ô-dā´shəs) adj.
Daring, fearless

© Great Source

contumacy
(kŏn´too-mə-sē) n.
A stubborn rebelliousness

© Great Source

dour
(door) adj.
Marked by harshness,
sternness, or ill temper

© Great Source

éclat
(ā-klä´) n.
Brilliant success

© Great Source

indefatigable
(ĭn´dĭ-făt´ĭ-gə-bəl) adj.
Tireless

© Great Source

---

irresolute
(ĭ-rĕz´ə-loot´) adj.
Undecided; wavering

© Great Source

obdurate
(ŏb´doo-rĭt) adj.
Hardhearted

© Great Source

obsequious
(ŏb-sē´kwē-əs) adj.
Fawning

© Great Source

pertinacity
(pûr´tn-ăs´ĭ-tē) n.
Stubbornness

© Great Source

stoic
(stō´ĭk) adj.
Unaffected by feelings

© Great Source

---

austere
(ô-stîr´) adj.
Severe or stern; somber

© Great Source

avarice
(ăv´ə-rĭs) n.
Extreme greed

© Great Source

florid
(flôr´ĭd) adj.
Flushed with rosy color

© Great Source

insatiable
(ĭn-sā´shə-bəl) adj.
Impossible to satisfy

© Great Source

inundate
(ĭn´ŭn-dāt´) v.
To overwhelm

© Great Source

---

myriad
(mĭr´ē-əd) adj.
Referring to a large but
undetermined number

© Great Source

parsimony
(pär´sə-mō´nē) n.
Extreme stinginess

© Great Source

prodigal
(prŏd´ĭ-gəl) adj.
Wastefully extravagant

© Great Source

replete
(rĭ-plēt´) adj.
Plentiful; abounding

© Great Source

voluminous
(və-loo´mə-nəs) adj.
Having great volume,
size, or number

© Great Source

LESSON 13 impute	LESSON 13 contrite	LESSON 13 clemency	LESSON 13 bilk	LESSON 13 abscond
LESSON 13 vindicate	LESSON 13 restitution	LESSON 13 reprehensible	LESSON 13 redress	LESSON 13 iniquity
LESSON 14 cryptic	LESSON 14 conundrum	LESSON 14 construe	LESSON 14 confound	LESSON 14 adduce
LESSON 14 rudimentary	LESSON 14 perspicacity	LESSON 14 patent	LESSON 14 paradox	LESSON 14 equivocate
LESSON 15 incongruous	LESSON 15 endemic	LESSON 15 eccentricity	LESSON 15 anomaly	LESSON 15 aberrant
LESSON 15 unwonted	LESSON 15 ubiquitous	LESSON 15 paragon	LESSON 15 outlandish	LESSON 15 mundane

abscond (ăb-skŏnd´) *v.*
To leave quickly and secretly, often to avoid arrest
© Great Source

bilk (bĭlk) *v.*
To swindle money
© Great Source

clemency (klĕm´ən-sē) *n.*
Mercy
© Great Source

contrite (kən-trīt´) *adj.*
Regretful
© Great Source

impute (ĭm-pyōōt´) *v.*
To attribute the fault or responsibility to
© Great Source

iniquity (ĭ-nĭk´wĭ-tē) *n.*
Wickedness
© Great Source

redress (rĭ-drĕs´) *v.*
To right a wrong
© Great Source

reprehensible (rĕp´rĭ-hĕn´sə-bəl) *adj.*
Deserving of blame
© Great Source

restitution (rĕs´tĭ-tōō´shən) *n.*
Compensation for a loss
© Great Source

vindicate (vĭn´dĭ-kāt´) *v.*
To clear of blame
© Great Source

adduce (ə-dōōs´) *v.*
To cite an example or means of proof in an argument
© Great Source

confound (kən-found´) *v.*
To mix up
© Great Source

construe (kən-strōō´) *v.*
To interpret
© Great Source

conundrum (kə-nŭn´drəm) *n.*
A self-contradictory problem; a dilemma
© Great Source

cryptic (krĭp´tĭk) *adj.*
Having hidden meaning
© Great Source

equivocate (ĭ-kwĭv´ə-kāt´) *v.*
To use evasive language to mislead
© Great Source

paradox (păr´ə-dŏks´) *n.*
Something with contradictory aspects
© Great Source

patent (păt´nt) *adj.*
Obvious; plain
© Great Source

perspicacity (pûr´spĭ-kăs´ĭ-tē) *n.*
Sharpness; acuteness of understanding
© Great Source

rudimentary (rōō´də-mĕn´tə-rē) *adj.*
Elementary; basic
© Great Source

aberrant (ăb´ər-ənt) *adj.*
Deviating from the expected course
© Great Source

anomaly (ə-nŏm´ə-lē) *n.*
Something departing from normal form
© Great Source

eccentricity (ĕk´sĕn-trĭs´ĭ-tē) *n.*
The quality of straying from what is conventional
© Great Source

endemic (ĕn-dĕm´ĭk) *adj.*
Common in or unique to a certain location or population
© Great Source

incongruous (ĭn-kŏng´grōō-əs) *adj.*
Lacking in harmony
© Great Source

mundane (mŭn-dān´) *adj.*
Commonplace
© Great Source

outlandish (out-lăn´dĭsh) *adj.*
Strikingly bizarre
© Great Source

paragon (-păr´ə-gŏn´) *n.*
Model of perfection
© Great Source

ubiquitous (yōō-bĭk´wĭ-təs) *adj.*
Seeming to be everywhere at the same time
© Great Source

unwonted (ŭn-wŏn´tĭd) *adj.*
Not habitual or ordinary; unusual
© Great Source

LESSON 16 **caustic**	LESSON 16 **pinnacle**	LESSON 17 **deplore**	LESSON 17 **mercurial**	LESSON 18 **commodious**	LESSON 18 **lofty**
LESSON 16 **deleterious**	LESSON 16 **raze**	LESSON 17 **disconsolate**	LESSON 17 **revel**	LESSON 18 **finite**	LESSON 18 **minuscule**
LESSON 16 **despoil**	LESSON 16 **stultify**	LESSON 17 **domineering**	LESSON 17 **sanguine**	LESSON 18 **gamut**	LESSON 18 **picayune**
LESSON 16 **effectual**	LESSON 16 **surmount**	LESSON 17 **halcyon**	LESSON 17 **tirade**	LESSON 18 **incalculable**	LESSON 18 **vestige**
LESSON 16 **obviate**	LESSON 16 **wrest**	LESSON 17 **lachrymose**	LESSON 17 **vex**	LESSON 18 **iota**	LESSON 18 **wane**

caustic	(kô′stĭk) *adj.*	Corrosive	© Great Source
deleterious	(dĕl′ĭ-tîr′ē-əs) *adj.*	Harmful	© Great Source
despoil	(dĭ-spoil′) *v.*	To plunder	© Great Source
effectual	(ĭ-fĕk′chōo-əl) *adj.*	Fully adequate; effective	© Great Source
obviate	(ŏb′vē-āt′) *v.*	To make unnecessary	© Great Source
pinnacle	(pĭn′ə-kəl) *n.*	Peak; most successful point	© Great Source
raze	(rāz) *v.*	To level to the ground	© Great Source
stultify	(stŭl′tə-fī′) *v.*	To make useless or ineffective	© Great Source
surmount	(sər-mount′) *v.*	To overcome	© Great Source
wrest	(rĕst) *v.*	To obtain by force or great effort	© Great Source
deplore	(dĭ-plôr′) *v.*	To condemn	© Great Source
disconsolate	(dĭs-kŏn′sə-lĭt) *adj.*	Hopelessly dejected or sad	© Great Source
domineering	(dŏm′ə-nîr′ĭng) *adj.*	Tyrannical	© Great Source
halcyon	(hăl′sē-ən) *adj.*	Peaceful	© Great Source
lachrymose	(lăk′rə-mōs′) *adj.*	Tearful	© Great Source
mercurial	(mər-kyŏor′ē-əl) *adj.*	Quick and changeable temperament; volatile	© Great Source
revel	(rĕv′əl) *v.*	To make merry; to celebrate	© Great Source
sanguine	(săng′gwĭn) *adj.*	Optimistic	© Great Source
tirade	(tī-rād′) *n.*	A long, angry speech	© Great Source
vex	(vĕks) *v.*	To baffle	© Great Source
commodious	(kə-mō′dē-əs) *adj.*	Spacious	© Great Source
finite	(fī′nīt′) *adj.*	Having an ending or a boundary	© Great Source
gamut	(găm′ət) *n.*	The complete range of something	© Great Source
incalculable	(ĭn-kăl′kyə-lə-bəl) *adj.*	Beyond measurement	© Great Source
iota	(ī-ō′tə) *n.*	A tiny bit	© Great Source
lofty	(lôf′tē) *adj.*	Elevated in character	© Great Source
minuscule	(mĭn′ə-skyōol′) *adj.*	Tiny; very small	© Great Source
picayune	(pĭk′ə-yōon′) *adj.*	Petty; trivial	© Great Source
vestige	(vĕs′tĭj) *n.*	A visible trace	© Great Source
wane	(wān) *v.*	To diminish in power or size	© Great Source

LESSON 19	LESSON 19	LESSON 19	LESSON 19	LESSON 19
apathetic	consecrate	credo	heinous	ingrate
LESSON 20	LESSON 19	LESSON 19	LESSON 19	LESSON 19
piety	sacrilegious	sanctimony	sanctity	timorous
LESSON 20	LESSON 20	LESSON 20	LESSON 20	LESSON 20
berserk	jubilee	juggernaut	kowtow	maelstrom
LESSON 20	LESSON 20	LESSON 20	LESSON 20	LESSON 20
mecca	nabob	saga	shibboleth	trek
LESSON 21	LESSON 21	LESSON 21	LESSON 21	LESSON 21
cavort	emanate	meander	retrogress	serpentine
LESSON 21	LESSON 21	LESSON 21	LESSON 21	LESSON 21
supersede	torpid	transitory	undulate	unremitting

apathetic
(ăp´ə-thĕt´ĭk) *adj.*
Indifferent

© Great Source

consecrate
(kŏn´sĭ-krāt´) *v.*
To declare as holy

© Great Source

credo
(krē´dō) *n.*
A statement of beliefs

© Great Source

heinous
(hā´nəs) *adj.*
Evil; abominable

© Great Source

ingrate
(ĭn´grāt´) *n.*
An ungrateful person

© Great Source

piety
(pī´ĭ-tē) *n.*
Religious reverence

© Great Source

sacrilegious
(săk´rə-lĭj´əs) *adj.*
Extremely irreverent toward what is considered sacred

© Great Source

sanctimony
(săngk´tə-mō´nē) *n.*
False show of righteousness

© Great Source

sanctity
(săngk´tĭ-tē) *n.*
Sacredness

© Great Source

timorous
(tĭm´ər-əs) *adj.*
Apprehensive; timid

© Great Source

berserk
(bər-sûrk´) *adj.*
Destructively violent

© Great Source

jubilee
(jōō´bə-lē´) *n.*
A gala celebrating a fiftieth anniversary

© Great Source

juggernaut
(jŭg´ər-nôt´) *n.*
An overwhelming force

© Great Source

kowtow
(kou-tou´) *v.*
To show servant-like submission; to fawn

© Great Source

maelstrom
(māl´strəm) *n.*
An unsettling or violent situation

© Great Source

mecca
(mĕk´ə) *n.*
A center of interest

© Great Source

nabob
(nā´bŏb´) *n.*
A wealthy person

© Great Source

saga
(sä´gə) *n.*
An epic tale

© Great Source

shibboleth
(shĭb´´ə-lĭth) *n.*
A word or pronunciation that is particular to a certain group

© Great Source

trek
(trĕk) *n.*
A difficult journey

© Great Source

cavort
(kə-vôrt´) *v.*
To leap or dance in high spirits

© Great Source

emanate
(ĕm´ə-nāt´) *v.*
To send forth

© Great Source

meander
(mē-ăn´dər) *v.*
To wander

© Great Source

retrogress
(rĕt´rə-grĕs´) *v.*
To go backward

© Great Source

serpentine
(sûr´pən-tēn´) *adj.*
Resembling a snake in form or movement

© Great Source

supersede
(sōō´pər-sēd´) *v.*
To supplant

© Great Source

torpid
(tôr´pĭd) *adj.*
Lethargic; inactive

© Great Source

transitory
(trăn´sĭ-tôr´ē) *adj.*
Temporary; short-lived

© Great Source

undulate
(ŭn´jə-lāt´) *v.*
To move with a smooth, wavelike motion

© Great Source

unremitting
(ŭn´rĭ-mĭt´ĭng) *adj.*
Never letting up; persistent

© Great Source

LESSON 22	LESSON 22	LESSON 22	LESSON 22	LESSON 22
extenuation	portent	pretentious	retentive	retinue

LESSON 22	LESSON 22	LESSON 22	LESSON 22	LESSON 22
sustain	sustenance	tenacious	tenement	untenable

LESSON 23	LESSON 23	LESSON 23	LESSON 23	LESSON 23
animus	corpulent	corpus	corpuscle	equanimity

LESSON 23	LESSON 23	LESSON 23	LESSON 23	LESSON 23
inanimate	incorporate	incorporeal	magnanimous	pusillanimous

LESSON 24	LESSON 24	LESSON 24	LESSON 24	LESSON 24
anonymous	cognomen	denomination	ignominious	misnomer

LESSON 24	LESSON 24	LESSON 24	LESSON 24	LESSON 24
moniker	nomenclature	nominal	patronymic	renown

extenuation (ĭk-stĕn´yŏo-ā´shen) *n.* A partial excuse
© Great Source

portent (pôr´tĕnt´) *n.* An omen
© Great Source

pretentious (prĭ-tĕn´shes) *adj.* Showy
© Great Source

retentive (rĭ-tĕn´tĭv) *adj.* Able to remember or store something
© Great Source

retinue (rĕt´n-ōo´) *n.* An entourage
© Great Source

sustain (se-stān´) *v.* To support; to maintain or provide for
© Great Source

sustenance (sŭs´te-nens) *n.* Something that supplies life, strength, or health
© Great Source

tenacious (te-nā´shes) *adj.* Holding stubbornly to something
© Great Source

tenement (tĕn´e-ment) *n.* A run-down, low-rent apartment building
© Great Source

untenable (ŭn-tĕn´e-bel) *adj.* Incapable of being defended, held, or occupied
© Great Source

animus (ăn´e-mes) *n.* A disposition
© Great Source

corpulent (kôr´pye-lent) *adj.* Very fat; obese
© Great Source

corpus (kôr´pes) *n.* A large collection of writings
© Great Source

corpuscle (kôr´pe-sel) *n.* An unattached body cell
© Great Source

equanimity (ē´kwe-nĭm´ĭ-tē) *n.* Calmness; composure
© Great Source

inanimate (ĭn-ăn´e-mĭt) *adj.* Not alive
© Great Source

incorporate (ĭn-kôr´pe-rāt´) *v.* To include as part of a whole
© Great Source

incorporeal (ĭn´kôr-pôr´ē-el) *adj.* Lacking physical substance
© Great Source

magnanimous (măg-năn´e-mes) *adj.* Generous in forgiving
© Great Source

pusillanimous (pyōo´se-lăn´e-mes) *adj.* Cowardly
© Great Source

anonymous (e-nŏn´e-mes) *adj.* Having an unknown name
© Great Source

cognomen (kŏg-nō´men) *n.* A surname
© Great Source

denomination (dĭ-nŏm´e-nā´shen) *n.* A united group of religious organizations
© Great Source

ignominious (ĭg´ne-mĭn´ē-es) *adj.* Disgraceful
© Great Source

misnomer (mĭs-nō´mer) *n.* An unsuitable name
© Great Source

moniker (mŏn´ĭ-ker) *n.* A distinctive nickname
© Great Source

nomenclature (nō´men-klā´cher) *n.* A system of names used in a science or art
© Great Source

nominal (nŏm´e-nel) *adj.* Insignificantly small
© Great Source

patronymic (păt´re-nĭm´ĭk) *adj.* Of or relating to the name of one's father
© Great Source

renown (rĭ-noun´) *n.* Great fame
© Great Source

LESSON 25 append	LESSON 26 pending	benediction	grandiloquence	LESSON 27 cadet	LESSON 27 caprice
LESSON 25 dispense	LESSON 25 preponderance	colloquium	indict	LESSON 27 caper	LESSON 27 chieftain
LESSON 25 expendable	LESSON 25 propensity	dictum	interlocutor	capital	LESSON 27 mischievous
LESSON 25 impend	LESSON 25 recompense	edict	loquacious	capitalism	per capita
LESSON 25 penchant	LESSON 25 suspension	elocution	soliloquy	capitulate	recapitulate

LESSON 28 coup d'etat	LESSON 28 dilettante	LESSON 28 élan	LESSON 28 entrée	LESSON 28 espirit de corps
LESSON 28 laissez faire	LESSON 28 noveau riche	LESSON 28 potpourri	LESSON 28 savoir-faire	LESSON 28 tête-à-tête
LESSON 29 abstract	LESSON 29 avant-garde	LESSON 29 eclectic	LESSON 29 expressionism	LESSON 29 grotesque
LESSON 29 hackneyed	LESSON 29 perspective	LESSON 29 representational	LESSON 29 surrealistic	LESSON 29 verisimilitude
LESSON 30 convivial	LESSON 30 ebullience	LESSON 30 felicitous	LESSON 30 irascible	LESSON 30 placid
LESSON 30 querulous	LESSON 30 sardonic	LESSON 30 surly	LESSON 30 truculent	LESSON 30 unctuous

Term	Pronunciation	Part of speech	Definition
coup d'etat	(kōō´ dā-tä´)	*n.*	A sudden overthrow of a government
dilettante	(dĭl´ĭ-tänt´)	*n.*	A lover of the fine arts; a connoisseur
élan	(ā-län´)	*n.*	Distinctive style; flair
entrée	(ŏn´trā)	*n.*	The power, permission, or liberty to enter; admittance
espirit de corps	(ĕ-sprē´ də kôr´)	*n.*	A spirit of comradeship among group members
laissez faire	(lĕs´ā fâr´)	*n.*	Noninterference in the affairs of others
noveau riche	(nōō´vō rēsh´)	*n.*	Newly wealthy
potpourri	(pō´pŏō-rē´)	*n.*	A mixed assortment
savoir-faire	(săv´wär-fâr´)	*n.*	Social grace
tête-à-tête	(tĕt´ə-tĕt´)	*n.*	A private conversation
abstract	(ăb-străkt´)	*adj.*	Not applied or practical; theoretical
avant-garde	(ä´vänt-gärd´)	*adj.*	Relating to an innovative group
eclectic	(ĭ-klĕk´tĭk)	*adj.*	Employing a variety of elements
expressionism	(ĭk-sprĕsh´ə-nĭz´əm)	*n.*	An art style emphasizing inner experiences
grotesque	(grō-tĕsk´)	*adj.*	Bizarre; distorted
hackneyed	(hăk´nēd)	*adj.*	Overfamiliar through overuse; trite
perspective	(pər-spĕk´tĭv)	*n.*	A particular outlook
representational	(rĕp´rĭ-zĕn-tā´shə-nəl)	*adj.*	Realistic depiction in the visual arts
surrealistic	(sə-rē´ə-lĭs´tĭk)	*adj.*	Oddly dreamlike or unreal
verisimilitude	(vĕr´ə-sĭ-mĭl´ĭ-tōōd´)	*n.*	Appearing to be real
convivial	(kən-vĭv´ē-əl)	*adj.*	Merry; festive
ebullience	(ĭ-bŏōl´yəns)	*n.*	Zestful; exuberant
felicitous	(fĭ-lĭs´ĭ-təs)	*adj.*	Well-suited; apt
irascible	(ĭ-răs´ə-bəl)	*adj.*	Quick tempered
placid	(plăs´ĭd)	*adj.*	Calm; complacent
querulous	(kwĕr´ə-ləs)	*adj.*	Irritable; tending to complain
sardonic	(sär-dŏn´ĭk)	*adj.*	Scornfully mocking
surly	(sûr´lē)	*adj.*	Ill-humored; gruff
truculent	(trŭk´yə-lənt)	*adj.*	Anxious to fight; scathing
unctuous	(ŭngk´chōō-əs)	*adj.*	Oily, slippery

WELCOME TO YORK MINSTER ...

York Minster is not only a wonderful building, it is also a living and diverse community. Whether you come here as a tourist or a pilgrim, we hope that, as you walk around, you will understand why the cathedral has inspired people of every generation since its completion.

CATHEDRAL OR MINSTER?

York Minster is the largest medieval gothic cathedral in Northern Europe. Not all cathedrals are minsters: not all minsters are cathedrals – but York Minster is both.

A cathedral is the mother church of a diocese. It is where the bishop has his *cathedra* or "seat", which is only found in a cathedral. York Minster is the cathedral church of the Diocese of York. A mynster was the Anglo-Saxon name for a missionary church – a church built as a new centre for Christian worship. The first Minster in York was built as such a centre in 627 A.D.

WE WELCOME YOU TO A LIVING CHURCH AND A WORKING COMMUNITY

There may be times when your visit to York Minster is interrupted by additional services (such as weddings or funerals). We hope you will understand this, and are grateful for your help in making these services as dignified as possible.

For further information please contact:
The Visitors' Department, St William's College,
College Street, York YO1 7JF
Tel: 01904 557216 or Fax: 01904 557218
Email: visitors@yorkminster.org   www.yorkminster.org.uk

5/22/05

WELCOME TO YORK MINSTER

The Cathedral and Metropolitical
Church of St Peter in York